W9-CAJ-938

SPITE, MALICE & REVENGE

SPITE, MALICE & REVENGE

An A-Z Collection of Every Dirty Trick in the Book

M. Nelson Chunder
and George Hayduke

GRAMERCY BOOKS
NEW YORK

Originally published in separate volumes under the titles:
I Hate You! An Angry Man's Guide to Revenge by M. Nelson Chunder, copyright © 1983 by Paladin Press
Mad As Hell by M. Nelson Chunder, copyright © 1984 by Paladin Press
Screw Unto Others: Revenge Tactics for All Occasions, by George Hayduke, copyright © 1987 by Paladin Press

This 1988 edition is published by Gramercy Books, distributed by Outlet Book Company, Inc., a Random House Company, 225 Park Avenue South, New York, New York, 10003, by arrangement with Paladin Press.

Printed and Bound in the United States of America

Library of Congress Cataloging-in-Publication Data

Spite, malice & revenge : the complete guide to getting even.
p. cm
Reprint (1st work). Originally published: I hate you! / M. Nelson Chunder. Boulder, Colo. : Paladin, c1983.
Reprint (2nd work). Originally published: Mad as hell / M. Nelson Chunder. Boulder, Colo. : Paladin, c1984.
Reprint (3rd work). Originally published: Screw unto others / George Hayduke. Boulder, Colo. : Paladin. c1987.

1. Revenge—Humor. I. Chunder, M. Nelson. I hate you! 1988. II. Chunder, M. Nelson. Mad as hell. 1988. III. Hayduke, George. Screw unto others. 1988. IV. Title: Spite, malice, and revenge.
PN6231.R45S67 1988
364.1—dc19 88-8116
CIP

Neither the authors nor the publisher assumes any responsibility for use or misuse of information contained in this book. It is sold for entertainment purposes only.

ISBN 0-517-67604-4
13 12 11 10 9 8 7

WARNING:

Spite, Malice & Revenge is intended for entertainment purposes only. Neither the authors nor the publisher will assume responsibility for the use or misuse of any information contained in this book.

Kissing

A man may kiss his wife goodby,
The rose may kiss the butterfly,
The wine may kiss the frosted glass,
And you, my friend, may kiss my ass.

CONTENTS

Hello . . .

Wonderful events can sprout when you plant the seeds of distrust in a garden of assholes. This, despite the critical view that revenge against bullies has lost its erection because we are pretty much an officially soft society. Back when Teddy Roosevelt, one of my all-time favorites, was president, a Moroccan sultan kidnapped an American citizen named Perdicaris. Not only did Teddy send a naval fleet to this one hostage's rescue, he also sent the orders: "Perdicaris alive and free or Raisuli (the sultan) dead and unburied." We no longer live in roughriding times, despite the mythical bullshit of Rambo and his PR man, Ronald Teflon Reagan. I mean, there are still MIAs and Khadaffi Duck still lives.

Happily for you and me, despite centuries of efforts by humanitarians to change our beliefs, the majority of people still cling to the primal urge to get even with someone who's done them a disfavor. All sorts of kindly folks have tried to wean us away from vengeance (e.g., governments seek to outlaw it) and, when that fails, attempt to channel vengeance into more acceptable forms of social expression, like war.

The truth is, in today's real world, hate, meanness,

(Continued...)

and violence rarely take a nap. America's favorite "sport" is pro wrestling, while tough guy contests are making a comeback. Some women even say they are sick of sensitive men and that they just want to get laid. Aren't the robber barons back where they belong — busting unions and terrorizing the slave labor? Mean is as American as apple pie, and, with that, I apologize to Stokely Carmichael for updating his line from a generation or so ago.

When I was on a talk show panel in Chicago, another guest, a fuddy-duddy who was also a psychologist, told me that my revenge antics were antisocial. To describe me to listeners he used words like "barbaric, destructive, childish, uncivilized . . ." I thanked him very sincerely. I was thrilled with that attention and description from this educated man. It's not every day you get such flattery from someone educated far beyond his own intelligence.

I recall something I had learned in the writings of Sigmund Freud, in which he noted, "the concept of revenge is seen, at best, as a childish coping mechanism to keep darker forces at bay, and, at worst, as a manifestation of serious psychic illness." By Sigmund, he's right.

Today, the people who study such things about other people think that the 1980s will be known by historians as the Age of Mean. Since the '70s were known as the Me Decade, the '80s will be known as the Mean Decade. Proof? Have you heard some nitwit TV preacher refer to AIDS as God's punishment of homosexuals? Seen some hardcore punkers slam-dancing? Told any Challenger jokes? An hour after the shuttle exploded? The Reaganistas?

When did *Newsweek* do a cover story on "The New Cruelty," or when did David Letterman start that new feature called "Cruel Pet Tricks?" Oh come, grow up, this is America. Norman Rockwell doesn't live here anymore.

To paraphrase Lamont Cranston's father, the weed of mean bears bitter fruit, i.e., bullies. Bullies come in all sizes, tempers, and ways of expressing their bullydom. With characteristic modesty I think of myself as a Bullybuster, someone who helps people get back at bullies, new and traditional.

Why do people want to get even? I think it's because we feel the world ought to operate fairly, and when it doesn't work that way, we react. Most people adopt the "helpless victim" or the "that's the way it is, hit me again" approach. That's the scared citizen who swallows the bully's challenge or the old person who stays inside his city apartment behind a door with three locks. The other response is to "take action," which means talking back, striking back, or, in our case, *Haydukery.*

While America is discovering the fun of revenge, we'll never get to the Big Leagues, though, to the level of the Turks, Sicilians, Mexicans, or Corsicans. To most Americans, revenge is fun, i.e., getting even. To the nasty Grown-Ups mentioned above it is serious lifetime, or deathtime, actually.

When I pooped and snooped as one of Uncle's mufti-clad nephews I worked with two "sergeants" whose names were "Smith," of course. I remember one of them telling me about a couple of the "indigenous personnel" with whom we worked in someone else's country. Here's what he advised: "Never, ever, get on their shit list, George. Those bastards will follow you into hell itself to get their revenge. If you die before they even the score, they'll dig up your dead body and piss all over it. If it takes till the day after forever, they'll get even with you."

Wonder where those indigenous dudes are today, now that we need them again?

How to Use This Wonderful Book

I have arranged these subjects both by method and mark, listing them alphabetically. In addition to using the obvious subject headings, you can also do a cross-reference of your own. Or you can adapt a method listed for one mark for another mark or situation. Thus, these subjects become as versatile as your own imagination.

While this mix 'n match versatility is a standard item here, the personalized nasty touch is still the best. Another effective part of this business is the anticipation of further damage after your initial attack. This is grand psychological warfare.

General Advice

Throughout this book I make universal reference to the "mark," which is a street label hung on the victim, male or female, of a scam or con or act of vengeance. In our case, the mark is a bully — anyone or anything — who has done something unpleasant, foul, unforgivable or fatal to you, your family, your property, or your friends. Never think of a mark as the victim of dirty tricks. Think of the mark as a very deserving bully, a target for your revenge.

Before you study any of the specific sections of this book, read these next few vital paragraphs. They tell you how to prepare before going into action.

1. Prepare a plan.

   Plan all details before you take action at all. Don't even ad-lib something from this book without a plan of exactly what you're going to do and how. If your campaign involves a series of actions, make a chronological chart, and then coordinate your efforts. Make a list of possible problems. Plan what you'll do if you get caught — depending upon who catches you. You must have every option, contingency, action, reaction, and evaluation planned in advance. Remember, time is

(Continued...)

usually on the side of the trickster. As Winston Churchill — who is one of my favorite heroes for many, many reasons — once said, "a lie gets halfway around the world before the truth even puts on its boots." Or, as that old Sicilian homily goes, "Revenge is a dish best served cold," which means don't strike while your ire is hot. Wait. Plan. Think. Learn.

2. Gather intelligence.

   Do what a real intelligence operative would do and compile a file on your mark. How detailed and thorough you are depends upon your plans for the mark. For a simple get-even number, you obviously need less intelligence than if you're planning an involved, time-release campaign. Before you start spying, make a written list of all the important things you need to know about the target — be it a person, company or institution.

3. Buy away from home.

   Any supplies, materials, or services you need must be purchased away from where you live. Buy far in advance and pay in cash. Try to be as inconspicuous and colorless as possible. Don't talk unnecessarily with people. The best rule here is the spy's favorite — a good operative will get lost in a crowd of one. The idea is for people not to remember you.

4. Never tip your hand.

   Don't get cocky, cute 'n clever, and start dropping hints about who's doing what to whom. I know that may sound stupid, but some would-be tricksters *are* gabby. Of course, in some of the cases this will not apply, e.g., unselling car customers at the dealership, or other tricks in which the scenario demands your personal involvement.

5. Never admit anything.

   If accused, act shocked, hurt, outraged, or

amused, whichever seems most appropriate. Deny everything, unless, again, your plan involves overt personal involvement. If you're working covert, stay that way. The only cool guy out of Watergate was G. Gordon Liddy; he kept his mouth shut.

6. Never apologize; it's a sign of weakness.

Normally, harassment of a citizen is a low-priority case with the police. The priority increases along with the person's socio-financial position in the community and with his or her political connections. If you are at war with a corporation, utility, or institution, that's a different ball game. They often have private security people, sometimes retired federal or state investigators. By habit, these people may not play according to the law. If you play dirty tricks upon a governmental body, prepare to have a case opened. But how hard it is followed depends upon a lot of factors. Understanding all this ahead of time is part of your intelligence planning before you get started in action.

The Eleven Commandments of Revenge

Thanks to my Apostle of Revenge, Dick Smegma, I humbly present for your perusal, belief, and adherence, the Eleven Commandments of Revenge. Stay faithful and you'll enjoy a lot of yucks without suffering the heartbreak of being caught.

1. *Thou shalt neither trust nor confide in anyone!*
   If you do, that person could eventually betray you. Even if it is a relative or spouse, don't tell them what you are up to. Implicated accomplices are OK.
2. *Thou shalt never use thine own telephone for revenge business!*
   Always use a public telephone or that of an unwitting mark so calls cannot be traced back to you or to someone who knows you.
3. *Thou shalt not touch revenge documents with thy bare hands!*
   Bare hands leave fingerprints! Wear gloves.
4. *Thou shalt become a garbage collector!*
   Once your victim places his trash outside his home/office for pickup, it is 100 percent legal for you to pick it up yourself. You can learn about

(Continued...)

your victim by sifting through his old papers, etc. The pros do it all the time.

5. *Thou shalt bide thy time before activating a revenge plot!*
   Give the victim time to forget about you and what he's done to wrong you. Getting even too soon makes it easier for him to discover who's doing it!
6. *Thou shalt secure a "mail-drop" address in another city!*
   You don't want revenge mail being traced back to your residence/town, do you?
7. *Thou shalt learn everything there is to learn about thy victim!*
   The best revenge schemes/plans are hatched by people who know their victim better than the victim knows about himself.
8. *Thou shalt pay cash all the time in a revenge plot!*
   Checks, money orders, etc., can be traced back to you. Cash cannot!
9. *Thou shalt trade with merchants who have never heard of you!*
   Do business with people only once when involved in a revenge plot. Possibly wear a disguise so they will have trouble identifying you in a legal confrontation.
10. *Thou shalt never threaten thy intended victim!*
    Why warn your intended victim that you are going to get even? When bad things begin to happen to your victim, whether or not you caused them, your victim will remember your threat, and he'll set out to even the score with you.
11. *Thou shalt not leave evidence lying around, however circumstantial.*
    If you are thought to be actively engaged in having fun at your mark's expense, the authorities may visit you. Thus, it would be prudent not to have any books by Hayduke or Chunder on your shelves at home or in the office.

Caution

The schemes, tricks, scams, stunts, cons, and scenarios presented here are solely for information and amusement purposes only. It would never, ever be my intent that you use this book as a working field manual or trickster's cookbook. I certainly don't expect that anyone who reads this book would actually ever do any of the things described here. I know that I never would.

This book is written solely to entertain and inform readers, not to instruct or persuade them to commit any nasty or illegal act. From my own mild disposition, I could hardly tell someone else to make any of these tactics operational.

There's an old Creole saying that sums it up well: *Weso geye kofias na dlo, e se dlo ki küit li,* which means something like, "A fish trusts the water, and yet it is in the water that it is cooked."

Please read this book with that reference in mind. Remember, it's all in good clean fun, isn't it? (That was a rhetorical question.) And, now, gentle reader, with all of the preamble behind us, let's get on with the *fun!*

Additives

When it comes to paying back her enemies, Carla Savage doesn't horse around. Her unbridled enthusiasm for redoing nasties has earned her my friendship, as if that's not enough. Carla is greatly into the (ab)use of Di Methyl Sulf Oxide (DMSO). It's colorless, odorless, and it will penetrate the skin carrying with it any of a variety of substances you might wish to add. DMSO is easy to get in most areas of the country.

Carla's suggestions include mixing DMSO with antabuse if you want to choke up your alcoholic mark. Mix it with horse liniment. Mix it with the chemical of your choice and coat your mark's doorknob, steering wheel, etc. Perhaps some odorous chemical could be mixed with DMSO and your mark's favorite sexual lubricant.

Or, if your mark is a real worm, Filthy McNasty has a cure. Buy some relatively mild cat worming pills. Grind them up and put them into the mark's food. They cause nausea and a really classic case of the runs. A fine added touch for this moving additive is to impair the mark's use of the proper disposal facilities. You can lock the room, lock the stalls, glue down the lids, etc. Or if you can, simply interdict the mark in person by engaging him or her in important business or personal communication of a nature that makes it tough to break away quickly. Enjoy the mark's discomfort.

Speaking of great physics, you can add some real kick to a jerk's or jerkess's drink by including citrate of magnesia, which has a peppy lemon-lime taste as a wonderful disguise. In a heavy enough dose, it's a real bowel-buster.

Phenolpthalein ($C_{20}H_{14}O_4$) is a white crystalline substance used as the active ingredient in chocolate-based candy laxatives. To use it you must first dissolve it in ethyl (grain) alcohol. Once dissolved, it may be used as an additive in various foods and drinks. The advantage, according to James Q. Carter, is that you don't have to rely on the hoary old chocolate candy joke. He says it's great for getting back at rude and/or noisy partyholics.

Another of Carter's ruesome additives is neutral red, a water-soluble, crystalline, red dye which will go in one end of your mark and come out the other without causing serious harm enroute—with the exception of creating bright red urine. Because of its red color, you need to use it in disguised drinks, e.g., sloe gin.

It's been a long time since my old pal Neal Abogado has turned up in correspondence. Always a foot soldier in the pharmacological trenches, Senor Abogado has come up with a use of Medroxygprogestrone Acetate, a regulated, prescriptive drug. "It's a powerful drug that deadens the sex drive in a real Big League way," Neal writes. "It's so strong that Mr. Stud goes from 'canis lupus' to 'penis limpus' really quickly. It's great to slip this to some slime who's been porking the wrong lady."

During a recent talk show, Linda from Pittsburgh told me about a bad time she had at the tail end of a date with a would-be Lothario who tried to turn the backseat of his car into the Quickie Dickie Motel. Since she knew this was his standard MO with all the girls at work, Linda rigged his car the following week by spreading industrial strength itching powder all over the backseat, plus in and around the driver's side seat.

Killroy suggests that you purchase some large, pure-niacin vitamin tablets from your local drug store. Pulverize a couple of them and put them in your mark's food. About twenty minutes later, your mark will experience hot flashes, and his skin will actually turn bright red. This trick is totally harmless, says Killroy.

Butyric acid is not so harmless, and apparently it is becoming a favorite additive of active tricksters. Recently, I heard from Tyra Pierce, a Missouri student, who knows some good uses for this solution.

"I'm kind of small and young looking for my age, so I get picked on a lot," writes Tyra. "I found a fun thing to do to tormentors is to load a syringe with 15 units of butyric acid, then shoot the stinky stuff into their dorm room locks, car door locks or places where the marks will put their keys or hands. That way, the acid has a chance of traveling to other locales to spread your revenge even more. Think about toilet topics!"

Thanks to the kindness of an unknown Missouri pharmacist, plus some practice, Tyra now knows that sulphurated potash smells awful, is inexpensive and is a lot safer to use than butyric acid. It's great stuff and does all the same things that the more expensive and esoteric chemical accomplishes.

Mr. D. from Austin is another pharmacologic phreak. His contribution to our field of applied science is a chemical known as sodium silicate solution, available at almost any drug store for no more than two dollars a bottle. When splashed on glass, the liquid soon dries and becomes virtually impossible to scrape off. Needless to say, any car windshield treated to a bottle of this stuff is ruined, as he has discovered in field tests. Keep in mind that the solution dries to a clear appearance, so you'll want to add coloring to make it more overwhelming. Also think about adding metal shavings, shreds of paper, vomit, dirt, dog doo, food scraps, etc. to your concoction. The nice thing about this stuff is that you can put the liquid in plastic bags for easy throwing, so that you may not even have to leave your car to make a hit.

Then, there is muriatic acid. Killroy cautions that this stuff is dangerous, so wear goggles and gloves when you go to have fun. Buy some muriatic acid concentrate from a chemical supply house. You may have to sign for it in your state, so think ahead and decide whose name and ID you want to use. Use the acid to etch nasty messages about your mark in someone's cement sidewalk, wall, etc. It can also destroy car finishes and sensitive metal parts.

more

Additives

There is some magic in the air. Or, as one of my old college friends, a fairly wild hangover from the 1960s, used to say as he dug into his stash . . . "Ahh, better living through chemistry." But, speaking of something completely different, that reminded me of a conversation my brother had with a certain M.M. in Florida.

It seems M.M. is in analysis—as in urine. He notes that if you add methylene blue to various drinks, it will pass through the human body without changing color. I had heard of bluebloods before, but never the other.

more

Additives

Although John was in Tempe, Arizona, when he told me about it, I believed him. Later, a doctor confirmed it; then I had my own medical advisor for this series, Dr. Chris Doyle, also verify it for me. Here's the story. A drug known as Urised, aka methylene blue, when ingested, turns the urine a bright, deep blue. It is medically harmless if directions are followed. However, if the mark has no idea he or she has ingested the stuff, the resultant blue piss might cause some psychic harm to the personality's well-being. It could be great fun for you to try on some mark. Dr. Doyle says it would be fairly easy to administer in powder form. He did caution against massive overdose, however.

Airlines

If you think my old Panama pal, Lt.C. Mac, was irritated at Eastern, or that Syd Prine was pissed off at his airline, listen to what Bonnie Parker III did when an airline lost her luggage for the second consecutive time in two flights.

"After playing the harried lady executive, followed by the coy flirt, then, by the pissed-off business traveler, all to no avail, I recalled something in one of your books, George. Never had roadkill looked so good," Ms. Parker told me one evening.

"My boyfriend thought I was really nuts when I made him take me out to hunt some obnoxious roadkill, which we quickly found, it being early spring. I gathered it into a big bag, took it home and stuck the plastic bag in my freezer. When the roadkill was good and hard, I wrapped it a bit more and stuffed it into an old suitcase I bought at Goodwill. I put tags on that suitcase in the name of an old, old boyfriend I hated and took it to the airport to check it on the next flight of *that* damned airline to my least favorite city, presenting my own ticket that I had bought moments ago in my old ex-boyfriend's name (using initials, dummy).

(Continued...)

"With the frozen roadkill-filled suitcase checked on the plane, I then cancelled my ticket, cashed it in, and left. The bag would arrive and as it would be unclaimed, *Dipshit Airlines* (not their real name) would have to store it."

Doesn't Ms. Parker III think well, for a normal person?

more

Airlines

I did a talk show in Ontario and found a delightful chap named N. J. Franchier. He had finally had it up to his rising gorge with the lack of service on some airlines and decided to *Get Even*. Here is his idea.

"I packed a zip-top packet of beef chunk soup mix with me in my carry-on luggage. When the time came for my stunt, I mixed some hot water with my soup. I quietly poured the soup into a throw-up bag, then pretended to be ill into the bag, making all the appropriate sounds. At the same time, my companion called the flight attendant.

"Just as the attendant was about to take my filled bag, I said, 'Wait a moment, please!' and offered the bag to my companion who dipped his fingers in, removed some chunks of meat and carrots and ate them. Before he helped himself to the tasty morsels in the bag, he politely offered some to the attendant and the others seated nearby who were incredulously witnessing this spectacle."

Now that is a great flight of fancy.

more

Airlines

Meanwhile, Sorethroat in Orlando, Florida, strings this bit of business together: He got on an airplane and sat quietly with a string hanging out of his mouth. At the end of the string was a small brass ring. Naturally, one of the people seated near him noticed it, but said nothing. A flight attendant finally asked him about the string/ring.

Sorethroat responded in the cultured tone of a studious academic, "I am a research scientist studying the effects of digestive juices on various foods. I recently swallowed a small basket containing samples of raw food. It's on the other end of this string, and I'm about to pull it up now for observation."

That statement cleared the aisles.

This stunt would also work on a bus or train as well.

Alarm Clocks

Everyone knows someone whose intellectual humor delights in rousting you out of bed at times you would prefer to be deep into the Land of Nod. Shauna from Phoenix has an alarming way of ringing in some revenge for these dastardly dips. Considering that most are friends, roomies, or others with whom you have close association, this is fairly easy. Borrow or otherwise obtain seven or eight cheap, loud alarm clocks and secret them all around the mark's abode — all within easy listening distance of where mark sleeps — *after* you have set each clock's alarm to go off in sequential order about four or five minutes apart.

Another idea for the semi-engineering minded came in a strange letter with a German postmark and signed simply Hun. What you do is basically the same type of revenge technique, only you open up the alarm clock if it is the older, wind-up, or geared one. Once there you change the pin settings of the alarm so that it is an hour or two ahead or behind that of what it shows on the face. If you're not technically minded, says Hun, you may just cut the bell connector or disable the bell/ringer wire. Either way, the premature, late, or lack of alarm

(Continued...)

dings the mark.

Funny, I thought it was the Swiss stereotype who doctored clocks?

more

Alarm Clocks

If you have access to your mark's bedroom, reset the alarm clock for a time he or she will be asleep. Or, if the mark must get up for work or school, reset the alarm for a later hour. Few people check the time settings, especially if it's a routine schedule situation. This timely tip came from Ron Canaveral in Florida.

Alarms

Apparently some of the Down Under folks lack a sense of security, as Peter Wanker writes from Sydney that his favorite Australian marks are installing alarms in their homes and autos. He notes, though, that a can of polyurethane foam will silence an alarm horn or bell quickly and quietly for whatever purpose you might have in mind.

On the same subject, that TAP columnist writing as The Stainless Steel Rat, notes that a lot of corporate travelers now carry those personal alarm devices that hang around a metal doorknob. If someone jiggles the knob, the alarm goes off.

"If you find one, hook a piece of wire or other metal object to the outside knob," the Rat writes.

This will cause the alarm to function. Hopefully, the mark will call the hotel desk and security people, which will create a big scene.

Here's a little extra. Before you cause the mark's alarm to go off, tie his/her door to the one across the hall so tightly that he/she cannot open it. Or, tie it to an electrical conduit, water pipe, fire hose or fire alarm.

Alum

Alum is the natural ingredient in unripe persimmons that causes your mouth to pucker. Powdered alum is readily available on drugstore shelves, too. Replace the mark's salt, sugar, or other seasoning with alum, and watch the fun. This is a good one to use on health-food freaks and in eating establishments. Thank the Indiana Cave Man for this tight-lipped wonderfulness.

Animal Scent

Hunters know deer musk masks human odor in the woods. Bob from Newport News has another use in which you make the mark's clothing, car, or furniture smell like a deer in heat. Bob writes: "A two-ounce bottle of the stuff applied to the mark's car seat and ceiling pads will render the vehicle an olfactory disaster area. If the mark locks the car, just use a large hypodermic needle to insert through the door weather stripping and squirt away."

Another good sport, Lucy Gagette, told me that the same product applied in liberal fashion to the bedding or eating area of your mark's pet cat or dog can promote some wonderfully antic animal psychoses. Perhaps, you could squirt this stuff on the pant leg of your mark to create a bit of involuntary sodomy for the pet.

Animals

Since I've always felt that animals are generally nicer than people, I find it fun to make those furry friends my allies when it's necessary to turn a mark's property into Wild Kingdom. Carla Savage, a truly neat lady, has the following stunt in mind. She purchases liquid animal scents from companies that manufacture them for trappers, hunters, dog trainers and other users. It's that fourth category she likes.

"It sure is a drag for some dumb mark, especially if he or she is a fussy cat or dog owner, to have the old property overrun by lust-crazed coyotes, foxes and ferals, wildly seeking that elusive female in heat whose scent has been sprinkled all over the place by me. Of course, these wild animals are also very liberal when it comes to adding their own bouqets to the collection of markings," Carla writes.

This neat lady has more uses for the lab-produced scents, adding, "The concentrated scent stinks awfully. Imagine getting it on your clothes, especially if you are a jogger in a town full of dogs. You wonder what the awful odor is, but you'll soon forget that as you are going to feel like the Pied Piper of Puppydom. A very tiny bit of scent will reach a dog's sensitive nose, even if it doesn't reach the mark's."

Saucy Sybil also came up with a splendid and unusual idea that uses a doggie to get even with some rotten person in your life. Get a glossy portrait-style photo of some truly ugly dog, put it in a nice frame and write the inscription "To my dear (add mark's name), with much love. Mother." Then send it to the mark, or better yet, have it delivered to the office.

Once again, and with accustomed literary fanfare, we welcome back Stoney Dale, the ex-professional wrestler who's as grand at chicanery as he is at ringling. Stoney's lived all over the country in his travels and had his share of nasty neighbor dogs who crap on his lawn, chew the garbage, scatter his papers all over the place and yowl all night when some bitch is in heat. He found a solution.

Buy one of those silent dog whistles, the kind canines can hear, but humans cannot. Set your alarm for 3 A.M. when your neighborhood dog owners are asleep, go out and toot quietly away on your new whistle. Soon, Stoney says, all the dogs start up, lights go on and owners yell at their dogs to settle down, ask what's wrong or call the police to report prowlers because the dog is acting so upset. Stoney says it works 100 percent well for him.

This trickster also adds, "To get back at a dog show sponsor, you might want to secrete yourself away from the crowd and toot away on your handy—and silent—whistle. Much to the dismay of the owners, handlers and judges, these highly trained dogs will run around in circles, bark, yap, cry and do everything but obey commands. It soon becomes a very comical mess," he relates.

Here is a nondamaging trick you can pull on a nasty dog. Normally, I am loath to suggest revenge on dogs, but this is a fun one. Bleaching peroxide will work on a dog's hair just as it does on human hair.

A number of people mentioned this one to me, but as I'd already seen *National Lampoon's Vacation,* I knew about it. You find a dead cat or dog—leave it to your imagination—and put a cutesy collar on it. Then, you attach one end of a leash to the collar and the other end to the bumper of your mark's car. Slide the corpse under the car. Hopefully, the mark will not spot the planted roadkill and will drag it all over town, or at least he'll drag it until an outraged officer of the law or vengeful citizen stops him one way or another. Actually doing this stunt is funnier than the film version.

Speaking of stench, I've described animal scents before, but skunk urine is the best, according to the experts, for smelling up a mark's property. Once the stuff is applied to a rug, car or clothes, you've provided nearly a year's worth of added nasal irritation to your mark's life. The experts say the best to use is natural, rather than synthetic, scent. See Sources.

Finally, don't rattle CW's cage out there in snowy Hastings, Nebraska, or he'll send you some rattlesnake eggs. Actually, they're the commercialized version of the old hooked-rubberband-and-washer-inside-the-envelope trick. Your mark

sees the envelope and thinks, "Rattlesnake eggs?" He opens it, the band springs and the sound scares the effluvia out of him. CW says this prepackaged version complete with printed label and "warning" is available from Good Time Gifts, P.O. Box 324C, Covent Station, NJ 07961.

Answering Machines

"Hello, I don't want to talk to you now."

"I'm not at home. Talk to my machine, instead."

The answering machine affair goes on—people and telephones, people vs. machines. For example, every kid on the East Coast at some odd time in his or her career works at "The Shore" during the summer. I did, and it was depressing . . . sex, drugs, and alcohol. That is enough to depress "Pub" who is a real resident of the seaside resort of Wildwood, New Jersey. So, he writes of neat ideas if you hate your mark's answering machine. Or, perhaps, your mark is the machine!

Find out what type/make/model of machine you need to respond to. Beg, borrow, or lift one of the little beepers that activates the answering machine in question. They are all rather interchangeable, according to Pub.

When you know your mark is going to be away and that his or her answering machine will be on, call, and then use your borrowed beeper to erase all his incoming calls. Or, erase only a selected few after you've previewed them. Or, listen to the messages and then revise them. Make up new return messages, or have a friend help you deliver them.

more

Answering Machines

I'm not at all upset by answering machines. In fact, often it's fun to give a purposefully garbled response or to give your message by skipping key words as if the machine were broken. Q107 from Toronto will often hold a small radio or Walkman to the telephone and play some garbage to the machine. Or he will tape and play a selected portion of a radio station giveaway telephone call that makes it sound as if the answering machine's owner has won a contest, maybe.

more

Answering Machines

The next time you are in your mark's home or business, take careful note if he has a telephone answering machine. If so, memorize the brand name (Sanyo, Code-A-Phone, etc.) and the model number.

Next, write to the manufacturer, explaining that you have lost or otherwise misplaced the owner's manual for that particular machine, and you'd like a replacement sent to you. Usually, the company will send you one free of charge, no questions asked.

Once you get the owner's manual, you can find out if the messages on the machine can be retrieved by remote control, using *any* touch-tone telephone. If so, you should be able to quickly determine the one- to three-digit code that allows you to play back your mark's personal messages, anytime you wish.

A word of caution, though, if you're going to do this intelligence-gathering bit: you will have to refrain from other means of messing with the machine, e.g., changing messages, etc. You don't want your mark to suspect that the answering machine has been compromised and that you're gathering goodies from it.

If you want to thank someone for this nice piece of advice, send a warm wave to Dick Smegma.

Apartments

This has to be Dr. Yaz's finest Yellow Brick Road. His mark lived in an apartment with a long, long hallway. The mark had to leave town for a business weekend. Somehow, Dr. Yaz and friends managed to appropriate a key to the apartment. And, with Dorothy and Toto's help, managed to lay an Oz number on the mark.

"We laid plastic covering down the long hallway, then under cover of night brought in many sacks of cement, which we mixed in the guy's bathtub, so we could pave his hallway. To finish off this boulevard, we painted the yellow line down the middle and scored the thing like bricks.

"As a finishing touch, we put up a big poster of Dorothy and friends on their Yellow Brick Road. It was on the door at the end of the hall so he'd see it at the end of his paved 'road.' "

One of the reasons Dr. Yaz and friends did this was because the guy was a jerk, plus, he annoyed young ladies who had no time for him.

Arrests

Using false identification in your mark's name, and, if necessary, your mark's "borrowed" car, get yourself arrested on a summary offense charge. Be polite and accept the summary. The twist is your false ID shows the mark's name with another address at some cutout mail drop. The trick happens when the hearing notification doesn't get to the mark, who obviously doesn't show up in court. He is tracked down through his license. He will really get arrested. By this time, the original cop probably doesn't remember what the mark looked like. So . . .

This is an involved stunt and has a minor degree of danger if you do it in a small, local jurisdiction. So, don't. I have seen it work twice in large, urban areas. Done properly, it creates a real nightmare for the mark.

Attacks on Haydukery

Early in 1986, a friend informed me that the State House of Legislators in Hawaii was considering two bills related to "harassment" and my readii g of the text of those bills showed that they are aimed at good clean Haydukery.

Like my president, I don't have to take crap from anyone! So, like my president, I see this, as he does most everything he doesn't like, as an act of war!

If these odious pieces of dubious legislation pass, you can be sure that Hayduke will strike hard, fast, and often. And, unlike my own advice, I am openly warning my enemies. Gosh, I really am a nice guy. Reagan didn't even do that for Khadaffi Duck or however that Libyan Mad Dog spells his name. Mad Dog? Didn't that used to be a cheap, mind-busting wine?

Anyway, governments and the people who form them are rarely to be trusted. As the wonderful Linda Ellerbee has said, "Government is like a pizza because when it comes to morality, they can slice it any way they want and someone else will have to pay for the cheese."

Auto Dealers

For the first time, we hear from an auto dealer who got ripped off, but who succeeded in getting back at the costly customer. RepoMan from Denver told me that a local real estate dealer bragged how he never made payments on any car and always avoided repossession. Using a fake ID, our RepoMan set up an appointment for the deadbeat with some friends who claimed they were selling their big business, blinding the real estate jerk with $$$ signs. While he was trying to hustle the business friends, RepoMan took back his car. At a prearranged time, the friends excused themselves for a brief conference, and left the office — which was not theirs — got in their own car and drove to their home 175 miles away, after calling local police to report a "breaking and entering" at that office. One wonders how long the real estate schmuck sat there before the police arrived and what he did when he eventually went out to where he'd parked "his" car?

Auto Keys

Sometimes the key to getting back at your mark is simple. As Major General K. Oss relates, "I have gotten hold of my mark's keys and simply filed off a point or two on each key, rendering them useless."

A friend of mine pulled this stunt on his girlfriend after she locked him out of "their" apartment over some misunderstanding about lust or something minor like that. No problem, except for all of his extra clothes, money and so on that was kept in this apartment, for which he paid two-thirds of the rent. After she relented and they agreed to split, he was able to do this minor Dremel tool job on her keys. He says it was good for two days of aggravation and accusation on her part. He maintained perfect innocence and kept telling her to leave him alone. Great!

Automobiles

One of the nice things about being published all over the world is the calibre of minds I meet. That's why I was glad to hear from Mark Death in Brisbane, Australia. Mark's first idea was to get a plastic spray bottle like you might use for fine-spraying laundry or for window cleaning, but, this time, fill it with automotive brake fluid and spray it all over the paint finish of the vehicle. Two coats, says Mark Death, and the car's paint will start to peel and crack.

Mark's next idea is a cheaper and permanent improvement on the locking gas cap for your mark's car. You might simply wish to use epoxy to coat the threads of his regular gas cap and seal it on forever.

While working as a petroleum transfer engineer, aka gas pump jockey, in the colds of Western Canada a long time ago, Dr. Deviant found a neat way to get back at a nasty mark's car tires. The Dr. explains: "I would use a hypodermic syringe filled with a water and sugar mix. I would inject the mixture into the valve in hopes that the freezing water would wreck the tire or that the sugar would mess up the valve. It always worked."

Sometimes the most simple things can really annoy

(Continued...)

and worry your mark. Larson Roberts likes it when his mark gets a new car or truck. "I spread a little puddle of oil under the new vehicle and smear a bit on the bottom of the engine or pan. The mark sees this and thinks he has a leak.

"Maybe the mark takes it back to the dealer and makes a pain of himself, or just pours in more oil at home. Hopefully, this overfilling will then cause real leaks and/or split seals," Larson says with a bright smile.

Over the past few years, I have heard many new ideas for filling a car with water and/or aquatic life. Until my Central American friend Bicho Cocha told me about this one incident, I had no idea someone would go to all of this trouble. According to Bicho, on their second date, it seems that the car owner decided he owned the sexual conduct of the young lady involved, due to meals and drinks. She did not agree. They finally reached an unhappy impasse, which he finally resolved by tossing her into the restaurant/motel swimming pool — in all of her finery — after she'd refused to go to bed with him. He also tossed their meals at her in the pool.

Better than even was the only way to go. She decided to create a Car Aquarium, and here is what she did. After extensive research, she learned where he parked his car, when it would be most open to attack, for how long, and with what effect.

Next, she opened the car and began to fill it in with rocks, plants (both real and plastic), and some tree limbs. Next, she shut the doors and sealed them with caulking. She then forced a hose into a window seal and ran a whole lot of water. She filled the car to the top of the window and left immediately.

As an added attraction, she alerted the local news media — especially television — about this odd car aquarium, tying it with some local, well-known charity, at the first pay phone she found.

Thanks to Dick Smegma I finally found out how

the term "bomb" became associated with automobiles. Here's how. It seems a plant supervisor not only stole a work improvement idea from two workers and claimed it as his own, but he also docked time unfairly from one of their pals because of a personal snit they'd had. Appeals and conversation on righting the wrongs never got beyond his own uncaring personality. He threatened suspensions, then firings.

Remember those five-gallon glass wine bottles and/or those huge bottles used upside down in office water coolers? These chaps got one of those and spent the next week filling it, instead of their urinal. Using a funnel, one fellow even managed to defecate in it several times as he had the runs badly. As a finale, another one ate the usual mix of pizza, vegetable soup and beer, then made himself vomit into the bottle.

Capping it tightly, they took this horrible mess to the supervisor's apartment complex and lugged it to the roof. Prior to doing so, they had determined that the boss parked his car head-on to the building and spotted the location. To aid in their aim, they spray-painted his windshield with phosphorescent paint which would show up in the dark — it being nighttime, of course.

Hoisting the huge bottle full of yukiness to the ledge, they lined up on their target with the care of a precision bombing crew. After making aiming allowances which a friendly engineer had calculated for them, they let it go over the edge. The bathroom bomb roared on toward the target.

The *crash* and *splash* had to be heard to be believed, one of the men told Dick. It smashed right through the windshield-target and exploded inside the car, showering the fermenting mixture of effluvia, excrement, and vomit everywhere in the vehicle's interior.

The car was less than six months old and was totally trashed. It was sold to a junkyard for parts — a $9500 Buick that brought less than $600 in return. The mark's insurance company refused to pay because of a technical error the guy had made in his coverage in an attempt to cheat the company. They said at work he became a beaten man and soon asked for a transfer. Bully for the bombers!

In another case of bully-busting, Zongie was afraid of his wife. A real termagant, she used to nail his ass every two weeks or so. Looking like Lyle Alzado in drag, she had only one pride and real love — her car, which she insisted on being hers and only hers. Bob from Newport News helped Zongie. Bob recalls, "We used Zap, one of the new acrylic cements for aircraft hobbyists, to stick the wipers to her car windshield. The best part was that she burned up the motor and had to get another one. She blamed it on vandals. In a way she was right."

Bob said their next stunt was a scientific experiment, "to see how long an automatic transmission will function with its cooling tubes crimped between the transmission and the radiator. In our one test, with 'Godzilla's' car, it took 15 miles to overheat the transmission, we figure. It seized and quit at 20. It happened when she was coming home from work on a fairly remote part of the roadway and she had to hike two miles to call for help."

Bob reports that when she asked Zongie for repair money, he reminded her she had always insisted it was her car. She paid. She may have gotten the point, too, as she started to act a bit more kindly to Zongie.

As an afterthought, Bob related that four tablespoons of common black pepper in an auto radiator will clog most of the cooling passages, causing almost immediate overheating. He said that will be their next zinger for Mrs. Zongie if needed.

Aunt Barby's been a friend of creative Haydukery for years, part of the price of living with the conductor of the Mount Lebanon Wind Symphony. Cutting off the quest for a motive, she gets directly to the right recipe that is without a doubt ideal for vehicular vermin, i.e., your mark and his car.

"It's quite simple," she says innocently, "you just add a cup or so of Minute Rice to the radiator of your mark's car. Not only have you gotten even, but you can even grain and bare it."

I think she meant something about shooting a moon. On the other hand, have a rice day with this.

Our recipe file of car radiator additives is piling up faster than vote fraud charges in a Mexican election. Krazy K adds dried beans, peas, or corn starch to our arsenal of additives. He also notes that we consider salt, too, as a long-term corrosive. In addition, Krazy K says you can add some fun things to the windshield washer tank as well, e.g., liquid detergent soap, ink, motor oil.

As an additive to the zapped windshield stunt to Mrs. Zongie's car, Dr. Deviant suggests you mix some alcohol solution in with the super glues to keep them from drying out. Seal well until needed, and then dump the solution into the windshield washer fluid reservoir of the mark's car.

Another nice additive for windshields was suggested by a bevy of beautiful pranksters, including Allen, Todd, Sally, Kristina and Chuck. The simple cure is to smear a lot of Vaseline on the mark's car windshield. It is a great dust and bug catcher, and otherwise makes clear driving rough.

Here's one we're borrowing from the old house, where this stunt was first used by some friends and me back in the early '50s on a nasty neighbor, before we had ever heard of the word "mark." It's the old dead-animal-in-the-home-heater-vent trick. Why not do the same thing with a mark's car? Put a dead squirrel or rat in the heater duct of the vehicle in winter? I don't know why not, so go do it.

What? Whaddaya mean I have no class or sophistication? I also have friends in Italy, too. Andrea Grosso wrote to tell me that Hayduke is big fun in Italy. He also passed along some stunts he has pulled in his country.

At one time a snobby acquaintance made fun of Andrea for learning English. He hassled him about it a whole lot. Andrea waited until his critic was in a bistro trying to impress some of the local talent to go for a ride in his new car. In the meantime, Andrea was unloading an entire cupful of stinky garlic sauce in that car's heating vent. It was a winter evening in Turin, Andrea added.

Andrea said the mark and his girl came out and got into his car. He started the engine and, in a few seconds, obviously, the heater fan as well. The car door flew open and the young woman exited, screaming curses and insults at the mark while she wiped stinky, saucey shrapnel from her coat.

Another good way to spruce up your mark when he or she is all dressed up with someplace nice to go is to put photo copier dry chemical in the air conditioning vents of the mark's car. This stuff really smears, especially if it gets warm and wet. Several readers suggested this idea.

Mr. Justice says that a cigar is more than a good smoke; it's also a fine way to bugger your mark's car. Take a good-sized, cheap cigar and slit the outer leaves to help the unraveling process. Then simply dump the stogie in the gas tank of the marked car. It may take weeks for the tobacco to shred into small enough bits to flow at least partially into the gas line, with predictable results.

Like herpes, this stunt just keeps giving. Mr. Justice explains that the mark "takes the car in and gets the gas line cleared, but there is obviously more cigar in the tank. Unless the mark gets the tank cleaned, there will be more clogging."

more

Automobiles

Next time you're in a grocery store parking lot and you see your mark's flashy new expensive foreign car, try to visualize this. According to Austin's Mr. D, you can arouse the mark's paranoid ire simply by putting a note like this on his car:

> Dear Sir,
> I'm sorry for the damage I've done to your car. I will gladly help pay for repairs.

Sign the note with a second mark's name and phone number, then retreat to a safe observation point. You should soon see panic break out as the car owner returns to find the note. As he inspects his beloved vehicle, he'll undoubtedly find a few nicks and scratches he never noticed before, and he'll blame your other mark. He may demand restitution. Or if the owner finds no damage, he'll at least be left in a state of bewilderment, and you'll be left with the enjoyment of having pulled off a harmless practical joke.

Mr. D adds, "You can also run this against one mark by picking some really sharp auto at random or choosing a car belonging to some local

Mafia boss, politico, police chief or some other bigwig who will go after your mark."

As a practical joke, a drinking buddy removed and hid the distributor cap from Sweet Rita's car. She paid him back a month or so later when the gang was out drinking. "He had a whole bunch of drinks, was pretty blotto and of course, should not have been driving. But, he insisted. So, while the others delayed him, I did the world a favor and also paid him back, all at once.

"I ran outside and quickly spray-painted the inside of all his windows a flat black with quick-drying paint I had been carrying in my car for just the right occasion. He stumbled out to his car, got in and started it up. He sat there for three minutes, running his windshield wipers. Finally, after five minutes, he stumbled back out of his car screaming about going blind. One of us drove him home."

Doug Hummel of Berlin has a grand idea to immobilize your mark's car. He'd been reading security books, where he spotted a device called "The Immobilizer." It is an antitheft device that causes your car to stall out in about five minutes or so if it is not started properly, like with your key. Surely, says Doug, this same device could be installed on your mark's car, then the fail/safe switch broken.

If some big lug or nasty nut has wronged you, CW has a plan to immobilize him, too. According to CW's formula, loosen some of the lug nuts on the mark's car tires, apply some liquid steel on the bolt, then retighten the lug nuts. That's bad, CW writes, because eventually even a jerk like your mark is going to have to have that tire taken off the vehicle. Hopefully, it will be when he has a flat in a dark, deserted place in the worst weather you can imagine.

If you feel truly destructive, our veteran correspondent Killroy has an idea for using scissor and bumper jacks. He says that lifting the rear differential with a scissor jack will mess up the rear end of the vehicle mightily. A bumper jack can be used to buckle up parts in all sorts of places on today's modern car.

Clear-cast resin, available in most hobby stores, mixed with a catalyst (usually included), then poured on your mark's car, will create a very hard finish that is tough to remove, he adds.

In a different vein, Farmer Bill from Pittsburgh had some problems with government bureaucrats. When they persisted, he placed fresh manure around the fresh air intakes of their government cars. I guess a little fertilizer in deserves a little on the way out, too. It seems a fair exchange to me.

Finally, some gentle soul who declined to sign his or her name to a nice letter provides an amusing idea for the crumb in your life. Take several handsful of cookies or crackers and crumble them into tiny, birdfood-sized tidbits. Scatter them across the mark's unattended car. It's a sharing and exchange situation in which the little birdies eat the crumbs, then drop something in return on the mark's car. This is a good recycling venture, too, and quite efficient as it takes you about a minute to pull it off and about an hour for your mark to clean his vehicular dumping ground. Repeat as necessary.

more

Automobiles

In *Up Yours!*, the author wrote about the Good Samaritan who breaks off toothpicks in car door locks. A fan named Steve offers a refinement of this. He says, "I put a bit of Loctite on both sides of the toothpick before inserting it. I don't push it in the whole way before breaking it off, but I snap it a bit short. Then I use the stub to push it in past the keyhole . . . kind of like countersinking."

A reader signing himself "The Big Con," writes from Cignetti, West Virginia, that he likes to do this same thing, only he applies this technique to the ignition lock.

"That's a real nasty one, something I would do only to someone who really deserved it," Big Con writes.

To pull off this next one, says Doug German, your mark either has to have two cars parked in tandem or have his/her car in a parking lot. Take fifty-pound test or stronger fishing line, wrap one end around the back bumper of the car, and wrap the other to the front gate of the vehicle in front. Wrap several layers of line. Doug reports one mark spent sixty dollars to replace his car's front grate after this stunt.

A simple variation on this same idea would be to attach a two-by-four stud, fulcrum-type arrangement, under the fender, slanted toward the rear of the vehicle. We can thank Bob Marchhairsani, a former university poster child from Philadelphia, Pennsylvania, for that idea.

Morton Downey, Jr., wasn't shy as he told me, "Don't even ask me why I did this to the guy, he was such a jerk. Trust me, this mark deserved it!"

Here's what happened. The mark had bought a new car and was a gas mileage nut. So, each night, Morton would add a few gallons of gasoline to the mark's car, unknown, of course, to the sucker. The mark took the car into the garage for the usual new-car checkup at five hundred miles. He bragged about his fabulous 70-MPG record. The service people looked at him oddly, as this car was rated by the EPA at 35 MPG.

"Then, I dropped the other pedal," Morton related. "I snuck around each night and siphoned out a few gallons, taking a little more each time. He had to get his tank filled more and more often."

By now, irate at the drop in gas efficiency, the mark took his car to the garage six times, screaming how his mileage had dropped through the 40s to the 20s and was now about 15 MPG.

Kilroy is a lot less kind. He starts his stunt with the hood of the mark's car already raised in symbolic surrender. While under the hood of your mark's car, locate the coil and attach a length of greasy bell wire to the negative terminal. Use old, greasy wire so it won't look out of place. Attach the other end of the wire to a ground. Your mark will not be able to start the car, and I don't know of any mechanic who can figure this one out!

Here's another of Kilroy's brilliant ideas. While driving through a parking lot, did you ever encounter someone blocking traffic as he or she waits for a car to pull out close to the store so as to avoid walking those few extra yards? Here's how to deal with them. Go to your local wrecking yard and find a car with an intact windshield-washer system. Purchase it, and install that extra system in your car. Take the washer nozzles that ejaculate water on the windshield and attach them to your car's grille—pointing straight forward. You may need some extra tubing to complete this task. It is available from your local aquarium store. Once the system is installed, fill the reservoir with thinned paint. The next time someone blocks you in the parking lot, you can flip on the switch and give them Kilroy's designer paint job on the rear end of their car.

Awards

A good sharp shot to the ego will double your mark over with embarrassment. You'll need access to a printer if you carry this one all the way. Make up a bogus award and arrange to have the certificate presented to your mark at some public gathering, like a company dinner or party. Make sure the local newspaper gets a copy of the story and has a photographer there. After all of the publicity, you might notify the organization that was supposed to have made the award about the imposter. This works well if your mark actually has some sort of association with the organization in question.

An abridged version of the same stunt cuts out the elaborate presentation and goes directly to the newspaper, i.e., simply give them a new release about the bogus award. If you make this big enough or serious enough, e.g., an honorary Ph.D. degree from some actual university, you could next tip off the newspaper's investigative reporter about this cad who is trying to pull a Janet Cooke on them. Nobody gets more indignant than a newspaper reporter who thinks some ordinary citizen is trying to take a literary dump in the hallowed halls of journalism. They're sensitive because it happens

(Continued...)

all the time. They've even established a name for this brand of hoaxing and paid lying. It's called public relations.

Bakery

At one time, a bakery had dealt unfairly with our hero, so he decided to get a rise from them by costing them some dough. He obtained several dead frogs and froze them. Then, he took them to various stores which carried the mark-bakery's products. Ahhh, but let him describe it.

"I'd pull a loaf of French bread out from its bag, poke in a couple fingers and stuff in one of my frozen frogs, or maybe just half of one. I'd put the other half in another loaf. I carefully smoothed things back over and went on my way. But, then, it's all for entertainment purposes only."

I like this chap.

Banks

A really snooty bank in a college town bought its way onto campus, opening a branch in the student union, by spreading cash both over and under the table. Everyone in the Establishment was happy, drinking well at the trough of greed. Meanwhile, as usual, the students got to stand at the other end of this financial digestive system, i.e., they got shat upon.

The bank soon instituted outrageous service charges for all sorts of routine transactions. They got nasty. They acted like they were, gee, part of the university administration. Some students decided enough was too much.

You have to realize that these students were mutants. They weren't like the collegiate vegetables, Falwell Freaks, Geeks, Greeks and other brain dead Pre-Yuppies who fester our campuses today. These mutant kids cared about honesty and fairness.

They got a lot of friends to go along with it because they promised free beer for each and every deposit/withdrawal slip presented that night. And, here's what they did.

They got a *huge* line of students, armed with $10,

(Continued...)

$20 and $50 bills, to go into the bank and open an account of some type. Then, each student would go back out to the end of the line, move forward, come back in and make a withdrawal. The bookkeeping department was in a shambles, its computers in a burnout frenzy. Bank officers were called in from the country club bar or the golf course. Chaos. Wonderfulness. Reform? That was asking for too much. Instead, they called the police and closed their bank for the rest of the day. But, stay tuned . . .

more

Banks

No lover of the honest life, and an ex-biker, Joey Kiechci says that you can get your mark in trouble by soaking a bank with secondary markdom.

"The deal is to write a note on the back of a deposit slip you know your mark will use. That's not all that tough to do if you think about it. Anyway, the note says, *'This is a stickup. I got a gun in my pocket and I'll blow your brains all over the wall unless you give me all the money,'* or something equally awful. As he innocently hands the marked deposit slip to the teller, he will not hear the silent bells, but he'll see stripes in his new wardrobe."

You and I know he won't really be arrested and will never see prison. But there will be a lot of hassle, threat, loud talk, and enough nastiness to share between the mark and his bank. Or, ex-bank, perhaps.

more

Banks

As Bartle Qinker points out, going through the bank's trash can be a revealing experience, as any garbologist will agree. He found bank employees' time cards, discarded loan applications and correspondence, and best of all, a complete set of microfiche cards with the names, account numbers and current balance of everyone in Alaska who banks with that particular institution.

"I had had a lot of trouble with this bank that was truly not my fault," Qinker writes. "So, I was thrilled to find one prize in the trash, a discarded direct-mail advertisement for a promotional gimmick. I checked some boxes on a pre-addressed card and ordered 250 promotional piggy banks for them."

Barbeques

Filthy McNasty suggests you add to the discomfort of your mark's next outdoor cookery by dumping a handful of powdered sulfur into the fire. If you also mix in ground red pepper, the guests will be reduced to tears as well as having their olfactory senses assaulted.

Barking Dogs

What's that, you say your neighbor's dogs bark? Your grandpa's old remedy used to be to shoot the dog with a BB gun. Here's a better idea. Call the neighbor and tell him/her you just spotted some kids lurking outside. Of course, you have to be sure the dog is just a barker, a mutt who likes to hear its own voice. Now, when the uncaring neighbor goes outside to check, you must lurk nearby with a lightly charged airgun and—you guessed it—nail the cacophonous canine's owner right square on her or his butt.

Bars

A. H. Sylvester, who hails from Incarcerationville, Colorado, is one funny lad. One of A. H.'s funnier brothers once had a beef with some bar owners because they'd fired him for no reason. He decided to fight fire with fire. He had a friend enter the bar with several vials of FFFG Black Powder which he used to load some of the explosive stuff in each of the bar's many ashtrays, mixed in with the butts and ashes. It made quite a fireworks show as folks in the bar unwittingly fused the booby traps with errant cigarettes. You can also bolster this type of action by adding some magnesium powder to the gunpowder.

Bathrooms

Leave it to Carla Savage, the love of my pen life, to attack a person's toilet. As she points out, whenever a building is going up somewhere, there is always at least one of those portable outhouses for the workers. What a grand target! Carla notes that these Job Johnies are always isolated, portable, and made of lightweight fiberglass. They make great receptacles (a.k.a. targets) for fillers, additives, booby traps, animals, additions or just about anything that comes to your imagination. What a way to get back at a construction company, land owner or developer. Hit 'em where they, ahhh, well. . . .

This is so diabolical that I wish I had thought of it. Filthy McNasty wants to get back at an especially awful restaurant, although this gag would work anywhere, especially if the bathroom is somewhat dark. Take a store mannequin, put a noose around its neck and string it up so that some innocent patron or employee will stumble into the room and discover the body.

Once upon a summer, James Q. Carter was hassled by a nasty security guard during some much-needed vacation employment, i.e., the guard didn't like college kids. This plant featured black plastic throne seats in the employee restrooms, so old James Q. got some black roofing tar and coated the potty seat in the guard's room just before this runty rent-a-cop came off duty. As our hero was leaving the plant an hour later, he heard all sorts of horror-rumors about other guards having to use naptha to clean up a hysterical colleague. It seems some folks never do learn how to wipe up behind themselves, while others do quite well. Touche, James.

A chemical engineer to whom I told this story said that Prussian Blue High Spot Indicator is also great for coating your enemy's toilet seat. It is highly "contagious" stuff in that it will spread all over everything the infected mark comes in contact with. Think of the fun at home, with the family, the wash, etc.

Of course, you can also just simply put on a coat of fresh paint the original color of the seat and neglect to post a "Wet Paint" sign.

Want to wash your mark's might right out? Killroy once had a landlord who refused to get the leaky faucets fixed and refused Killroy permission to do his own work. Our hardy trickster stole into the landlord's place, unscrewed the aerator from several of his faucets, packed them with hard clay and put them back in. The man went nuts trying to figure out what had happened to his own water supply.

Beaches

The next time you go to the beach, Filthy McNasty says to take along about two hundred empty bottles and corks. When launched, each corked bottle should contain a neatly printed note that says something like this:

> Scientist studying local ocean (or lake) currents will pay you $10 for the return of this form to him. Please indicate where you found this bottle and what time of day you found it. Your $10 reward will be forthcoming within the week. Just send this form to:
>
> Full Name of Mark
> Mark's Full Address

You can do the same stunt using helium-filled balloons, too. As a final twist, Filthy says to make it look like a promotional gimmick for a sci-fi-movie that's in town. The card will have little space ships printed on it, plus this message:

> UFOs have landed! To hear the voice of a genuine Martian and get free tickets to (whatever), call (123) 555-1212, 24 hours a day.

The number you use, of course, will be that of your mark—hopefully, the home telephone. Getting calls like this at work could create some hassles with co-workers and the bosses.

Filthy also has a grand way of scaring the kapok out of obnoxious surfers and other beach bums who can ruin your surf 'n sun days. It's called "Shark Alert," and here's how Filthy works it: "I use a radio-controlled electric model boat with the top half (cabin and deck) removed. In its place is a large, realistic plastic replica of a shark's dorsal fin. The motor, receiver and battery section are sealed shut and waterproofed. The receiving antenna is folded along the fin and secured with epoxy.

"Wade out beyond the waves and send it on its way. Go back and find a secluded spot. With your transmitter, make it circle around the swimmers and surfers while controlling its movements. Your accomplice in the water will sound the alarm, shouting, 'Shark! Help!' and pointing to the deadly dorsal fin slicing through the water. While splashing and waving frantically, he'll scream, 'Swim for your lives!' "

Filthy then quickly guides the shark to a remote location down the beach to be recovered for use again.

Filthy adds, "With some stage blood and phony wound makeup, plus some accomplices to be 'victims' and 'first aid volunteers,' you can make a real production out of this stunt. You can really stick it to a resort area."

Billboards

Billboards, the most obnoxious form of advertisement because it uglies and clutters our countryside, deserve any and all of the fun we can do to them. William Board, who has a grand name, is a Truth in Advertising spokesman in California who claims to have altered more than 15 billboard ads in 1985 and 17 more in 1986. He says he's never been caught in three years, despite police stakeouts demanded by uptight Establishment heavies.

Board claims many cops are on his side and have helped him by tipping him to troublesome stakeout sites. Most of his alterations are of a political nature involving nuclear energy, U.S. policy in Central America and California's most disgusting export, Ronald Reagan.

His usual MO is to scale the billboard and artistically alter the wording or picture on the board to satirize his mark. His ethical rules demand that he attack only those who attack or victimize others. According to most press accounts, William Board is a bit of a folk hero in that region.

Bird Calls

Here's a nice musical duet for which we can thank Janie McGeary and Len Jenkins. You take a turkey, crow, duck or goose call into a sedate restaurant, church, funeral home, rest home or other highly inappropriate place to which you owe a nasty or two. Start calling from a place of concealment. Call and move out, call and move out. Don't overdo this one on the first mission, though. Come back again and do it again sometime soon.

Bitches

Saucy Sybil had a nice way of putting down a bitch and giving her disposition a well-deserved ride. As Saucy recalled her fun, "We had this particularly awful woman in our office, a real gossip and a mean, nasty bitch. Using a public messenger, I sent her a broom at the office with a note explaining that I wanted to be sure she was never without transportation.

"Everyone in the office knew about it, and she was never a threat to anyone again. She soon left that office, possibly riding the broom she so richly deserved."

Bitchy Calls

Everyone who's ever worked anywhere the public can call to complain has faced the Bitchy Call — you know, taking the red ass for something you didn't do, know nothing about or have any control over, anyway. Marching to the relief of beleaguered timorous telephonics is Joe Prosnick with his solution.

"You answer the telephone and as soon as you establish that it's a certified bitchy call, you start to get snide and abusive. If asked, you identify yourself with the name of an employee who passed away recently."

Joe adds, "I'm a newspaper photographer and we get a lot of crackpots who call to bitch about what we publish. We all use the name of one of our colleagues who died several years ago — then, we abuse the crackpot. The loony calls the editor and relates how rude and awful this Mr. Blank was."

Most editors are used to crank calls and figure the bitchy caller has made it all up, and they deliver another return message. By definition, a bitchy phone call is regarded as one which is unreasonable, shrill, demanding, whiney, insulting, illiterate, or from a politician or a TV preacher.

Blood (Fake)

My thanks to Dr. Foge McCutcheon for this sensational substitute with so many uses. Combine ferric chloride and potassium thiocyanate solutions to produce a bright red liquid that looks just like blood.

Blood (Real)

Wait, don't be squeamish. Good grief, I was twenty-two years old before I knew there were other uses for a hemostat. Read what the Indiana Cave Man has to say about this topic, as I think you'll like the vein his humor runs in.

Get some real animal blood from a slaughterhouse. Freeze a large chunk of it, and keep it packed in dry ice until you're ready to stash it in the mark's desk drawer, filing cabinet, briefcase, locker, safe deposit box, mailbox, etc. It's especially effective if the enclosure is lockable and the mark is absent. When a pool of blood is discovered dripping from a locked container, someone is *sure* to call the police, who will harass the mark for several hours, after which he has a nasty mess to clean up. The boss's rug is an ideal place for a mishap to occur. If you can't transfer a brick of frozen blood into the mark's possession, use a large syringe, enema set, etc., to inject the liquid.

Body Fluids and Semifluids

According to the McGeary Codicil to the Panama Canal Treaty, "Vomitus is not littering." That's all very good for the diplomatic crowd, but it doesn't stand a very tall statute when someone performs bodily functions in your car — a classic tale of many American males of high school age. Nanker Phelge wrote to tell me that he had a good way of really paying back someone who not only barfed in his car, but was so drunk that he also voided his bladder at the same time.

"This brainless creep kept telling me he was OK. I wanted to stop to let him go to the side of the road, but, *noooo,* he was fine," Nanker says. "A minute later he unloads it all in the backseat of my car. Nice. The next day he was blaming me for the whole thing, muttering about how my driving made him sick. He was feeding us a line, so I decided to feed him back.

"I have this formula for 'Golden Shower Gravy' which makes a fine substitute for regular, therapeutic chicken soup. Start with some dehydrated chicken soup mix, then add pee to fill and flavor. Bring to a hard boil, thicken with a small amount of flour, stir for one minute, cool slightly, then serve to your mark."

(Continued...)

Nanker did this the following day in the mark's own home . . . then, told him about it fifteen minutes after the guy had scarfed down the soup.

"At least this time he decorated his own place," Nanker closed.

Bolts

Want to help your mark by stripping some of the vital bolts on his equipment, home or other property? Kilroy suggests you use a sixteen-point box end wrench two sizes larger than the bolt; torque it down very tight.

Bombs

Even unreal bombs are fun, especially if you are a master of disguise. You can buy empty cases for practice bombs at most military surplus stores and fill them with materials that look like explosives. Many high explosives look like brown wax or plastic wood fillers. Other experts have said that brown sugar looks like an explosive, too.

Buy an empty practice bomb case and fill it with bogus explosive. You'll have to paint the outer case for realism, too. Most practice units are blue, so you need to paint yours flat black, with an inch-and-a-half yellow band about six inches from the end.

Partly bury it nose-down in the ground of your mark's lawn, or lean it against the door of his or her office. You can also hide it so that it will surely be found—in the broom closet or basement of the home or office.

Caution: Leave no fingerprints or other trackable clues, as police and military bomb-disposal people have little sense of humor about this sort of trick. A very understandable emotion, I'd agree.

Books

I bet someone in CW's family knew a frustrated librarian. Or perhaps, some jerk borrowed a book from him and never returned it. Anyway, here is a unique payback, courtesy of CW. Next time you're at the home of your mark (a.k.a. your book borrower), take along some glue and slip into his/her library. Glue some selected pages together in various volumes of the mark's books. Also, get your own books and secrete them outside.

Boomboxes

This teenage punk, wearing the livery and hairstyle of his ilk, sauntered along West Fourth Street carrying a monster box, the volume of its rock music matching the level of a Concorde on takeoff. He gazed at Walter Zapper, walking in the opposite direction.

"If you don't like it, Square, what you gonna do about it?" The punk felt secure. He was mistaken.

Walter had his right hand inside his raincoat pocket. In the palm of his hand was a black object about the size of a pack of cigarettes. Walter pressed the thumb switch. The noise from the box stopped abruptly. What came out of the box now was not rock music, but a wisp of smoke. The rat didn't know his radio had been zapped by a radio beam from Zapper's raincoat pocket. All he knew was that the wiring and insulation were burning.

No, it's not a joke or a made-up dream. An MIT electronics engineer, Walter Zapper is quite real and his hobby is using his talents wisely and well to take away, electronically, as many of life's annoyances as possible. Walter is somewhat of a legend to a few folks in New York City, where he also has a device which trashes

(Continued...)

automobile horns, one for manipulating the ON/OFF DUTY signs of taxi cabs, and yet another for controlling the electric windows of automobiles.

Born Agains

The Rev. Martin Newcumer Holmes, a lay minister in the order of St. Mattress, has published a list of different ways to harass Born Agains who are bothering you. His list appeared in *Overthrow* magazine, an excellent publication. The list:

1. Shout "Bring back the Roman lions" at them.
2. Have a mass Bible-burning at one of their street meetings.
3. Request that the church grant space for a mass divine bisexual penetration, i.e., orgy.
4. Make a citizen's arrest of any Born-Again preacher you find, charging him with promoting obscenity.
5. Tell them loudly that you're a born-again pervert.
6. Tell them you're a gay activist and you would like to teach Sunday School to lead their kids in the right direction.
7. Spray-paint a lavender hammer and sickle on the church doors.
8. Telephone the preacher at 4 A.M., stating the Communists are "out to get" you.
9. Have a mass nude baptism in the name of born-again perversion.

10. Disrupt a church service by exclaiming that the Bible is a bunch of racist and sexist fairy tales.
11. Ask them if God has a penis or a vagina.
12. Pass out tracts stating that Jesus can be seen via the use of LSD, peyote, or mushrooms.
13. Tell them you have X-ray vision which allows you to see through their clothes.
14. Squirt them with a solution of DMSO and LSD.
15. Stamp their right hand or forehead with the numbers, "666."
16. Start your own O.R.G.A.S.M. chapter (Organization of Religious Groups Against Sexual Materials). Pass out explicitly written antiporn literature written in the style of a sleazy skin book.
17. Call in on any religious audience participation programs on radio or TV and give every detail of your depraved life before being Born Again.
18. Organize a Jump for Jesus rally with the local parachute club.

Bovine Effluvia

I was going to use *Bullshit* for this category, when my editor gently reminded me that we now live in religiously conservative times and that the pious pulpit-pullers would probably flock to the bookshops and torch my tomes if I used anything but God-Squad approved language. Thus . . .

I learned about this product from Tom, a friend in the newspaper business who quickly produces it for defensive use when cornered by what passes as the sports editor at his newspaper. You must understand that the target of my friend's spray is the most obnoxious person in the universe — trust me, I've met him.

This six-ounce spray can has a delightful label clearly stating *Bullshit Repellent* and you can use it to disperse even the most stubborn and prolific verbal excrement, e.g., witness my friend's use of it to vanish the idiot editor.

Seriously, though, some enterprising chaps have been reading my books. I'm happy to report that more and more honest American business folks are selling ideas founded upon my philosophy, and, ahem, ideas. I love it. The latest is a *Crap-o-gram,* which is just about

(Continued...)

as it sounds. These folks will send your vexing pain in the ass of a mark a nasty, insulting message along with a gift-wrapped box of fake cow manure.

Bumper Stickers

I travel a lot and see many bumper stickers. I also have had samples sent to me by readers and friends. Some of them aren't very pleasant, although I found most of them to be funny. Some were so obnoxious that my editor refused to allow them in my last book. "They offend people," I was told. Hey, I thought that was my point. Oh well . . .

Here are a few that may be less offensive, but no less visible, on the back deck of someone's vehicle. To avoid offending the pressure-sensitive, I will try it this time with your imagination's cooperation. We'll play complete the sentence. I furnish the first part of the bumper sticker and you use your own mind, creativity or nastiness to complete the statement. Here we go...

MICROWAVE THE ____________!
I'D RATHER BE KILLING ____________!
JESUS WAS ____________!
I ____________ MY ____________!
I MURDERED MY ____________!
PISS ON ____________!

That's the ticket then — now you can make up your own.

Bureaucrats

Tor and Snow Dog are back again with some good, clean fun for entertainment purposes only. Have a bureaucrat who's screwed you? Does a dog have fleas?

This trick will take a little work, but it is worth it. You can't get a bureaucrat fired, but you sure can make her or his life difficult. Do some research and find out what law, bill or whatever provides the funding for the offending agency. The next time these chronic do-nothings turn a deaf ear to you, inform them in your most official manner that they might be interested in knowing that you have been circulating a petition to repeal the law that provides their funding. If you can sound convincing, and you have done your homework, this really gets results. It's been tried with great success on agencies such as the Southern California Rapid Transit District. Of course, actually drawing up and circulating the petition can't hurt, either.

Another way to get to a bureaucrat is to file complaints against him. But file your complaints with other, related agencies. A dim-witted mail carrier, for example, might be reported to the Department of the Treasury for losing federal checks. Since the government keeps records of everything, this will be reported and might make things interesting if the victim tries for a promotion or transfer. Such complaints are also usually most effective if sent directly to the head of the particular agency.

Tor and Snow Dog also suggest putting your offending bureaucrat on the mailing lists of groups advocating the violent overthrow of the U.S. government. With the sociopathic paranoia of the Reaganistas, this is guaranteed to get success. They write, "You might give money in your bureaumark's name to one of these causes. Or at the appropriate religious or other national holiday, give his or her boss an inspirationally inscribed copy of something like *The Anarchist's Cookbook.*"

Finally, our cuddly California couple wants to know, have you ever asked to talk to someone with authority, only to be told that he is not in? The next time someone feeds you a line like that, casually ask who would be in charge in the event of a "disaster." If you get some lame answer instead of a name, why not "arrange" a disaster to see who or what crawls out of the woodwork?

The disasters can range from setting off the in-house fire alarm to placing an ad stating that tickets for a "secret" event (Rolling Stones concert, Frank Sinatra farewell appearance, give-aways of appliances) will be available at the location. Just happen to be around when the fertilizer hits the ventilator, and then go after the person who takes charge—mercilessly and unrelentingly. That's your head bureaumark.

One of the deadliest weapons in the bureaucrat's arsenal is the memo. I get copies of a lot of memoranda, but this one caught my attention because of its put-on potential. Just add a bit of devilish imagination, catch my drift, eh? Think forgery. Think imagined scandal. Think drugs. Think after-hours porno production parties. Think it, then memo it with copies to all, being sure to sign your favorite mark's name to the invention.

Burials

The Philly Phantom has a great idea for deadhead marks, the type of jerk, if the world were a bottle of mouthwash, your mark would be a case of halitosis. Apparently, the Philly Phantom knows people like that. He writes, "When much else failed to get a reaction from this jerk, I finally called four different burial plot companies and set up interviews for my mark at his home. I later did this for a burial vault sales company, too. Maybe, he got the idea someone was after him?" Actually, in Philadelphia, that's a fairly good assumption, right, Mr. Bruno?

Buried Treasure

Jim Murray of Columbia, South Carolina, relayed a funny idea on a WIS radio talk show. Bury a few trinkets of lookalike gold on the mark's property, and then create the publicity that *real* valuable stuff has been found there. If the mark has a farm or large, open land, so much the better. However, I can see this one also being used for a city tenement building. Think about this a little bit.

You can also use buried treasure to terrorize other people. If you're in a treasure-hunting area, such as a beach or fairgrounds in which people armed with metal detectors prowl after busy weekends, add some excitement to their lives.

Bury a small unlocked box in a shallow hole and tamp it down well. You might even tamp some sod on it if necessary. The treasure hunter finds the treasure and eagerly digs it up. The payoff is now up to you. Here are some suggestions from Lucy Chamber, the lady who suggested all this nastiness in the first place:

1. The small box is festooned with official-looking United States Government Radiation Warning stickers.
2. The small box contains an especially disgusting piece of roadkill.

3. **If you can specify which individual mark will open the small box, you could stuff a recently dead house pet belonging to that mark into the box.**
4. **If the treasure hunters are little kids, you could fill the small box with porno pictures the rug rats can take back to mommy.**

CB Wars

Moronic barbarians that they are, CBers tend to fight among themselves. There are many documented cases of heavy violence resulting from arguments over stepping on messages, use of a particular channel, or because a CBer caught up with someone who had bad-mouthed him on the air or jammed his transmissions. If you know the internal details of a CB war and have a CB of your own, there are things you can do to escalate the conflict:

1. Jam selectively so that the jamee blames some other mark.
2. Tape-record and rebroadcast "select" transmissions or create new ones.
3. Build a short-range jammer from a cheap toy CB walkie-talkie. Hide it near the mark's house, where it will jam "his" channel. Use a large battery so it will run for a long time. Remove all fingerprints. Enclose a nasty note to the mark, in case he finds the jammer. Sign some other mark's name.

Ca Ca

If you're having neighbor problems, Mr. D from Austin says to take note of the times they leave their homes or cars unoccupied and unguarded. When you need to use a restroom and one of the neighbors is out of pocket, play "Santa Claus" by using his chimney as a toilet. Or leave "orphans" at his front door. Or perform the ultimate humiliation by taking a dump on the neighbor's car and sliding up and down the windshield to wipe.

Calcium Carbide

We had an old uncle back East who used to be a deep miner in West Virginia. In the old days, mines were lighted by carbide lamps, and many hardware stores in mine country across this nation still sell carbide, along with helmets that have carbide lamps built right into the hat. It is also used by nocturnal hunters and campers.

Calcium carbide is available where camping supplies are sold. It looks like crushed rock. It produces large volumes of acetylene gas when it comes into contact with water. The acetylene contains hydrogen sulfide and other impurities, and it has a nauseating smell. Here are some uses:

1. Distribute carbide in the mark's locale. It reacts slowly with atmospheric moisture and produces a long-lasting, low-level stench.
2. Add carbide to the mark's potted plants. It will really take off next time the plants are watered, and it will probably kill the plants as well.
3. Carefully dry the bowl of a water fountain or sink, or the floor of a shower stall; add carbide. Watch the fun when the mark turns on the water. Caution: acetylene gas is explosive in a wide range of mixtures in the air. A plastic trash bag filled

with acetylene and oxygen from a welding set sounds like a stick of dynamite when ignited. Use a long fuse.

Camp Counselors

After the last two books, I heard from all sorts of camp counselors who wanted ideas on how to get back at the obnoxious little peckerheads who infest summer camps because their parents wanted the time free from these past sexual mistakes. Actually, Jason Vorhees was first in line with ways to get back, but, he's found his own groove, so we turn to Captain Video, who, in addition to his experiences in minor league baseball, is also a camp counselor.

"It's an old trick, but fun. If you have a truly rotten kid who won't adjust to the regular drill and rule, some night fill his hand with shaving cream, then tickle his nose. If that doesn't work to settle him, check out his shampoo.

"If it is white or cream-colored, replace it with condensed milk or Elmer's glue thinned with solvent, or use Nair. If it is orange-colored, you can use cooking oils and jam," says Capt. Video.

Capt. Video says that you should not get caught or even put under suspicion for revenging the kids. "Remember, camping isn't fun, it's a business for someone and you don't want to piss off the director and get

(Continued...)

fired. Always try to get your pranks blamed on the second worst kid in the outfit."

Candy

Here's another horrible idea from our Aussie friend, Tug Wanker. He says to add some internal twists to the *Up Yours!* suggestion of turning human fecal matter into candy, using dog droppings instead.

"If you have a mark who has abused an animal, this is very fitting revenge. You help the animal because it can't help itself," Wanker says.

"Get some dog crap and let it dry. Put on rubber gloves and cut the stuff into small squares. Melt some milk chocolate and pour it over the feces. Once dry, wrap the pieces in foil and place in an empty candy box. In addition to the immediate effect, the 'candy' is likely to give the mark a case of internal parasites. Ask any veterinarian about this."

I did ask, and I got some of the strangest looks you can imagine, along with "You can't be serious. Do you realize how sick that could make someone?"

It all sounds like good news to me.

Car Dealers

Mot Rot has an excellent idea to help prospective buyers decide whether to buy from your mark—the salesperson.

"A water pistol full of motor oil and black coloring that's squirted through the front grille of a showroom vehicle in question gives the buyer a lot to think about when he peeks under the hood," Mot reports.

Car Pounds

I bet nearly all of you have had or will have your car towed away. It isn't one of life's fun experiences. It's where you learn fast about the tough, real world of uncaring greed. But, there's a brighter outlook, thanks to Kilroy.

"Want to get even with the car pound? Want to get a free paint job?" he asks.

Here's his scam. Park your car in a towaway zone. It is soon towed. It's vital that your car was never towed there before or the authorities will grow suspicious at what's about to happen.

Late that night, using one of those old-fashioned, pump-type fire extinguishers or a garden sprayer filled with paint, shower all the cars in the pound with odd and grossly colored paint. You can travel the outside perimeter of the fence, spraying the paint up, over, and around.

If the yard has a guard dog, feed it drugged meat, then spray it, too. Even if they put up a legal bluff, the yard is really responsible for your car and all of the others while they are impounded. That is why these yards are bonded. They will have no choice but to fix your car to your liking.

"I have personally done this one," Kilroy notes. "It is one of the most profitable and rewarding acts of vengeful vandalism I have ever experienced. I've always gotten what I asked for."

Cassette Tapes

According to many of my music phreak phans, mass-produced music cassettes are getting worse in terms of quality disregard, i.e., more and more turn up defective. How to get even? Macho from New York City talked with a store manager who refused him a refund or even a credit for a truly defective tape he returned. It went like this:

MACHO: This tape's defective.

MGR: It's open. How do I know you didn't just copy it and are now returning it — to cheat me?

MACHO: Simple, play the tape for yourself. See, it's defective.

MGR: No credit. Take your tape and leave.

Macho did. But, he later came back with a hand-held portable magnet and proceeded to "help the manager by making certain nobody would ever victimize this manager's tapes by copying them."

According to Macho, a friend who worked in a nearby store told him that the manager had been having some bad scenes with punks and other badasses who obviously had brought defective tapes, too, as in *nothing* was on these new tapes . . . no music, nothing.

Castration

Don't only threaten to de-ball a mark, show him "proof" of past surgical escapades! Send him a brief, untraceable note explaining in detail how you castrated another jerk who messed with your life. Enclose two dried prunes or slightly made-up or disguised apricots in the letter. You might stain the end with some actual blood and let dry a few days before mail delivery to your mark.

Ms. Lisa was bullied at a party, followed home and bothered further by a wanna-be romeo with all the suavity of a puke-ridden leisure suit. After three civilized attempts to get him to leave, she told him she was calling the police. He said he would hurt her body, badly. Since she knew his name and address, she locked herself in her room and did call the police. One week later, she had her good friend from an old line Corsican family complete the stunt mentioned in the previous paragraph. I think this mark is now selling trusses to penguins at the South Pole.

In another instance, a lady told me about a friend who had narrowly missed a nasty rape by some drunken "students/athletes" from the local state university, well known as a football factory. In turn, one of her friends

(Continued...)

knew how to get back at the potential rapists, chemically.

She told me, "There is a very nasty chemical which is available legally which will turn a rapist into a eunuch very quickly with regular dosage. It does what our courts won't do — chemically castrate the rapist."

Cement

Mr. Science came up with a good one from the halls of Ace McCutcheon High School. He says that an ounce of regular table sugar placed in 100 pounds of concrete cuts its bonding strength significantly.

Ace adds, "I read this in a consumer alert bulletin that the CIA was mailing to peasants in Nicaragua who might have this problem due to the Contra influx into their lives."

According to Ace and Mr. Science, the concrete mix's calcium combines with the sugar instead of carbon dioxide and you get calcium saccharate, which is soluble.

I've always wondered about that, but they say it really works.

more

Cement

If you have, can get, or can buy access to a load of wet, ready-mix cement bound for the mark's construction site, you can add fluorescein, road-kill, feces, or butyric acid, as appropriate. Better yet, add some large bones, human if possible, to the concrete, and be sure no-nonsense authorities are notified just after the load arrives and is poured.

Charcoal Grill

The Tennessean has a bang-up idea for your mark's next cookout party. He says to take an ordinary twelve-gauge shotgun shell and cut it apart at the wadding. This way you'll get rid of all the BBs. Use good-quality electrical tape to wrap around and around the shell husk. Mix Elmer's glue with charcoal dust and keep recoating the taped-over shell until you get something that looks amazingly like a charcoal briquet. Put it back in your mark's charcoal bucket or bag. You could also put several of these little time bombs in there. There's nothing like starting that next cookout with a *bang*, eh?

Charity

I thought it would be nice to add something positive in this case. Could we volunteer the mark for all sorts of religious and other charity work? Let's pretend to be his or her secretary calling to volunteer the *biggie* for some community service. Or, using official letterhead, let's do the same thing. Try to make the service as common, little guy and/or demeaning as possible. Try to tie up his or her weekends. Usually, the majority of "marked" upperfolks will just do their day in the barrel rather than raise too much fuss. On the other hand, if they bitch too much, it hurts their reputation even more. Heads you lose, tails I win.

Chemicals

Rooftop warfare comes easily in NYC and can lead to fun, as Chuck Slender tells me. From the twenty-third floor of a midtown building, he did just that, filling a large bottle with hydrochloric acid which he'd purchased in a pool supply shop. He then dropped in a few chunks of aluminum and capped the bottle tightly.

The combination of the two forms a very dark gas cloud that smells as bad as it looks. Chuck had a shill on the street below near the movie theater to which they owed a chemical revenge for the nasty it had done to him and his friends. When the crowd outside the theater was long and impatient, it was "bombs away."

Chuck says, "We let that sucker fall into the street right near the crowd. This huge, dark cloud formed out of the explosion and began to drift toward the crowd. My man on the street shouted *'Poison gas!'* and told the people to run for their lives."

The police and fire people were there in minutes, and closed the theater and several streets in the area for a two-hour period. Chuck and his friends, meanwhile, had gone elsewhere.

Thanks to Macho, our guerrilla advisor from NYC,

(Continued...)

we now have a single source for a whole lot of disgusting chemicals with which you can do terrible things to your mark. Here is his shopping list:

1. *Rotten Eggs Scent.* This bargain carries the strong aroma of sulphur.
2. *Skunk Repellent.* Safely keeps skunks out of your yard.
3. *Dog/Cat Repellent.* Safely keeps dogs/cats from making messes in your yard.
4. *Skunk Scent.* Actual skunk essence. Its horrible, pungent odor is sure to linger on and on.
5. *"P" Scent.* Fermented fox urine. Smells musky and is stomach-turning.
6. *Fart Spray.* Absolutely the most disgusting odor imaginable. In an aerosol spray can, a one to two second burst will "perfume" a room thoroughly. Experiment *outdoors.*

According to Macho, all of these are available from On The Nose.

There are other uses for chemicals which don't seem quite as nasty. For example, photocopying does more than just make its mark on the American literary scene, creating copyright bandits of us all. Thanks to my faithful researcher from Canada, Dr. Deviant, a new and positive use has come from these delightful machines.

He reports, "I worked in a reprographics department, where the copy machines are, and learned from personal experience that the dry toner used in most of the machines is really a pain to work with. If you get it on your skin, you must rinse it away with cold water immediately; if you use warm water, it bonds to your skin like it does to paper."

Oh, my, that info got Dr. Deviant's mind rolling. He suggested all sorts of uses for the chemical, which is easily available from office supply shops. It might be the second generation chemical of choice to mix in with powdered soap at a least favorite restaurant or plant washroom. Could it be molded into a bar of "homemade soap" now that homemade soap kits are cheaply available? Could it be mixed with bathwater perfumes and softeners? Could it replace the dye-in-the-showerhead from an earlier volume? Or, your turn now . . .

Chickens

After reading Ted Shumaker's contribution, I'm not sure I will ever order Chicken a la King again. A fisherman, Ted takes along a glass jar that's full of chicken intestines to use as bait. He once tightly sealed an extra jar, stuck it in his car trunk and forgot about it. The chicken intestines fermented and exploded, sending a mixture of chicken guts-'n-glass shrapnel all through his trunk.

"I had that car three years and never did get the awful smell out of the trunk," Ted says. "No spray invented, no cleaner—commercial or otherwise—worked. No freshener hid the odor. It was awful."

As a youngster I cleaned my share of chickens and I can vouch for what they smell like fresh. I can only imagine the fowl odor described by Ted. Perhaps, Chicken Tartare would be on order? Forget it, it was a joke.

Churches

Not too long ago, I did a radio talk show in Orlando, Florida. A lady who said she wanted to be known as Fragrance called in to talk about the Catholic Church. She was an older lady, the type you always thought of as straight and no-nonsense. Delightfully, I was very wrong. She was wonderful.

"A long, long time ago, my sister and I put a strong ink in the Holy Water, and because the church was very dark then with little lighting, a lot of people ended up with the ink-spot look."

There was no suggestion for this, it's just neat that a truly senior citizen has the same sense of humor to share all these years later.

Cigarettes

Jim Fisher runs a very cool radio talk show out of WOC in Davenport, Iowa. That reminds me of a great idea from Donald Murphy of that city.

"This guy bums smokes all the time . . . disgusting, cheap jerk. I took some filtered Kools and buried a matchhead in the middle of a Kool for the next time he bummed one from me.

"That mixture of sulphur and menthol didn't really flame, but it ruined his taste buds for a couple days," says Donald.

Classified Advertising

I read my newspapers most thoroughly and found these two classified ads running a few times. I wonder if they are straight? If not, I am sure each crafty reader can immediately create a great scam from each.

1. Tired of finding time to do your grocery shopping? Let me do it for you. I will shop, find all the bargains, then deliver to you. Phone ____________.
2. I would like to talk seriously with anyone who was foolish enough to buy contact lenses from ____________. If you were taken, too, call ____________.

If you're feeling smug by now, let me introduce Panama's own R. P. Ork, who knows which classified buttons to push, sending his mark down the slide to confusion and unhappiness. Ork says, "I find that for guys, the two greatest things to advertise are guns and cars, especially if you sell mint classics of each at a fair, or less, price.

"Everyone reading the ad is looking for a bargain or better. So, give better to him. And, stick it to your mark, too. It's easy," says Ork.

Here's Ork's order of battle for this one. Select a weekend you know your mark will be at home and, hopefully, be entertaining guests or be otherwise busy. Then, place your ad in a newspaper or have it read on the radio for him.

"Let's advertise an S & W .44 mag, with 8¾ inch barrel, new-in-box, for just $300. Say it's a sacrifice to make a mortgage payment," advises Ork.

"Or, advertise a collector's model Ford T-Bird, 1957, better-than-mint, for only $7,000 because of a divorce settlement due now."

According to Ork, the stinger here is that you advertise on the weekend when the mark can't readily stop the ad; you don't include a telephone number, just an address, and you ask people to come at an hour you know will be upsetting to your mark. Also, your mark will have to argue with the newspaper or radio station about not paying for the advertising for which he's being billed.

Clothes Dryers

There's an even neater topping than pizza for your mark's dryer. Some hilarious reader with great measurements, signing the letter 177-38-1380, sent me the idea of spreading a half pound of Limburger between the barrel and the housing of the dryer unit. He says you can also toss in a dead squirrel for good measure.

Coin Boxes

Filthy McNasty wants to crowd coin boxes. When you board the bus, buy a paper or use a pay machine of any sort, make certain to bend the edges of your coins somewhat before insertion. The resultant grind of your crimped coins will make the machine's action sound like a couple of Ginger Baker rimshots and eventually jam the works. You can add some super glue if you like, much as a gourmet adds dressing to a salad.

Coin-Operated Machines

Tired of being ripped off by her local car wash whose machine ate her quarters but refused to give her fair service, Little D grumbled to the absentee owner by letter, which was ignored. She found out the guy also owned a local Laundromat and that those machines were also ripping off people.

All of the coin-operated equipment had coin trays where you deposit your quarter in the round depression, then slide the handle in to deposit the coin and supposedly activate the process. Note that each tray has a hole in the coin tray to permit you to poke your finger up to retrieve your coin if you change your mind before the money goes into the machine.

Buy or borrow a number of small, cheap padlocks and lock one through the hole and edge of each coin tray on each machine in any place that is ripping off people, says Little D. It closes down the operation immediately, causing the mark lost revenue and even more irritated customers.

Dick Smegma has another solution. He suggests super-gluing slugs or actual coins into these coin trays, which also voids the operation.

College Bookstores

No kidding, I went through college, although it was 77 years ago. I remember that one of our biggest rip-offs then was buying new books from the campus bookstore, then, "selling" them back again at the end of the term for a pittance of the original price. It seemed a rip-off then, and, according to the students from whom I get calls and letters now, it is still the same old thievery. Here's my solution.

Pretend you're the instructor for a particular course. Call in, and then follow up with a memo on purloined or recreated memohead. Make it seem that "you" want to order a new book for the next semester. The store will do this, and the real prof will have no idea about any of this until the next semester. Your used book from the semester before will be very, very valuable to the students now taking the course. Your thanks for this idea go "Two Radio Guys From Denver."

Communist Propaganda

Listen to Radio Moscow/Havana/Peking on a shortwave radio. Write down their mailing addresses and send them letters of great praise from the mark requesting QSL cards, program schedules, and other literature. They read these types of letters from listeners over the air, so send "good ones" from the mark, making him sound like an active supporter.

The mark will receive a big load of propaganda and will also get his name recorded in the computers of the CIA, FBI and other interested institutions filed under possible Commies, subversives, and other bad stuff. This is useful against politicians, those in the military, bigots, Moral-Majority types, and marks who have security clearances.

Computers

A group signing themselves "Seniors Who Can't Spell" evidently know their computers well. They suggest that the addition of a small strip of magnetic tape to the little door that the disc goes into will screw the computer into a frenzy of nonfunctionability. Use black tape, they add.

They also report that the Radio Shack TRSDOS word-processing program Scripsit has a fun loophole. If you overload the memory with unnecessary material, it creates unprintable documents. This program keeps all blocks of words using the "Move" command in memory but does not record them in the usual place. An expert will have to come in to repair this mischief.

Tyra Pierce has been covering the collegiate scene for me and reports some fun things to be done with student versions of plastic lifelines to the computer commander—ID cards. If your school uses nonphoto ID cards with magnetic strips and is in any way lax with security, you have it made. Simply get your mark's student ID number, almost always a Social Security number, and pretend you are him or her. Go to the correct office, cry and moan about someone stealing "your" wallet with "your" ID card in it, pay your five dollars and get a new card out and activated—all in the mark's name. At the same time, this process automatically destroys all verification of the old card—still securely in the possession of the unsuspecting mark. You can now do the whole bit on this person. You are that person in the computer's memory. And, best of all, as far as the computer is concerned, the mark, as represented by that old card, has ceased to exist.

In the same sense, this type of scam will work on the cards used in bank machines or department store credit departments. But as bank and store credit security is tight, you had better work on the card itself. Why not try to get hold of the mark's card long enough to use a bulk eraser to "clean" the magnetic strip, then return the card—all without the mark's knowledge. Hassle will be the order of the day when the mark tries to use this essentially blank piece of plastic.

more

Computers

Some lonely people are so happy to get phone calls that they might be two minutes into the thing before they realize all the one-sided monolog is from a machine, a computer-generated call, usually from a business. When these machines are programmed to make a pitch and provide you the opportunity to respond to a recorder, Arizona Mary has a fun way to give them the business. She pretends she is a computer, too.

"It took a bit of study and practice, but I can now talk just like an electronic, machine-generated voice. I talk to the machine in machine-talk — varying my message, depending upon what it said to me. It's fun and can sometimes mess up the human who will have to listen to the other end of my lines."

A neighbor of Mary's is not so kindly. A hacker by serious hobby, he has a lock 'n trace device on his equipment that runs down the location and number calling him as a computer-generated "junk mail" call. If this becomes enough of a nuisance and he wishes to play get-even, he puts his own computer on the call-generation mode and ties it to the company's regular business line.

"This way, I can tie up their normal business line or

(Continued...)

their 800 number for sales orders if it's long distance. It's a fun payback," according to Herr Hacker.

more

Computers

Jimmy Carter, no, not that one, is a fine duster, suggesting if you have a grudge against a computer-using operator that you sprinkle a bit of fine sand on the hard discs they use for data storage and retrieval. At best, the disc will shatter, and at high speeds, those little pieces will scatter all through the unit.

Are you savoring the down time already?

Condoms

I was going to slip this on as a stunt under the automobile section, but I figured condom would attract more attention. Now that I have yours—attention, that is—here's the deal. This one came in from The Tennessean out there in Savannah. Unroll a fresh condom and place it inside the gas tank of the mark's car, pushing it down in with a wire. The Tennessean says the rubber will float around in there until it gets sucked up into the gas line, in which case it won't get too far, causing the engine to die. Sometimes, the condom floats free and the car starts again and runs. Sometimes, it doesn't. Either way, it's fun for you; hell for the mark.

When it comes to releasing a flood of feeling about friends and marks, Florida's E. G. doesn't fool around. He fills a strong, brand-name quality condom with a gallon or so of iced water and then gently lays it down next to his mark who may be sleeping or in a drunken stupor. The next loud step is to have the alarm go off or the telephone ring on that appropriate (other) side of the mark.

Condoms

New uses for the ubiquitous condom continue to pour in from tricksters who use rubbers for more than putting that macho circular indentation in their wallets. Our prolific Mr. Heffer from Missouri recalls some uses from his college days of bunk beds and not-so-considerate dorm colleagues.

"You know the bastards who party all night, then come in sloppy drunk, make noise, fart, vomit, all that?" It was a rhetorical question. "Here's my strike-back. Fill a large condom with about two gallons of cold water — yes, it will all fit. Elevate your mark's bed slightly at the bottom. Place the condom under the covers at the foot of the bed.

"The drunken mark slides in, breaks the condom and is flooded to the crotch with cold water. Hopefully, he will piss the bed at this point, too."

Mr. Heffer's alternative idea works with bunk beds. He ways, "This time carefully — and, I stress carefully — place the water-filled rubber between the mattress and springs of the top bunk. The light needs to be out, of course, and you need to be sure your mark is in the lower bunk. It would help, too, if the mark's top-

(Continued...)

bunk roomie gets to bed after the mark. Great idea, huh?"

more

Condoms

I wonder if anyone ever uses condoms for their historically primary function anymore? In any case, Alan from the North has a grand stomach-turner for us. Simply slip a condom over your mark's doorknob and coat it generously with a copious supply of Vaseline. Hopefully, you will do this so the mark discovers your trap at night or when the lights are out—an added touch you could take care of.

If you think I'm an evil degenerate, I thank you for your kind thoughts. But you ought to meet the Gripper. A graduate of the Hole-in-the-Rubber Academy of Everyone's Junior High School, he mixes super glue with alcohol, so the solution stays liquid until heat is applied. A small amount of this solution applied to a "lubricated" condom is a devastating experience. One smart lady loaded one up, so to speak, for a nasty guy who had done her wrong. It was their last act together, as he spent the next few days in the hospital. I like the Gripper and hope to hear from him again.

Contests

It's easy to either hold a contest or to enter a mark or someone in the mark's family in the contest. It's also a grand way to gain public ridicule for your mark. According to the renowned psychologist, Solly Barkloudly, people who are overweight, ugly, stupid, or all three, really are upset by this, despite what they may proclaim, or what you may read in the cheerleader press. You can use this to your advantage.

If your mark has a daughter who looks like a beach ball with arms, enter her in the Goodyear Blimp Lookalike Contest and inform the mark you have done so. If you have lazy or stupid people at the desks of your local newspaper or radio station, take advantage. Name the mark or someone in the mark's family as the "winner" of some award in a dubious, insulting contest. When in doubt, remember Les Nessman of the TV show *WKRP in Cincinnati?* Very realistic show — I worked at a radio station just like it for a year.

Contra Aid

To ease the hygiene problem facing El Presidente's favorite freedom fighters in their invasion of Nicaragua, Phyllis Schafly's Eagle Forum organization has donated "personal cleanliness kits" for distribution to our Contra surrogates who run their cross-border terrorist attacks from Costa Rica and Honduras. In each kit are breath mints, toilet paper, a Spanish-language Bible and "inspirational literature" featuring messages from El Presidente and Mrs. Schafly. No, I am *not* kidding you; it's all true.

Here is where Pablo Digno de Heno comes into this big picture. Not only does Pablo disagree with the Reaganista aggression against Nicaragua, he is also interested in doing what he can to defeat it. That is why Pablo's group has put together units of a subkit which he has infiltrated into Mrs. Schafly's parcels. Included in Pablo's subkits are:

- Small packets of marijuana imprinted with the Presidential seal and the logo, Reaganista Gold
- Two packets of condoms with instructions in Spanish saying "For prevention of future Contras left behind during pillage." The packets are signed with the

(Continued...)

legend, "For a good time when in the U.S.A., call Phyllis Schlafly," which is followed by the Eagle Forum telephone number.

- A packet of wallet-sized color photos of Somoza with instructions for passing them out to villagers in Nicaragua.
- A document awarding the bearer an officer's commission in the Somoza National Guard.
- Conterfeit Nicaraguan cordobas (money) with Ronald Reagan's picture on each bill.

Pablo estimates that several hundred of his kits got through, disguised with the real units, and found their way into Contra hands.

Who is Pablo Digno de Heno? He's a U.S. Navy vet. A pacifist? Not on your life! This man's a serious collector of serious right-wing causes. But, he just doesn't like to see stupidity repeat itself.

Controversy Clearing House

Thanks and a tip of the Hayduke homburg to Vonnie Bruce for this grand idea to clutter a mark's mail and telephone with controversial communication. She based it upon a woman with whom she once shared an apartment. The woman in question was a legend in her own mind and spent hours verbally reminding everyone how great she was. Vonnie's big chance came during one of those people-in-the-street interviews which a large radio network played nationally.

"They asked me about abortion and I replied, 'Americans haven't been told all the facts about secret, tax-paid abortions for the mistresses of TV stars and politicians,'" Vonnie related. "I went on whetting audience interest for about twenty more seconds, and then said, 'If you want more information on these secret, illegal abortions that you're paying for with your tax dollars, contact. . .'"

At this point, Vonnie gave the audience her ex-roommate's home address and telephone number as the information source. She says that three radio stations called the confused markess for more interviews, and she was getting dozens of calls and letters daily.

(Continued...)

This same routine will work for many other types of issues. Just pick something which is very emotional, controversial and polar. And be sure you are the "voice of an authority" on the subject. Reporters, radio and TV people are very gullible with stuff like this (see *Media)*.

Corporate/ Institutional

Obviously, the ideas here can be used elsewhere and otherwise, but for now they go under this category. I included this category because a lot of talk-show callers asked me how and what to do with nasty co-workers. Here are some suggestions.

You can always order printing, photography, repairs, or other types of services for the mark and/or the mark's department. The success here is to keep each individual order small, as in $200 or under. The range of revenge here is limited only by your imagination. One caller told me she ordered her mark six different luxury items that would look suspicious to a corporate comptroller or auditor, e.g., Omaha steaks, personally monogrammed clothing, booze, etc.

Everyone in personnel departments worries about not violating various privacy and other related laws when it comes to employee evaluations or job applications. A Hayduker spends time thinking of ways to include illegal and obnoxious items on such forms. After completing your modified form, see if you can bootleg it into the system where it will show up randomly.

Or, as an alternative, you can prepare *and* complete

(Continued...)

such a form for someone else, then submit it to the appropriate office for processing. See them go bonkers when they discover the awful items. It might be fun to use a secondary mark as the person "who" filled out the form.

You need to include items of specific information on these forms that flagrantly violate racial, sexual, ethnic, religious and privacy laws. Do it grossly; if they wish to know your sex I am sure you can furnish crude words for that, too.

Creative Editing

Go on, admit it. You've always had a hankering to play Steven Spielberg, Chuck Barris, or one of those other biggie movie producers. When you act on that urge, do it so as to win an award for embarrassment to your mark. Kick him right in the Oscars.

Everyone is into home movies or home videos these days. Your idea is to get hold of your mark's prize films or videos and do some creative editing. It would be great fun to insert scenes with John Holmes and his Mr. Johnson doing fun things with Serena, Seka or Jesse St. James. You can edit in a few flash frames, so it looks like subliminal seduction, or you can cut in longer scenes for total outrage. Or, put out a casting call to some of your more outrageous and less-inhibited friends so you can produce your own blue loop to be included with the mark's family scenes.

Later, when the offending footage is shown during family gatherings, plan to have or include some shill in the audience to either yuk-up and encourage the mark's guilt or to berate him for such poor taste. This scam works wonderfully well with some person who is very obnoxious about dictating his fundamental religious

(Continued...)

beliefs on you. Or, you might use one of these brain-locked zombies to add to your own mark's woes if he is not a zealot.

Credit Cards

If you bother to read the back side of your bank-generated credit card, you will notice a policy about disputed charges. That refers to a situation in which you dispute a charge item or amount on your bill, or that a company did not credit you for a return, never sent the merchandise to you, or whatever. There are formal steps, involving only your writing a letter, to create an "in dispute" situation for that transaction and amount only, meaning you don't have to pay until the dispute is resolved.

Perhaps, you can find out that your mark has a disputed transaction. If you know the mark's card number, you can easily call the bank and tell the credit card service representative that everything is okay for the deal, that "you" want the dispute status removed and it's alright to charge that amount to "your" account. By the time the mark catches up with the affair at the next billing cycle, it will be far too late for a simple resolution.

Credit Zap

According to Neal Abogado, who has a lot of experience in the business world, it is simple to get back at some scuzzball who's stuck you with unpaid bills or who has used his position to unjustly damage your credit standing or budget. According to Neal, it is fairly easy to infiltrate credit bureau operations in a small community.

"Use a fake name to rent a mail drop and open a phony checking account, complete with printed checks. Join your local credit bureau," Neal notes. "Then, using your phony business address/mail drop, run a credit check on your mark. It will cost you about ten bucks to do this. Pay for it with one of your checks and make sure your check doesn't bounce. Don't scam the bureau with bad paper.

"When you get the credit check printout of the mark, you will have the name, location and account numbers of many of his or her credit transactions. You can take it from there as a whole range of rotten things are open to your choice."

Please note that much of what was just presented may violate local, state and national laws. But then, what doesn't?

Crickets

Crickets are great assets. Infesting your mark's habitat with myriads of crickets can be an investment with unusually high yield. These little guys can be caught in the field near your place and kept in small cages, or you can buy them at most bait shops. Not only do they chirp loudly and hop around, they eat holes in many fabrics. Also, a cricket can look like a cockroach to many people. It seems to me that crickets would be good to use against die-hard environmentalists who refuse to use insecticides.

Cult Stuff

While sharing a few glasses of Scotch 'n Bile with Chuck Manson down in Dallas last fall, we got to discussing his old family ties in California. He told me that one of his ladies came in one visiting day to pass along a keen idea. It seems that one of the late Nixon administration's top White House press people had recently been reborn as a Manson Family member and had this thought.

"He said it would be a really peachy-keen idea to sneak into your mark's office or home and replace all of the family portraits and pictures displayed there with group photos of the Manson Family itself, or members of the family engaged in bizarre sex acts," Chuck told me.

What? You thought Chuck was still in jail? Naive, naive, naive. Those California cultists stick together. Actually, following a highest level political decision, Chuck was secretly freed and replaced in prison by a "specially trained CIA lookalike." Someone has plans for Chuck both in Central America and with the 1988 reelection campaign.

Customs

One of the neat things about the Customs Service today is that they will investigate almost anything, regardless of what it is, as Dick Smegma so informed me. He adds that if you know that your mark is returning to this country on a specific date, including flight number, airline and arrival time, all you have to do is get a message to local customs officials at the arrival city informing them mysteriously that "John Mark" will be attempting to smuggle "something" into the country. You need not give out any additional details.

When your mark arrives, regardless of who he is and who he knows, I can guarantee you that he will be given a *thorough* searching. The more the mark protests and gets pissed about it, the more persistent do the customs people become, only they will remain maddeningly polite about it all. The best part is, even if the mark appears to be clean, if the customs inspector's suspicions are aroused, a file will be opened and this beef will follow the mark on each departure and arrival.

Dates

I can't understand why someone would want to get rid of a date or gross out someone else's date that very night. But if you do, Morton Downey, Jr., has a workable plan acquired from his own experience during a double-date dinner in a fine restaurant.

"It was a situation that called for a quick gross-out and riddance, believe me," says Morton. "While the other folks' attention was diverted, I stuffed a bunch of fried onions up my nose and into my mouth. I then faked a huge, loud, animated sneeze, spraying the target-date with mist, slime, and solids. The after-action report was that I still had a variety of the onions hanging out of my nostrils and mouth. The stunt was totally effective; she split."

Dating Service

Call your mark's employer while your mark is not at work and ask to speak with him. The receptionist will explain that he is not in the office at the moment and ask if she can take a message. You then identify yourself as a representative of the local computer dating service and explain that he will not be able to use your computer dating service any longer until he pays his long overdue account. Obviously, this works best if you use the name of a real computer dating service in your area.

According to Killroy, you can embellish this scenario by altering the reasons why the mark is no longer welcome. Perhaps he did something awful, like peed or took a dump in a host's hot tub, joined some middle-aged ladies for a shower or streaked through a country club dining room wearing only a jockstrap—and that fastened over his head. Your only limit here is your imagination and the mark's employer's gullibility.

Dead Animals

Even without Stephen King, pet cemeteries are a big business. But I can easily think of other uses for dead animals. "Advertise for them and buy their bodies." In every telephone directory you can spot an ad for an animal disposal and/or rendering company. Why not set up your mark in the same business? A series of small ads in the local newspapers will do it. In addition to listing the telephone number to call, with business hours you know are inconvenient to the mark, you can also tell people about your special "Bring Right Down to the Plant" feature, listing the mark's home address.

This gives new meaning to the concept of 101 things to do with a large, dead plow horse.

Desk Drawers

Thanks to WOC radio's Jim Fisher in Davenport, Iowa, I learned of one manager who was frustrated with his terminally dumb office help and their attempts to ruin his career and decided to play musical drawers with his staff.

"I arrived very early one morning and switched their desk drawers around from desk to desk. Then I left and called in at 8 A.M. that I'd be in a bit late. I had a great breakfast and then walked in to find all the stupid jerks in a mess over whose drawer belonged in whose desk. They were still trying to figure it out thirty minutes later," says the manager.

"I often thought how much fun it would have been to add a bit of super glue to the trick!"

Diesel Engines

Our buddy Jimi the Z is also back from his hibernation with a fine tip for properly tuning your mark's diesel engine. Simply give the nuts holding the lines to the injectors a one-eighth twist to loosen them. Do it to all the engine's cylinders on one side only or to every other cylinder. Jimi says the idea is to start just a small leak. At 3,000 psi, this will make a hell of a mess on the engine, enough so that it might not start.

Dog Droppings

If you have a dog owner who allows his pet to poop on your premises, a WOC radio listener in Davenport has a grand idea—give the gift back.

"Borrow some paper from a local store or use your imagination. Wrap the fresh crap in lots of paper stuffing, put it in a decorator box, and gift-wrap it," advises the listener. "Put on a nice bow and card. Then have the package delivered, or mail it to your mark. Hopefully, the mark will fish around in the packing for the present."

Is that what the Pointer Sisters meant by a soft touch?

Dogs

He is a former NYC cop who now lives in Sarasota, Florida, and he likes dogs "unless they bark at night or dump in my yard — but, I'd never really harm them like some folks do." Instead, he makes a tasty treat, involving a little meatball which surrounds a lot of canine-sized portions of Ex-Lax.

"The next step is to make sure you shut them in the owner's yard, house, apartment, or automobile. Or, if you have another mark in your neighborhood, you can leave the soon-to-be-pooping pup with him."

Relax, animal lovers, this really does not hurt the animal, only cleans it out thoroughly and messily. Just be certain you give a child-sized portion. Who knows, maybe the mutt has worms and this will help clean that out, too. And, you can always think of your mark trying to clean that up.

Our ex-cop reminds, "This works great for the mark who lets the dog roam all over the place. You're helping out by taking the doggie home."

Doorknobs

We call this one the Skull's Wake-Up call from MP school. He noticed how many of his rotten mark enemies — really bad people he needed to get even with in a hard fashion — left their porch lights on all evening. Perfect. All you need is a light bulb adapter with an outlet on it, plus an extension cord that's been stripped of six inches of insulation at one end.

Wear insulated gloves, unscrew the lightbulb, replace it with the adapter, and then fit the bulb back in the adapter. Carefully wrap the stripped, bare wires around the mark's doorknob. Carefully plug the plug into the adapter. You've now left a shocking wake-up call for when the mark opens the front door.

At this point, Skull says you're free to ring the doorbell, knock loudly, or just let nature take its course. Your options depend on many factors about who will be approaching that live door, when, and from what side.

more

Doorknobs

Doorknobs and small alcohol burners make interesting companions. You can obtain a small burner for a very nominal sum in any hobby store. Construct a wire frame for the burner and hang it on the outside of your mark's doorknob so that the flame from the burner makes strong, direct contact with the knob.

The idea here is to do this for fifteen or twenty minutes before the mark will open the door, either on some schedule, such as jogging or work, or because you have pushed a doorbell button. Within those fifteen or twenty minutes of cooking, the heat will radiate to the inside knob, which your mark will soon grasp. It's not a really nice way to start his or her day!

If this idea warms you up, you'll have to hand the credit to Kilroy.

Drinking Fountains

A generic thought about plumbing fixtures could concern drinking fountains and goes like this.

"No children, dwarfs, or other handicapped folks work in my office. Yet, the other fountain is about eighteen inches off the floor, making it tough to drink from," writes our composite complainer.

"So, I bought a very official-looking custom sign (from a mail-order house in another state) and placed it above the fountain. It read:

UNISEX URINAL/BIDET
DRINK AT YOUR OWN RISK

Also, according to Norton Worthen, an unemployed commode designer, you can use a small hex wrench to turn a fountain's nozzle so it will spray the user in the face—hard.

"You can also adjust the flow so that the person has to suck on the device itself, which means you could treat that part of the unit with chemicals and other awful things," Worthen relates.

Other suggestions came from The Indiana Cave Man, who suggested wrapping fluorescein, potassium permanganate, or another potent dye in a nylon stocking and cramming it into the nozzle area on down the pipe behind the nozzle.

Finally, Ruthless Love, a member of the Pagans, a great bunch of bikers, suggested putting something terminally disgusting into the fountain's bowl, e.g., old vegetable soup tinged with butyric acid, a week's collection of nose blow, some dead rodents, the severed head of a house cat, a dead bird, an obviously used condom, a dirty woman's used panties, etc.

Drugs

A lot of people have written to tell me how great a high you can get with Yohimbine HC1, an active alkaloid found in yohimbine bark. According to others, it has excellent additional properties as well; the Crazy Chemist says it is a great aphrodisiac, as I reported earlier. I'm glad to spread the good word. You can buy Yohimbine HC1 from the Inner Center. But, as it is a sacrament of their church, you will have to become a member. See Sources.

Want to play "Pretend Pot?" It can be great fun if you want to involve parents, police, school authorities and other potential buffoons. When you burn dried strawberry leaves, they smell just like pot does in the smoking mode. RT with the dts says to use your imagination with this one.

Let's get real again. Deanol is said to be a safe, natural stimulant that imparts a feeling of happiness. Its chemical name is dimethylaminoethanol (DMAE). It is inexpensive and at this writing is readily available over-the-counter from chemical supply houses. Fencamfamine is a stimulant which is also available over-the-counter. It is medium priced and produces, I'm told, an effect somewhere between cocaine and speed.

Nature lover Annie Fellantori holds a Ph.D. in the study of psilocybin cubensis, or magic mushrooms, as our street friends know them. These delightful headbenders can be chopped into your mark's salad, which should soon Caesar on him. Knowing better, you can take them recreationally.

So much for fun. Let's get nasty. South American Indians can't be too far wrong, especially when they make such good poisons. Dieffenbachia, or "Dumb Cane," is a very popular decorative plant often found in hotel lobbies and larger homes. It is also popular with the Indians, who use the plant's extract to poison their spear and arrow tips. A bit of the poisonous, milky liquid on a person's tongue renders him mute for a period of minutes—thus the name "Dumb Cane." All this from those folks who gave us curare.

According to Filthy McNasty, Lobelia herb may be bought at most natural food shops. Added to food, it will cause the mark to toss it all up. Or if you want to send your mark on a long trip, grind up and sprinkle some Heavenly Blue morning glory seeds on his food.

Then there is the hard logic of a contributor known only as Cold Steel, who sounds to me like a nurse. Cold Steel writes, "Hospitals use narcotics, it's a fact of life, right? Every drop of every controlled drug must be strictly accounted for, and this fact gives the seasoned trickster another target. Simply tip off the local narcs that a drug ring is operating from your favorite hospital. They *will* investigate."

On talk shows and in the mail, I get a lot of complaints about the super-sniffer dogs the narcs use these days to hassle righteous folks about drugs. Uncle Bill Basque has a solution. First, these dogs have very sensitive noses. Second, with the proper materials, you can render their sensitive noses useless for days, all without really harming the dog.

For example, while eating his hashbrowns in Dallas one evening, Bill told me that ammonia and bleach powders or smelling salts spread on the floor where the animals will be working wipes their sniffers right out.

more

Drugs

Planting drugs predates even old me. But, because he is an ex-cop, Mr. Justice has a more pragmatic twist to the stunt. The ingredients you need are some oregano, spearmint shavings, and some small manila or glassine envelopes of the type favored by stamp collectors and drug dealers. You mix these ingredients well and pop them into a hiding place in your mark's car. Try for something really exotic, like under the seat. Now comes the fun.

Mr. Justice explains, "Call the local police and give them some imaginary name or the name of one of the mark's friends — be prepared with a real address, too. After you have identified 'yourself,' tell police that Mr. Mark is dealing drugs out of his car. Personally you don't care about a little grass for adults, but now he's selling PCP and bad coke to little neighborhood kiddies."

Mr. Justice's next instructions are to hang up and split the entire area with great, but not suspicious, haste. The police will quickly send a zone car to the mark's address — which you gave them — and a search will be made of his car. A field test may come out negative, but

(Continued...)

the minty smell of "PCP-laced grass" will merit a further investigation "downtown." This means your mark will be taken into custody and the ingredients will have to be lab-tested.

Mr. Justice says the same scam will work if you want to make your mark out as a numbers runner. All you need here are some homemade or real numbers slips and some amount lists. In both cases, not only will the police be interested, but so might those who really do deal in drugs and numbers. Perhaps, then, some other enforcers will come to visit your mark and discuss his new business.

Drunks

If you ve ever suffered through drunken captivity in the military, college or hunting camps, you'll appreciate Tyra Pierce's fine revenge. This is for every guy who's had to endure late nights and early mornings with a troupe of untrained amateur drunks doing their things.

Buy a few cans of cream of something soup—it doesn't matter which. Set them in the hot sun for a few days until the contents cook ripe. Do the same with two cans of beer. Mix the two together and put them both back in the sun for some additional curing time—maybe a day or two. Don't smell this vile mix, just bottle it, cork it and set it aside until your drunken companions or neighbors do their next thing.

When the louts eventually settle down, here's what you can do with the mixture. But let Tyra tell what he did, "I snuck into their room after passout time and poured this mixture over the toilet and the bathroom floor. Then I left, dripping the rest out into the room toward some beds. I quietly closed and locked their door from the inside as I left the area. When they stumbled around later in the morning and found the mess, they naturally assumed it was one of their own. It started a small civil war."

WARNING:
Many of the techniques in this book may be illegal; therefore this volume is offered for entertainment purposes only.

Eating Out the Slobs

A wonderful waitress from Davenport told me a great way to correct pigs who hassle the ladies who wait on them in restaurants:

"If the guy is a real jerk and just won't let you alone, then it's time to get someone else to distract him awhile. Usually, you have one waitress who has a great, healthy chest, or one who knows crude jokes, or one with Jane Fonda Class Legs. While the jerk has his mind caught in his pants zipper, you run out to his car and run a line of dirty grease on his steering wheel and heavy syrup on the car seat. He is a sloppy slob in your place, so let's pay him back accordingly. The punishment fits the crime."

Ecotage

Years ago, when concerned people started saying *hell no* to the greedy grabbers of profitable progress, somebody combined the terms ecology and sabotage to come up with *ecotage.* My own mentor, Edward Abbey, invented the term monkeywrenching in his book, *The Monkey Wrench Gang,* and it's been quite a progression. That's why I consider David Foreman a soil brother of ours. David publishes *Earthfirst,* the magazine of the environmental activist. He also has written a field manual called *Ecodefense: A Guide To Monkeywrenching,* which is basically how to sabotage land rapists.

I gladly share the beliefs and dreams of these fine folks and happily share anything they can use from the Haydukery involved in my books. Probably the best endorsement I ever heard for them came from a public relations whore for the logging industry who said, "Foreman's publications all carry a disclaimer about using the ideas, but, that's like handing out hand grenades and saying, 'we don't advocate you use them, but here they are.' " Isn't that great?

Or, as my own great pal, Uncle George, might say,

(Continued...)

"By God, let's turn the Alaskan pipeline over and see what's on the other side."

So far they sound like my kind of Give 'em Hell Harry Truman ass kickers; then, I called David Foreman. It seems he has a staff of flunkies, one of whom sounded uptight as he fussed about "David's image and associations." My request for information and a copy of Foreman's manual for review in *this* book would "have to be checked and considered."

A day or so later, one of the foremost of the Foreman minions called back to refuse all cooperation with me. I was told that association with me and my book would not serve in Mr. Foreman's best interest. I was crushed.

Still, I believe in what David Foreman is doing, as our roots are common and he plucked the weed of "monkey wrenching" from the same garden of ecological warfare (aka ecotage) as I did. My only regret is I can't give him a fat, wet kiss, right on the lips, in front of his horrified court of staff remoras.

Electrical Appliances

Kilroy has a home decorator's suggestion on how to help your mark exercise the circuit breakers and his or her own health, and also make an appliance repairperson richer.

"Cut the plug off a favored appliance—after you detach it from the wall receptacle. Tie the two wires together and tape with electrical tape to prevent a visible flash. Plug the armed cord into the outlet behind a piece of heavy furniture and wait for him/her to turn the appliance on. After your mark resets his blown circuit breakers umpteen times, a frustrated phone call will ring out for the expensive repairperson."

More from Kilroy: This time, unplug the mark's TV, stereo, vacuum cleaner, etc. Push a straight pin through the cord to create a short circuit. Use wire cutters to cut off the protruding ends of the pin so that the mark can't see the pin. When the mark sticks the plug in an outlet, there will be a big flash and puff of smoke. The fuse blows or the circuit breaker opens, leaving the outlet dead.

If the mark is a true nerd, he will refuse to believe that something is wrong with his precious equipment and will probably try plugging it into another outlet or two before giving up and going to a repair shop. Line cords rarely go bad, so the repair shop will probably replace many of the appliance's expensive guts before testing the cord. It's standard practice in even the best repair shops to charge the mark for everything that was replaced while attempting to find the trouble.

In the meantime, the poor mark (now there is a contradiction of terms), will be screaming, "Watt's wrong with my electrical circuits? Has the devil possessed me and my home?"

The Indiana Cave Man has invented a splendid tool for electrical chicanery. He calls it his Handy Dandy Fuse Popper (HDFP). It's an ordinary male plug with its terminals shorted together with very heavy wire, probably ten or twelve gauge. You simply shove this plug into selected outlets in the mark's home or office, and then remove it promptly after it does its ominous task, which leaves the mark with a dead outlet. This is fun, as it does nice things to the minds of paranoid marks.

An electric company's watt-hour meters are sealed against tampering by a special plastic or metal padlock-shaped device which is easily removed with a pair of wire cutters. Removing the seal is illegal. If you remove the seal from the mark's meter, he'll never notice, but the meter reader will. The power company will probably replace the seal once or twice and say nothing, but if the seal repeatedly disappears, the mark will get in trouble about it.

If you want to be less subtle, you can simply rip off the seal and metal retaining band, unplug the entire meter assembly, and smash it to the ground, simultaneously depriving the mark of power and getting him and the power company angry with each other. The company may even hold him responsible for the costly device.

You could also remove the seal and meter while the mark is away, tamper crudely with the insides, and replace the meter. The mark won't notice, but the power company will, and they'll come down hard on him.

Here's another idea: Remove the mark's meter and exchange it with some other mark's meter. Choose meters with vastly different readings. Both marks will get whopping bills—the mark whose meter reading was less than last time will get charged for 100,000+ kilowatt-hours, because the power company's computer will assume that the meter made a full revolution. If you leave the swap as is, the power company will accuse the marks of hanky-panky. If you undo the swap after the meter reader has made his rounds, the billing fiasco will be repeated next month, and the only evidence will be a couple of missing seals. Trying to convince the power company that *they* made a mistake will keep the two marks busy for weeks!

If the mark's electric service is in an isolated area, shoot the meter with a bow and arrow, crossbow, or shotgun when there are no witnesses around. You could also stick a Nazi pike or some other symbolic spear into it. When the meter is replaced, attack it again. After losing a few meters, the power company can legally refuse to supply service to the mark.

Electronic Equipment

Piezoelectric spark-shooters are made for lighting gas flames. They're inexpensive and available where camping equipment is sold. When the trigger is pulled, many thousands of volts are generated which jump a half-inch gap at the end. The volts could shock you, but only very mildly. Modify one of these sparkers by extending the tip and surrounding shell with a pair of wires, needles, etc. Insert the end into the mark's electronic equipment and start shooting sparks into the integrated circuits. This causes untraceable device failure and is especially effective against computers, especially while they are operating. If this idea shocks you, thank the Indiana Cave Man.

Enemies

One of the finest pieces of advice I got came from this wonderful lady in central Florida who told me, "Always forgive your enemies; nothing bothers them so much."

Excrement

For some reason I have always liked this word. Perhaps, it goes back to Miss McDowell's trowel. I wonder if Howard or Jack would remember? Mick, do you recall? Anyway, Rick has a new use for human effluvia, and that is to smear it on the air conditioner intake of an apartment or office. I wonder if one uses a spatula or other special applicator? Otherwise, it could be very uncomfortable trying to squat in there — oh, never mind.

Excrement has always been a fashionable material for terrorizing a deserving target. Our own OSS and the British SOE used it in their secret wars against the Germans and Japanese in World War II. Today, terrorists often use it in their symbolic wars against everyone. A police friend told me that cultists, kid gangs, and other street slime often will take a nasty dump in the office or home of some rich, powerful person after breaking into and stealing from the place. I bet you might be able to come up with ways a good bullybuster might adapt the same tactic and make it work for the good guys.

Finally, according to the Hombre of Justice, human feces mix well with chocolate or coffee ice

(Continued...)

cream and because of the freezing later involved, the odor is eliminated. This stunt gives new meaning to the order, *eat shit!*

Exotic Weapons

Did you like those exploding arrows that Sylvester Stallone used as Rambo? Want some working plans to make the same type of arrows, Claymore mines, shotgun rockets or a mortar of your own? All of these are guaranteed to work. An outfit known as Kephart Publications sells the plans and claims the finished products are cheap and easily made in your own workshop — no machine-shop tools or skills needed. Are they legal to complete and own? That's for someone else to worry about.

Explosives

Dr. Demolition calls this explosive his 35mm Killer. Here is what you need:

1 lb. of potassium chlorate
¾ cup of 350 mesh (fine) aluminum powder
1 cup Hercules Blue Dot coarse gunpowder
$^{3}/_{32}$" rocket fuse
15 empty 35mm film containers
1 mortar and pestle for mixing

Here's what you do: Mix them all together using a mortar and pestle or plastic tray — anything not likely to create a spark. Also, do not allow any aluminum dust to get into the air; that stuff is dangerous.

After thoroughly mixing, use a small plastic spoon to fill the film cans. Fill fully, then tamp tightly with the ceramic pestle. Cut six inches of fuse for each bomb, prick a tiny hole in the film can lid to feed the fuse through. Before you screw on the lids, be sure you seal the threads with a super-glue. Also seal the fuse hole.

You are now ready for destruction. Dr. Demolition says that each one sounds like two M-80s going off together. Note: These are *not* waterproof, but they *are very dangerous!*

Explosives and Bombs

Steve Tedeschi sends me the formula for what he claims is he loudest M-80 possible. He notes that his research turned up the formulae and methods that the fireworks industry used years ago when they made the old-fashioned M-80s. He also claims these are more stable and less prone to decomposition than other formula M-80s. That means it's safer to save these for a rainy day trick, I guess. Here's Steve's formula:

Potassium Perchlorate	50%
Antimony Trisulfide	25%
German Dark Pyro Aluminum	25%

You load the mixture in a standard-sized fireworks container, approximately 1½" by ⅝", and seal with proper end caps and fusing. Steve writes that in his fifteen years of making fireworks, this is the loudest he's heard of the hundreds of combinations and compositions. He also notes it has 100 percent reliable ignition with cannon fuse.

Going from the chemical to the comical, we run across the Indiana Cave Man, who wants you to meet a dead rat in an explosive context. He tells how to make a "Dead Rat Slop Bomb."

Stuff a dead rat, pet or other small varmint into a glass jar, add two inches of water, screw the lid on *tightly,* hide it behind the mark's sofa or in another appropriate location. Decaying organic matter releases awful gas which will explode the bottle after a few days. Delay time depends on temperature and initial conditions. This slop bomb has the advantages of high potency and long delay. It's especially effective if it contains the mark's pet or portion thereof, as lots of potential exists here for making it look like the mark's kids did it. Pint or quart mayonnaise jars are ideal.

Unknown to all but a few of the world's population, Hastings, Nebraska, is the home of *Shotgun News,* a grand wishbook for gun collectors. It's also the home base for CW, who is still running free and has some new ideas.

"One of the worst things I know is my truly awful stink bomb mixture," our bombastic chemist writes. "Take a quart jar with a rubber seal. Add a quarter inch of crystal Drano. Add one or two inches of water. Let it sit in a warm room for about an hour to allow the gases to cook with the lid on. Let the gases cool, then open the lid and add six egg whites—only the whites. Add a quarter cup of Methylene Blue, then fill the jar to about an inch of the top with water and seal it. Let it sit for four to six weeks.

"You use this bomb by shaking the container really well, then placing it where you wish. You can pour it (be careful of splashback), throw it, open it or leave it sit until the action wrecks the rubber seal and lets the odor seep out. Devastating," notes CW.

Then, there is the Masked Revenger, who surely does have a deep well of patience. For nearly a year, he put up with some college-dorm bozos who stole from him, got sick on his clothing and insulted him by just being there. When he did *Get Even,* he did so with a bang.

"I'm sensitive enough not to inflict personal injury, so I guess this falls into the calcium carbide class. But here goes," he writes. "Purchase a can of calcium carbide, a bottle cork, a disposable syringe, a small amount of hydrogen peroxide, a length of bell wire, a long, skinny balloon, then find a high voltage/low amperage power source, such as an electric fence transformer.

"Punch two holes in the cork and insert two pieces of stiff wire in the holes, leaving enough for leads on one side of the cork and just enough for a spark gap on the other. Epoxy all these so there are no air leaks.

"Inflate and deflate the balloon several times to stretch out the rubber. Powder a couple grains of carbide and put it into the balloon. Be very certain the inside of the balloon is totally dry, then slip the end of the balloon over the cork and clamp it securely with a plastic tie.

"Wait until the middle of the night when the mark is totally asleep. Stick the balloon under his/her door as far as it will go. Then push the syringe through the cork and fill the balloon with the hydrogen peroxide. This will combine with the calcium carbide to provide *fun* gas and leave enough good old O^2 to ensure ignition.

"Clip the power supply wires to the wire leads coming out of the cork, and as the balloon inflates all the way, simply complete the electrical connection. If the *Barrroooooommmmm* shock doesn't knock you senseless, take your power supply with you and run like hell."

According to the Masked Revenger, in his initial tests in a closed, empty dorm room, the device shook rooms two doors away. In actual use, it also leaves very little physical evidence as most of the contents are destroyed. It does leave behind a very strong odor.

Farm Animals

Everyone loves to see farm animals. In the spring, entire families spend weekends gazing at tiny sheep and cattle. If your mark owns a herd of cattle or sheep, you can surely give the fans a message. Using epoxy spray paint, which won't harm the critters, spray obscene messages and sexual commands on the sides of the animals. This paint is very hard to remove from their fur and is very readable, especially if you use the Day-Glow varieties.

You could probably accuse your mark of some form of participatory bestiality, such as identifying small sheep as his offspring or using spray paint on the side of a cow to say that your mark was the worst lay she'd ever had. Stuff like that can be funny, especially when the little rug rats start asking mommy and daddy what all the words written on the animals mean.

Fart

Despite the Establishment's prissy attitude to the contrary, farts are a great Hayduking device. Ask anyone who ever served in any armed forces or served time in most any nation . . . *farts 'r us,* and they can be fun. According to the more stiff-spined critics, only juveniles, fools, Uncle Gerry, Chris, the Colonel, Uncle George, myself, and a few others find farting and belching amusing. That assumption is quite incorrect. The classic literature is full of flatulence and eructation. The venerable Mark Twain devoted an entire book to the classics of farting. Farting and belching belong, so let's enjoy them.

With this in mind, I offer the following two treatises. In St. Petersburg, Florida, Joseph St. Pierre was awarded $25,000 in a lawsuit against the McDonald's hamburger chain. Among the problems St. Pierre claimed were caused by meat at McDonald's was "chronic uncontrollable gas."

"From the time I get up in the morning to the time I go to bed at night," he told the jury, "I do nothing but pass wind." St. Pierre also told the panel that friends refuse to go to dinner with him and his fellow employees

(Continued...)

"won't stand in back of him."

The *Times of India* published this item:

The daily output of flatulence from a single sheep contains enough methane gas to power a small truck for forty kilometers, according to a New Zealand scientist, reports Reuters from Wellington.

Dr. David Lowe told a conference of meteorologists that New Zealand could solve some of its fuel problems if it found a way to harness the less savory by-product of its seventy-two million sheep.

"He said the total daily methane output of New Zealand's sheep was one thousand tons. If a sheep was put on the back of a utility truck with a bale of hay and connected to the engine 'with appropriate fittings,' it could run the vehicle for about forty kilometers a day," he said.

As if these literary references to flatulence were not enough, we now learn that the conductor of the Mt. Lebanon Wind Symphony is becoming a fashion entrepreneur, announcing in all of the trade press, "This spring I will be bringing out my new line of pre-farted underwear for those willing to make such a daring fashion statement."

Singing Sam used a fart to get back at a mark through an answering machine. The mark had the usual pompous message, which Sam had a girlfriend change for him while the mark was away for a week. The new message started with someone sounding like the mark saying, "Hello, I'm out of town and want you to listen to this brief message directed personally at you before you leave your message. Here's to you. . . ." This was followed by a very loud, authentic, long and wet fart that rumbled the machine.

Farting and Beyond

According to Professor Frank Snakeoil, director of Anal Athletics at Mercenary University of Propaganda (MUP), there is a perfect escalation to farting in the general direction of your mark. The next step down the evolutionary ladder is to actually take a dump — loudly and graphically — in your pants in front of the mark, his family, friends, associates, whomever. Then, take off your pants, hand them to the mark as you make a very brief speech about how appropriate the award is, turn and leave. Hopefully, a loyal colleague will have proper escape clothing and vehicle just outside for you to hasten your immediate departure.

Fast Food Places

This one is sure to generate a bad taste somewhere. Pick a food chain in your area with lots of outlets. For example, drive up to one branch of your local McFastfood. Order something. Pay the two dollars, or whatever, and drive to their next outlet. Order something different and much more expensive.

When the young lady gives you your bill, pay and leave. Drive back in thirty seconds and present the first bag of goodies and your larger check. Ask for a mammoth refund. Then enjoy your discount meal.

Fireplaces

This one also works well with wood stoves and comes to us with the goodwill of the Tennessean. Actually, it's also an old World War II trick from the British Special Operations Executive. Maybe the Tennessean is an old SOE man?

Take a piece of firewood from your mark's woodpile or get one log like the type he uses. In your home or shop, drill a one-inch hole about twelve inches deep. Insert an M-80, some other large firecracker, or a cut-down skyrocket into that hole. Repack with shavings and sawdust after using Elmer's glue to fasten the explosive device in the cavity. Close the end with glue and/or putty. Smear some light clay on that end of the log and allow it to harden. Replace the special "log" on top of the mark's woodpile. You may never hear about it, but the mark surely will.

Fluorescein

Remember that orange dye marker my friend George Hayduke and some friends used in a community swimming pool to teach some bigots a lesson? I didn't know this, but the technical name for that substance is fluorescein, and it's available at chemical supply houses. You can also get it by buying surplus dye-marker kits at an Army/Navy store. It's an intense yellow dye which turns bright green in sunlight. It's harmless, but upsetting, especially when it's put into a village or private water supply, ornamental fountain, swimming pool, etc.

Here are some ideas for its use from The Indiana Cave Man. He uses a salt shaker with closable holes. If the mark is a housewife or janitor, sprinkle some fluorescein on the tile or linoleum floor. The more they try to mop it away, the greener it glows.

If you sprinkle it into a carpet, it is almost impossible to get rid of. Normally highly water-soluble, it really stains porous items. The Cave Man also suggests that you add butyric acid to the fluorescein and place the mixture in a newly poured, wet concrete area, such as a porch, patio, or flooring slab.

You can sprinkle it on clothes (for sweat to mix with) or on bathing suits. Sprinkle it on doormats so kids track it inside. Put it in the bottled water at the office.

Food

Boise Jim had had it. He was tired of the horrible food served in his school cafeteria. "It was so bad," he wrote, "that even Reagan's EPA was concerned about cleaning up the place." Jim didn't wait for the bureaucrats.

"I found my salvation in a coin machine in the rest room of a local bar. I bought some cheap generic condoms. I thought I might add some spice to the clam chowder," Jim says.

Ever the gourmet, I wondered if Jim meant Manhattan or New England. Nevertheless, here's how he slipped the condomint into the chowder.

"It was a buffet line, serve yourself. As I poured clam chowder into my bowl, I simply touched the ladle to the opened rubber, and presto—it stuck. I just put the laden-ladle back in the tureen. About two minutes later, some young cutie poured the rubber into her bowl. Her reaction was certainly funnier than that of the stiff teachers."

The same bit of creative cookery works well in any buffet-style eating place. Remember, where you serve yourself, you may always serve others.

more

Food

My gracious, we actually have a celebrity contributor. He plays in the backfield for a great Super Bowl team caged in Chicago. His team nickname is Sweetness and his nom de guerre for this book is Mr. Loose. It seems the Bears get on each other a lot and Mr. Loose takes his share of abuse. One day he discovered the paraffin wax that the team trainer uses for heat-treatment of injury. It has a reddish color and when melted looked just like red glaze. Mr. Loose quietly dunked some of the team's pre-game doughnuts in this wax and when it dried and hardened, the result was a glazed donut lookalike. Some taste in humor, that Mr. Loose.

In another stunt, he found that artificial fat tissue, which the trainer uses to pad the hands of the linemen, looks like cheese, although it's made of rubber. It was no problem to slip a couple of pieces into the sandwich of one of Mr. Loose's main tormentors. So much for celebrities. Now, consider this.

Whenever the gang got together, they always assumed or bullied Betty into doing the cooking. Never any thank-yous or compliments on the cooking,

(Continued...)

although it was excellent, beyond the usual patronizing waves. Betty tried all sorts of nice ways to spread the chore around. Finally, she began to put bits of cotton in the pancake batter and other additives to the various other foods. The "hints" worked and Betty soon joined the diners as someone else volunteered to cook.

Miss Illmanners handled the same basic problem by including unusual hors d'oeuvres, such as mouse paw, bunny tail, mole face, or toenail d'human, in her finger food. Same result. All of this recalls similar solutions listed in my earlier books.

Gift and gag shops are fantastic sources for the paraphernalia of Hayduking. For instance, Chris in Urbana called in on a radio talk show to tell me that he used a sheet of plastic cheese in a sandwich to get back at a food-hogging roommate. The guy ate it. I wonder if his stool resembled those little white puff-things companies use as packing?

Food Stamps

Marty and Mike have a really hip Illinois collegiate radio audience, and these folks taught me a lot of fun things to do to evil people. For example, Jeff called in to suggest that you offer in a local newspaper classified ad, "FREE FOOD STAMPS" or "DISCOUNT FOOD STAMPS — CHEAP!" and list your mark's telephone number. As a touch, you might request late-night calls due to "shift work."

After Jeff hung up, another caller volunteered the delightful idea that the feds would probably be very curious about who was giving away or selling food stamps. Gee, gang, a bonus!

Furniture Stores

Ever been had by a furniture store and been refused relief for wood that rots or splits, or upholstery that fades? The Chainsaw Queen had that happen and did something very subtle. She secreted a screwdriver on her person, and then she and a very loud, noisy, garish and sexily dressed young lady friend went to the store that was about to be in trouble.

"While my sexy friend asked questions and created the diversion, I unscrewed a whole lot of support screws out of a whole lot of furniture, especially expensive and somewhat frail pieces. Our hope was that some human tank would come in and plop down to bounce-test the strength of the furniture.

"We didn't have to wait long . . . it happened twice while we were still there. We left, holding back squalls of laughter."

Fuses

So you have loud, unruly neighbors who play the stereo too loud and long. Or you live next to a garage band that practices during the hours when Dracula stalks. Filthy McNasty will help you. Use super glue to disable their fuse box. Or turn off their power and quickly padlock the fuse box shut.

Another fusionary idea was shot from the brain of Bullet Bill. He likes to raid his mark's box of spare fuses, putting clear nail polish or clear paint on the electrical contacts. Bullet's other idea involved a photo. He writes, "I taped a picture of a dynamite stick to my mark's fuse box, along with a note which read 'Next time, I put explosives in here and when the lights go out in the house and you open this box, your lights go out too. BOOM!' It was great, according to his sister who was my accomplice."

Garbage

If your city is having a garbage collector's strike, and they're about as common today as business failures, here's a way to use the strike to get one up on your mark. Obtain as much of your mark's trash as possible, making sure you add as many especially gross and disgusting things as you can (like human feces, used sexual accessories, child porno stuff, etc.). Collect this yourself, and set it aside, as Julia Child would say. Let it develop character and odor.

Now write some nasty protest letters to various civic leaders in your mark's name. Get abusive and threatening. Mail the letters. Put carbon copies and other items containing your mark's name and address in your simmering garbage bags. Take these bags to the city park, a freeway overpass, city hall, or the mayor's home. Bomb the stuff there and get away quickly.

Nature, law, and official retaliation will take their course.

more

Garbage

Mad Mike wrote to tell me that he got back at a crooked boss by taking my advice about the weights and measures seals on gasoline pumps. He closed that station quickly, so he did. Mike also passes along a new tip on garbaging your mark.

It works best if your mark has a large family and several garbage cans. On garbage night, wait until your mark hauls his three or four cans out to the street for morning pickup. A few hours later, when all is quiet and dark, carefully put all of his full cans back where he normally stores them. He will find them there in the morning and wonder. You can probably do this several times as the garbage piles up and up. Won't it be fun in the truly hot weather of full summer?

Garden Hoses

Does your mark take terrific pride in his garden? If so, back pour some weedkiller or defoliant into his water hose and replace the nozzle. Also, threadlock is wonderful stuff, as water, oil, gasoline and many solvents will not touch it. There are many suggestions for using this product, including garden hoses/spigot hook-ups, home/apartment plumbing appliances and installations.

Killroy says that it's great fun to run your mark's garden hose into a nearby tree and afix the nozzle to a branch pointed at the faucet valve. He has done this many times, and it always proves to be very irritating to your mark when he goes to turn on the faucet.

Gas Stations

If you know a true creep who owns a gas station, one in a chain of a major oil company, for example, Mot Rot knows a good pay-back. Mot says that the underground storage tank for unleaded gas at the mark's station is a fine place for you to dump your leaded gas.

Mot reports, "Leaded gas found in an unleaded storage tank is very illegal and conviction carries a heavy fine. Modern tests can easily determine even small amounts of lead." Mot says to put this modern technology to work on your behalf.

Gasoline

In March 1986, there was a general strike in Panama. Among other things that happened, the refineries were shut down. So pretty soon the local gas stations ran dry. The U.S. military personnel were able to gas up at the PX station, only to find out the next morning that their purchases had been siphoned off during the night.

Two U.S. Army officers from the Logistics Directorate, Major George Alexander and Chief Warrant Officer Don Maulden, experienced such losses. They understood the plight of the poor Panamanians and were genuinely concerned for their health — concerned, that is, that someone might suffer irreparable body harm as a result of improper siphoning techniques.

In the spirit of international harmony and understanding, George and Don each left a five-gallon gasoline can in his driveway that night. Each contained about four gallons of gasoline.

Each also contained five pounds of sugar.

Next morning, the cans were gone. As the officers related their experiences to our roving colleague, M. Nelson Chunder, their countenances shone with beatific

(Continued...)

radiance that can only be known by those who have unselfishly shared their possessions with others less fortunate than themselves.

Gelatin

You salacious creature, you read the contents and turned to this page first thinking of kinky things to do with gelatin mix. What I have here is much more funny, and it's from my Italian friend Andrea.

It's summer and really hot. Your mark is sleeping without pajamas, as, in the nude. You take several small packs of gelatin powder and lightly sprinkle the powder all over your mark's body, mixing little blips of one color here, another color here. Andrea, who's done this one, says body perspiration melts the powder and causes all sorts of fun colors to form on the mark's body. It will stain both body and bedding, that's for sure. Thanks, Andrea, I will think of you next time I buy gelatin.

Getaway

One author, Ronald George Eriksen 2, has a book called *Getaway* (available from Paladin Press). Some of his ideas may help remove you and your vehicle from the scene.

1. Have thorough knowledge of the area you are driving in.
2. Predrive all avenues, and note possible escape routes and side exits.
3. Avoid getting boxed-in in traffic.
4. Always park so you have a fast exit from your parking space.
5. If possible, drive on major thoroughfares.
6. Know the locations of police stations, hospitals, military outposts, etc.
7. Check rear-view mirrors frequently.
8. Be wary of groups of men in uniform (jogging suits, janitor outfits, etc.).
9. Look for walkie talkie units.
10. Never trust anyone with your automobile key.
11. Avoid construction areas.
12. Keep your gas tank at least half full.
13. If suspicious people are observed loitering about your vehicle, avoid it.

If you think, though, that you are being followed, using Ronald Eriksen's book, here are some modified suggestions to lose that tail. As some of these are fairly extreme and involve illegal and perhaps unsafe techniques, please be sure you *do* have a tail before you start this drill. There is no sense in attracting undue attention to yourself and your vehicle.

1. After running a red light or driving the wrong way on a one-way street, watch to see if anyone follows.
2. While traveling on a freeway at high speed, suddenly cut across four lanes of traffic and make an exit.
3. After rounding a blind curve, make a bootlegger's turn and take off in the opposite direction.
4. After turning a corner, pull over and park. Take note of all vehicles passing by.
5. Go through alleys, dirt roads, sidewalks, or cut across people's lawns.
6. While driving over a long undivided bridge, suddenly make a bootlegger's turn.
7. Have a *very* trusted friend follow you to detect any surveillance.

Goldfish

Little Billy Gondorrhea once needed to get back at a nasty friend who killed his pet rock. Billy put some Jello mix in the mark's goldfish bowl. Another fishy stunt was pulled by Bullets Morepage, who got some freshly deceased goldfish free from a pet store. She made them into a disguised sandwich for her mark and smuggled it into his packed lunch. Another bullet was fired in the name of revenge.

Golf Balls

There was this rumor going around back when we were kids that if you put mothballs in your vehicle's gasoline tank it hopped up the power of the car. I don't know if that's true, but the following idea that came in from several people surely is true.

Put an ordinary golf ball into the gas tank of your mark's car. The ball rolls with the motion of the vehicle, going "bump" each time it hits the edge of the tank in any direction. Your mark will keep wondering, "What in hell is that soft bump, bump, bump I keep hearing?"

Some of the newer cars which use unleaded gas probably don't have a large enough opening to fit a golf ball. How about a ball bearing? Or several ball bearings? They'd make a louder bump anyway.

Golfers

Kilroy told me about getting even with this gruesome slob who used to bug, bait, and cheat at golf. It's a good story, even though the actual payoff is typical of two-dollar-haircut humor.

"This obese sap used to think he'd lose weight and get strong carrying his light golf bag and a few clubs around when a bunch of us played on Sunday afternoon.

"Trust me, the guy is such a horror show he gives slobs a good name. Anyway, I placed a ten-pound iron weight from an exercise set in the bottom of his bag. By the fifth hole, the guy is muttering and bitching about his bag getting heavier and heavier. That gave me an idea.

"The following week I wrapped another weight in a towel and put it in the bottom of the bag. This guy staggered through the nine holes, sweat popping out of his fat face, giving his porcine pallor an unhealthy pall.

"He didn't show up the next week."

Gossips

The rationale behind gossip is understandable if you agree with the explanation of Pauli Hayworth, one of the oustanding liberal feminists of our time. Ms. Hayworth explains, "On the evolutionary scale, Woman and the Bird are far superior to Man. That is why, of course, Man was forced to invent the telephone wire, to accommodate his two biological/intellectual superiors."

Pauli revealed how she uses the neighborhood and office gossips to help fight her wars against rude people. "It's not at all complicated. I just call the gossip and ask him or her to answer some questions I have about the mark. Of course, I don't use my own name . . . I usually pretend to be an insurance investigator or reporter.

"I ask the gossip how long Mr. Mark has been on the drug rehab program. Or, I ask if the gossip knows if Ms. Mark has been fired again for homosexuality — stuff like this," Pauli explains.

Pauli never fails to be amazed how quickly the words get around.

Graffiti

Here is some arousing new literary mulch for the spray-paint and marker crowd. The following graffiti are new from my own collection and that of other Movement loyalists. Credit is given where appropriate. You'll find no special order to this collection, and you are welcome to borrow and use each as your own. Spray in peace, as they say.

GETTING UP EARLY IN THE MORNING IS WORSE THAN GOING TO BED WITH A MAN WHO DOESN'T KNOW WHAT HE'S DOING

—Diane, in Jessick, IN, 1983

PISS ON DISCO
I SNATCH KISSES AND VICE VERSA

—Woodland Lounge, a biker's bar in PA, 1982

SPERM BANK NIGHT DEPOSIT
SIT ON A HAPPY FACE

—O'Hare, Chicago, 1982

NEVER STEP IN ANYTHING SOFT
THE BIGGER THEY ARE THE HARDER THEY HIT

—Paul Wilson in CO, 1983

CONSERVE PAPER, USE BOTH SIDES
—Jimmy Watt in Washington, 1983

VOTE NO ON PROPOSITION YES
—R. Wilson Reagan in NJ, 1983

WE'RE SNOW BLIND . . . DO ANOTHER LINE
—P. Chico in Salvador, 1983

REALITY IS FOR THOSE WHO CAN'T HANDLE DRUGS
—John Mitchell in Eglin AFB, 1976

I GAVE HER A DIAMOND, SHE GAVE ME A DISEASE
—Tracy in PA, 1982

PABST IS MY BREW HEAVEN
—David in Honduras, 1983

I'M RIPE, EAT ME
—Mick in St. Louis, 1983

BUILDERS HAVE GREAT TOOLS
—Paul Wilson in Boulder, 1981

HUMPTY-DUMPTY WAS ON THE GRASSY KNOLL
—R. Nixxon in Dallas, 1963

HOW DO *YOU* SPELL RELIEF? F-A-R-T!
—Uncle Gerald in Pittsburgh, forever

I'M NOT WEARING UNDERWEAR,
FILM AT 11

—D. Hazinski in Atlanta, 1983

GOOD SEX IS NEVER HAVING TO
SAY YOU'RE HORNY

—Dreamers Everywhere

more

Graffiti

I started out using these as fillers for half empty pages, then a lot of people started sending me their favorites and on radio shows, readers called in to say they were using the graffiti from my book to make their own statements. Once more, the scrawl of the wild:

- WHEN GOD MADE MAN SHE WAS ONLY KIDDING
- IT'S A BITCH TO BE A BUTCH
- DULL WOMEN HAVE CLEAN HOMES AND MINDS
- SAVE THE BALES (pro pot message)
- I NEVER SCREW ON THE FIRST GRAM
- I COME AT NIGHT AND AM GONE BY MORNING
- THE DRUNKER I GET, THE PRETTIER YOU ARE
- TODAY, I'LL DO IT FOR LOVE, BUT TOMORROW IT'S $50
- STICKS AND STONES MAY BREAK MY BONES, BUT LEATHER REALLY EXCITES ME
- EXTRASENSORY PERVERSION — DON'T

(Continued...)

CUM IN MY MIND

- WHAT DOES IT SAY ON THE BOTTOM OF COKE BOTTLED ON LESBOS? USE OTHER END
- TRUE AMBITION — TO BE A 50-FT WOMAN'S GYNECOLOGIST
- SOME WOMEN ARE BORN TO GREATNESS, OTHERS HAVE IT THRUST INTO THEM
- I ♥ SOIXANTE-NEUF

Gravesites

OK, enough light humor, it's back to heavy time. If you really want to shatter your mark, as in really do the sucker in, here you go. Borrow some very uninhibited friends, truck them to the gravesite of your mark's close family. Using a Polaroid camera, take pictures of your associates performing sexual and scatological acts upon the gravesite and stone.

This is a long story involving a racial bigot, some family cruelty that broke apart a young couple and their child, and, finally, the death of the bigot. The bigot's adult son was just as evil, by the way. Photos were taken showing an interracial couple doing fun things with each other on the old man's grave. Faces were not shown and the people were not local. A printed message was attached to each photo and they were disseminated to the appropriate media and local gossips:

> Here is photographic proof that Elmo Hateblack is a member of the Church of Satan. He is performing Black Mass with Mistress Charlatan, high priestess, on the grave of his father, Elmer Hateblack.

Elmo is, of course, the son. Phew, this one really

(Continued...)

made some tight sphincters in that town. Who gets credit for this messy masterpiece of black humor? Dick Smegma.

Greeting Cards

Finding fame in Madison Avenue's advertising industry is the sort of ambivalent feeling a dehydrated person gets when he finds a bucket of warm spit in the desert. But, that's not how I felt when I discovered that two young advertising executives, Barbara Davilman and Nina Tassler, had commercialized my *Get Even* concept with their own business venture called Bittersweet, Inc. The moonlighting ladies came up with nasty "greeting" cards for the same sorts of rounders I go after in my books.

My favorite of their cards shows a cute young couple, obviously nude, standing coyly behind some bushes. The headline reads, "Do you remember that wonderful time when. . . ?" Then, the kicker comes on the inside panel, "Oh, never mind That wasn't you." Great! I don't have their address, but the card line is Bittersweet, Inc., in New York.

Grenades

Nothing new and different here, as anyone who can read an army manual on making his own weapons can figure this one out. Suppose you really want to trash the inside of someone's apartment or automobile. Take an M80, cover it with auto body putty or epoxy, then dip it into a dish of BBs. The result is a truly effective fragmentation grenade. Thanks, and a tip of the hat over toward the Right in the direction of Ed Sasquatch.

A safer and more fun grenade update comes from us from Killroy. To make a first-rate paint grenade, go to your local hobby shop and purchase some Clearcast resin ball molds. They are *very* thin glass, inexpensive and shaped like miniature vases. They come in various sizes and can be filled with paint, then corked or sealed. You do the rest.

Guns

There are many new gun laws in place. Play on the ignorance of your mark and advertise him or her as a gun dealer who is selling guns which are now classed as illegal. List fairly cheap prices, but, don't be too unrealistic. List the mark's address and phone number. Always remember to include the magic phrase, "I've discovered a *big* loophole in the federal gun laws." That line insures *strong* government interest in your mark.

If you have a mark who's an obnoxiously anti-gun person, you might wish to do one of two things. (1) If you have the money, make a hefty cash contribution in his or her name to the Citizens Committee For The Right To Keep And Bear Arms. Or, (2), you may wish to make a hefty pledge in the mark's name. I would accompany this donation/pledge with letters to the editors of your local newspapers and one or more of the gun publications. For addresses, see the Useful Addresses section of this book.

Actually, this is a success story, but I wasn't sure if I ought to place it there, or in the humor section. I decided to call a fool by its own name, and so placed it here. Enjoy, as the contributor, Von Henry, is a good

(Continued...)

guy, and, as the Rev. Paul Wilson once wrote, "Guns . . . you're only caught dead without one."

Von Henry relates how someone he knew wished to get back at a person who was the head of his state's version of the Anti-Handgun Gang. He needed to get back at him for another reason, but used this affiliation to wipe out his mark. This may be a useful object lesson.

Von says his pal wrote a batch of letters to various people and groups using the mark's name and letterhead. The first batch went to groups like Handgun Control, Inc., and informed them that he had seen the truth now about gun control and it was the work of the devil, the International Communist Conspiracy and was related to the spread of AIDS, child molestation, unions, and democrats.

Next, he "had" Mr. Mark write to groups like the NRA, CCRTKBA, and others pledging undying support and enclosing small cash contributions. He requested literature, membership information, and info on how to form a local fund-raising group.

The third batch of mail to go out under Mr. Mark's name went to both state and federal officials, legislators and congressmen, demanding a repeal of the Gun Control Act of 1968. In this letter he also threatened to raise funds and to work to defeat any "communist-loving, sonofabitch traitor" who opposed his views.

Finally, Mr. Mark "sent" letters to a variety of newspapers in the state accusing nearly everyone in that state, except himself, of being a communist/fascist/homosexual/democrat. He managed to make the KKK seem like a Desmond Tutu fan club, he was so rabid. Horrendously, many newspapers print letters without checking and in this case, it happened.

I am pausing now only to let your imagination try to cope with the fallout this campaign caused in terms of legal, moral, personal, political and paranoid confusion, and quandry. My salute goes out to Von Henry and his friend for a job well done.

Halloweeners

Mike "No More Mr. Nice Guy" McCoochen did the following to pay back some teenage hooligans who enjoyed smashing little kids' pumpkins in the street.

Mike rigged a light socket to a board behind a huge pumpkin. He attached an M-80 to the filament of a 150-watt light bulb. This socket was attached to a switch which disconnected the flow of electricity when pressure was applied.

"When the nasty mark lifts the pumpkin, the pressure switch causes the filament to ignite the M-80, plus it turns on a large floodlight beamed on my porch," Mike chortled.

Mike cautions against setting the target pumpkin near where innocent children could stumble into the ambush. He tried it this past Halloween and reports the counterbullying worked wonderfully.

Hand Grenades

These are great little framers. Let's cover the basic use plan first and then get to the decorating details. It makes a great extra for a neighborhood or community Easter egg hunt activity, or Halloween trick or treat bag, although it really will work anytime. Scatter a few of your modified hand-grenade cases around where the kiddies are likely to find one or two and bring them to mommy and daddy. Or, if you can arrange to meet some Halloweeners at your mark's home, dump one or two in the children's bags.

It won't be long until an official Police Easter Egg or Witch Hunt will begin. At the height of the panic, when the ever-present news media are there, you or your accomplice should inform some reporter (never reveal your identity) that the mark—point out his house—is a mercenary and has dozens of rifles, bombs, and grenades stored in his place.

Now, here's how to make an empty practice grenade look real. You can easily buy them with real fuse mechanisms at most surplus stores. Unscrew the top; in some grenades, though, there is already a hole in the bottom. Fill the unit with some nonexplosive (see Bombs section) which is not easily identified. Plug any holes tightly and seal with super glue. Paint over any of the blue-painted body with either flat black or olive drab paint (also available at surplus or hobby shops). Put a yellow band about half an inch wide around the neck if you wish, although not all live grenades have this band, I'm told. Screw the fuse back on, set the pop-off handle, and replace the safety pin.

Your grenade is now safely armed for some fun. But, as with the fake bogus bombs, don't get caught. This is a heavy one with the authorities despite its basically harmless prank nature.

Hangovers

Don Wildmon is one of those friends with whom you don't want to go out overdrinking. He has a massively creative sense of evil. His favorite is when someone has a world class hangover, i.e., the kind that makes you wish you were the poster child for immediate terminal illness.

"You find the worst, most horrible rubber monster mask possible at a costume shop and hold it until this moment of submental hangover melange, when the mark is tossing between the line of malt madness and mindless malaise . . . and decides to take a shower," Don says.

"The next move is to make it to the shower before your mark and install the mask over the shower head so that the water will pour out semi-normally through the eyes, nose and mouth of the mask. Then, you unscrew the lightbulb in the shower room so the area is in semi-darkness.

"The mark will stumble in and manage to adjust the water . . . all drunks have that guidance ability. As soon as some degree of new wakening is witnessed by you — hiding in the shadows — HIT THE LIGHTS!"

(Continued...)

The result is usually physical freakout of a level achieved by Jason Vorhees while he terrorizes third grade girls seeing their first *Friday the 13th* movie on the VCR while mom and dad are out for the evening. The effect is embellished, by the way, if you can somehow introduce red dye to the water flow.

Help Lines

I thank Ray from Kansas City for sharing this scary, but very effective, stunt. I will change some of the details to protect the source, but in essence, here's how it happened.

A man was in the process of a nasty divorce and was living alone in an apartment. About 11:30, a police tactical squad burst into his room, subdued this terrified guy, slapped a strait jacket on him, and hustled him off to a psychiatric hospital. He was almost hysterical, which added to the effectiveness of the situation.

He was shot with drugs, after having had his stomach pumped, then strapped into a bed for observation. After an hour he was told that *he* had called the Human Suicide Rescue Hotline and reported that he'd taken poison and, further, was going to blow up the neighborhood with a TNT bomb in his apartment, or shoot any police who came looking for him.

It took him another hour, plus several confirming telephone calls, to get across that this was a hoax. He was released with very little apology. In fact, they were angry at him for being "the kind of person in his situation who would get taken advantage of and make fools

(Continued...)

of the authorities.'' No apology — get out. He found his apartment had been tossed and torn by the police bomb squad, plus his landlady was evicting him on the spot because of the incident.

The guy figured his estranged wife had somehow engineered the entire thing. She, of course, was out of state with tight alibis and acted insulted, threatening to sue him if he dragged her into the thing.

Wow . . . that's heavy duty! But, if anyone can use it, you have K.C. Ray's blessing.

Highways

Kepler McGeary, one of the Wild Bunch from Idaho, decided one day to tie up traffic badly on his least favorite freeway to his least favorite city. He borrowed a heavy dump truck full of municipal gravel while a friend drove another. Together, they headed to the pre-chosen bottleneck spot far between exit ramps, as they had planned the event well in advance after much thought, checking of alternative routes, maps, and potential rescue efforts by authorities. Says Kepler:

"We reached the spot and swung our rigs head to head, blocking three of the four lanes. We already had a long line of cars behind us — we started out just as morning rush hour did. We quickly dumped our loads of gravel which totally jammed the entire parkway. We both quickly left the cabs of the trucks, and with a valve buster let the air out of tires on both vehicles. We then fled to the next ramp where a colleague picked us up."

"Nobody saw us escape and there were no clues as to what happened. We got away with it and blocked traffic for four hours that morning. Made TV, too. I think the city fathers knew what had happened but didn't want the public to know."

Hit 'n Run Drivers

Some brainless driver once struck the car of Major General K. Oss and immediately chose to become a hit 'n run statistic. Unwise, as the general witnessed the event and obtained the license number of the foolish one. He easily traced it using techniques from a book that personal modesty forbids me to mention here. Here's the drill after you find the guilty party.

"With a bit of effort you can remove the hinge pins on your mark's car door, as I did," the general explained. "The door is then carefully reshut for the mark to open and spill to the ground. Or, it may hold, hopefully, even after the mark's reshutting. The door will then fall off when the mark takes the next corner. Perhaps, the mark will not be wearing a seat belt and will join the door in the roadway."

Hitchhikers

Ever since one of them deliberately vomited a ripe pizza in his car, Ray Domino has hated hitchhikers. He was also robbed by a hitchhiker of a gold pig head, a family heirloom he had on a necklace. "The bastard took my wallet, too, but I really missed the pig's charm."

So Ray now goes out of his way to bother abusive hitchhikers. He carries an arsenal of antihitchhiker ordnance in his battered old VW, including water and paint bombs, shaving cream pies and bags filled with itching powders and other irritants.

"In my other car I am building an auxiliary windshield wiper reservoir and hose to be aimed horizontally off the bumper so I can drive slowly by and strafe them with whatever mixture I choose to include in my reservoir."

If I were you, I'd stay out of Ray's way on the open road.

Hookah

I put this one in to educate all you druggies who know only the crude slang term "bong," when what you really mean is a hookah—the true name for that delightful smoking device. On the other hand, maybe you're from New England and thought I meant something else. Nonethess, the Sonic Boomer has this really fab idea for a bong bomb.

"This doper had done something really bad to some really nice people and some corrective behavior was in order," says the Boomer. "I added some methyl alcohol to his bong instead of the customary water. Flooosh, it was meltdown time."

He added with his hearty, humanitarian laugh, "Nobody got physically burned, but I suspect he had to change his shorts after the flash went off."

Horns

It's dangerous, silly, risky, but funny. Mr. Death says if you want to keep your mark awake at night or otherwise harass him during the evening hours, horn in on his time. Our Australian friend says to buy cheap bicycle horns that use batteries to make their awful sound. Buy a dozen of them. Hide them in and around your mark's home, office and/or apartment. Run around and insert batteries into each and keep on moving . . . quickly.

Another way to drive a mark horny is to put a cheap timer device on his car horn, so that it will be set off ablaring at 4 or 5 in the old A.M. This is a nice way to get back at someone you know who tailgates and is always quick on the horn trigger for other drivers.

Hospitals

Most hospitals give newly admitted patients an informative brochure, folder or packet of materials outlining such subjects as visiting hours, treatment procedures, mealtimes, etc. According to Cold Steel, our in-hospital spy, an enterprising trickster could add some new items to these patient packets. One item could be a real or bogus business card for an attorney whose specialty is medical malpractice; nothing freaks out a hospital administration more than the thought of a lawsuit. It will tighten their pucker factor a hundredfold. You could also include information on drug connections inside the hospital, how to have sex with nurses, interns, custodians, etc. Or advertise an in-house hooker/gigolo service. Use your imagination.

A few words of caution, though. Hospitals, even bad ones, are in the business of patient care. You must never, ever, do anything that will put any patient in jeopardy in any way for even a moment. *You* might end up in old St. Wimpus some time. So, be careful there!

Houses

A grand cop turned writer, Joseph Wambugh once shared a talk show with me. He told me a true story about a true prick of a precinct captain whom nobody liked. When the jerk and his wife went on a two-week vacation, some jokesters advertised his house at a very low price and actually had it sold before the owners returned. It created one hell of a fiasco that eventually reached city hall.

Speaking of homes, once a builder screwed Killroy over, not a smart move! Killroy poured a bunch of used motor oil over the drywall in the mark's new construction job, making it impossible to paint over. It added up to costly replacement time. Or to paraphrase the Archduke of Kissinger, one man's vandal is another man's freedom fighter.

IRS

Tax reform. Remember that rich folk rip-off that went through Congress like a dose of salts in 1986? True tax reform, honesty that would help you and me instead of the rich folks who buy this country's politicians and lawmakers, is about as likely as William Perry getting a job as a jockey. Left with that, let's use what we have.

Office supply stores sell Taxpayer File Systems, a filing system for your papers, bills, receipts, and checks. It's your own file-stop center for all of your income-tax related papers. Buy one of these and create a file for your mark. Put in a bunch of miscellaneous papers, receipts, dubious claims, and weakly documented deductions. Make it a mess. Make it look like fraud. Make it insulting. Then, around April 10, bundle up the whole thing and send it to the IRS with a cover letter. This letter should be smug, insulting, and cocky. Tell them to figure out the deductions. Include a very sloppy 1040 return for your mark with lots of obviously weak and illegal deductions. Insult the IRS. Caution: Remember my rules when doing something like this as you're dealing with a *very heavy* federal outfit. Be cool and cautious. But, have fun!

Impersonations

Vaughn Meador and Rich Little have inspired a lot of Haydukery. For example, one of my old pals, who was a radio reporter in the early '60s, used to call his buddies at the *New York Times* and *Washington Post* whenever a nasty story about JFK would appear. He sounded more like JFK than the President. Anyway, pretending to be JFK, my pal would lambaste the newspaper guys, then start to get personal about their wives and girlfriends. It made for fun. Is there a lesson in there for you? I hope so.

Speaking of JFK, the men who conspired to have him murdered in Dallas also used impersonation to make a patsy out of an innocent dupe named Lee Harvey Oswald. They used at least one, maybe two, Oswald look-alikes to do bizarre things in that area so people would remember the man and the name. Is there a lesson in there for you? I hope so.

Impersonate your mark or hire someone to impersonate the mark. Do awful, rotten things in the mark's name. In addition to the people who killed John Kennedy, this stunt is a favorite trick of such fun folks as those at the CIA and the KGB.

Incinerators

If your rotten landlord's place or your least favorite school has a master trash incinerator, it is fun to dump empty aerosol cans into the chutes and listen to the explosive fun that follows about ten seconds later. Don't use cans full of paint, though, or you get a very dramatic pyrotechnical effect when they explode, as in major firebomb time.

A caller from Cleveland had such a tough time getting her landlord to clean up apartments as he ignored her completely. She went to a dozen barber shops and collected a lot of human hair, as in two garbage bags full. Have you ever smelled human hair burning? If not, take my word for it, hair smells worse than a whole body barbeque. Anyway, my caller from Cleveland dumped all of this collected human hair into the incinerator of her building. Within three hours, state and federal agencies had the landlord under close investigation.

Insurance Companies

If your mark works for one of the uptight companies in the insurance industry, Jimi the Z says you're in luck. From experience, he knows that most of these ripoff corporations automatically discipline or terminate employees who make any sort of public dissent or uproar with the legislative or regulatory bodies that deal with the insurance industry. Thus, you could have your mark supposedly write a nasty letter to the editor of a newspaper or magazine, a complaint letter to a regulatory agency, a kudo letter to the Consumer Advocate in your state, or have the mark quoted in a newspaper- or magazine-piece critical of the insurance industry. The fun and nasty games of mistaken identification and paranoid charges and countercharges will give you many guffaws. You can work this same one in the banking industry and the military as well.

Interoffice Memos

If you've ever been in an interoffice political war you know the destructive power of memo missiles. Our Jimmy Carter, as opposed to Georgia's Mr. Peanut, adds to your office arsenal with a forgotten weapon — the envelope. Jimmy writes, "As most of these interoffice envelopes are frequently reused by crossing off the last name before readdressing it, you can use this fact to create paranoia or to spread blame for a nasty and/or anonymous memo to some secondary mark."

Simply send a nasty, filthy, gross or totally insulting memo to your mark, but use the envelope listing the previous address of another mark. The mark adds two and two and comes up with a major error.

Intestines

Kansas City's Ray had an uncaring neighbor who used to toss garbage into Ray's yard. Bad form. Ray tossed it back after trying to reason with the neighbor. No luck, the guy just didn't care and kept dumping. Ray has this friend who works at a meat slaughtering and packing plant across the river, over in Missouri. Ah heck, let's let Ray finish his story. "So, we picked up two barrels of guts from the plant, and that night we spread them on the neighbor's porch. You gotta know just how hot it is in Kansas City in the deep summer. I don't know which was worse, the flies or the stink."

Was Ray bothered again?

"The guy called the police, but, hey, I was at work, and had a great alibi. In fact, I really sympathized with the guy, pretended while the cops were there that I was a great buddy and caring neighbor who was really upset with this awful deed. What a blast. He quit bugging me. No more garbage in my yard."

Jammers

Exercising his reader's rights, the Stainless Steel Rat is back with his version of a simple, homemade "fuzzbuster," an FM signal jammer. You'll see his diagram following these instructions. The specs include an output of 50 to 900 MHz, using 9 to 16 volts and drawing 5 ma.

Barney Vincelette has to be one of our more delightful tricksters. A veteran of the *Real People* TV show, this guy lives in a house coated with luminous paint and illuminated with black light. He lived in more conventional apartments, but he got upset with people running loud TVs and stereos at uncivilized times of day. That's when he designed and built jammers which work well. Here are his diagrams, with his welcome to help yourself.

There are a few jammers available commercially too. A fun guy I know bought one from Johnson Smith and used it to block out a period of closed circuit instruction in the company he worked for. He simply carried it into the meeting room in his briefcase. In another instance, our old pals, Some Very Funny Seniors, spirited one in the false ceiling of their school auditorium, disrupting a planned TV show that would have gotten some very lazy teachers out of the classroom for a few hours.

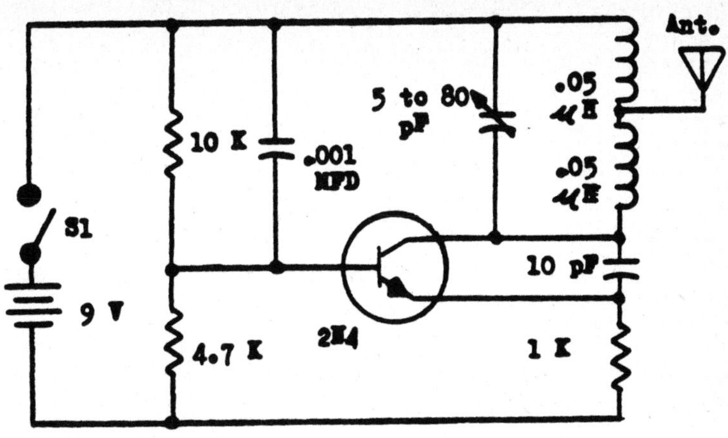

The Stainless "Steal" Rat

Job Interview

It's a simple, basic bit of monkey warfare, but as President Reagan has showed us so often, all is unfair in war, politics or American business. Here's a neat thing to do to the competition, according to Annie Fellantori, who actually is a straighto potato herself.

"If your mark is going on a job interview, call the place he's interviewing and cancel the interview. Or move it back, making the interview time earlier by two hours. That way, the mark shows up late," Annie says with a hard, evil look that could open a clamshell at a hundred yards.

Jocks

At last, an up-to-date athlete who has something new to stuff in your mark's jockstrap — Nair. According to Todd from Phoenix, sweat really does the trick, activating the ingredients which turn your mark back to his prepubescence. Hair today, gone today, is Todd's motto.

Another jocularity comes from athletic supporter Jock Worthen, who gets off on nasty photos. The idea here is to use copied photos of jock or underwear ads with normal models. Or, you can take your own photos with grossly fat models, female models, or whatever. The next step is to composite your mark's head/facial photo on the body of whatever or whomever you've chosen to wear the jock. Whatever way, your mark loses, especially if the photo gains exceptionally wide circulation, like at grade schools and junior and senior high schools with appropriate warnings. I like that portrait, do you?

Junque Mail

After the last book, I got a very uptight-assed letter from the Direct Mail Marketing Association complaining about the nasty things I had written about "direct mail" (aka junk mail), and explaining how vital this commercial mail is to the American economy, how much it means to the lives of the elderly and shut-ins. In this book I vow to dress up my style somewhat. Thus, I will no longer use the term junk mail. It is now as you see it above, junque mail.

Schizoid Sam has come up with a different way to deal with the creative cretins who fill your mailbox with their ploys to transfer funds from your pocket to theirs. He writes, "I always respond to their requests for my financial support to aid their questionable causes. I check the highest amount requested and send them either Monopoly money or one of those 'Dear Name, you may have already won $1,000,000' bogus checks that other junk mailers send out. I figure this is fun, insults them, and I add $$ injury to that by using their postpaid envelopes to return my nastiness in."

Jury Duty

Nobody has caught up with him yet, but authorities in one Pennsylvania county are looking for a man who had called six women and, posing as a court official, ordered them to report for "emergency jury duty" at the courthouse at 5 a.m. the next day. He told them they would be fined if they did not appear. Each did so. The friend who sent me the newspaper clippings about the incident said that authorities were looking for a possible co-worker or neighbor, which sounds to me like they have nothing to go on. It's a cute scam for all involved.

Ketchup

Dr. Davenport, from the town by the same name in Iowa, does not like rip-off restaurants that serve less than diet portions at porker prices. He says they are bloodsuckers, and he has found an appetizing way to deal with them.

"I carry a tampon into the restaurant. While waiting for service, I push it down into the table's ketchup bottle. Or, if I can spirit away several bottles from the service area, I fill up a few bottles. I always leave the string hanging out," says the doctor.

"I always move to a new table or another part of the establishment after doing my thing. Then I watch the ketchup customers and their reactions when they discover what I've done."

If you're worried about professional credentials to carry out this operation, don't. Dr. Davenport's hobby is amateur gynecology.

Keyholes

My friend Bob has had a long and experienced career in the snoop 'n poop field, marred only by his own strong sense of ethics and moral honesty. He managed to share a device that must have come from the hardware division of the Nasty Toy Department: a key-in-a-sleeve device used to jam a lock, usually a door lock. The idea is to slip the bronze outer portion into any keyhole that will accept it. Turn the chromed key and remove. The bronze half is now totally "locked" in the keyhole, blocking all attempts to insert a key into the lock. Actually, the device is a secondary security lock, but it can be put to our evil uses as well.

Keypads

According to The Stainless Steel Rat, a writer for TAP, many installations use touch-sensitive keypads as electronic locks and alarms. They are simply a numbered keyboard like a touch-sensitive phone dial, which you've no doubt seen on TV spy shows.

When nobody is around, wipe the pads free of all fingerprints, and then apply fingerprint dust on the entire surface. The next time some authorized person uses the unit, you can come forward from your observation post and discover the three- or four-digit opening code. A bit of mini-experimenting will open the unit quickly.

Or, according to the Rat, if you want to have some fun with this device, instead of beating it, just push the * and # buttons at the same time. These two buttons have a panic button or emergency function in most units, the Rat notes, and this will bring all sorts of people running.

Keys

Another of Mr. D.'s harassment techniques is far-fetched but worth a try if you're bored with the usual. Due to the possibility that this might prove a little risky for your target, he suggests that you be more careful than may seem necessary. Here's the trick. Collect various keys, particularly house keys, and place them on key rings. Tag each ring with a label showing your target's name, address, etc. You might also list a high-dollar occupation, such as gun collector, jewelry connoisseur or diamond specialist. The tags should be roughed up to look worn from use, and the keys should be slightly tarnished, rather than suspiciously shiny and new.

Judiciously deposit the tagged keys in a number of locations around the scuzzbag areas of town. The idea is to entice interlopers to visit your target's home and possibly try to break in. The chances of such luck are nil, but even if honest citizens contact your target upon finding the keys, all is not lost. You will have placed your target in the unpleasant position of wondering what the hell is going on.

Labels

Many tricksters now use the Dymo Label Maker to create anonymous messages for their marks. As James Q. Carter writes, "It's a lot easier than cutting letters and words out of newspapers and pasting them on paper." Carter also uses his homemade labels for mark's store windows, walls and display areas, issuing such consumer warnings as Rip Off Artist, Price Gouger, Sodomist, Thief, Pervert, Inept or whatever he thinks describes the mark. He also knew someone who sent a message to his mark using a label maker to create a tape reading "B-O-O-M! This could have been a letter bomb." Oh, and don't forget to wipe your prints off the plastic tape, he adds.

In a like sense, the Indiana Cave Man suggests that doing your own silk-screen printing is easy and inexpensive. Print some large official-looking, adhesive labels, something to the effect as follows:

CRIMINAL EVIDENCE
Impounded by the
FEDERAL BUREAU OF INVESTIGATION
TAMPERING WITH EVIDENCE IS A FELONY
Maximum penalty $10,000/5 years imprisonment

for disturbing this seal without permission of
FEDERAL PROSECUTOR'S OFFICE.
(add appropriate long-distance phone number.)

Use these stickers to seal the doors, trunk and hood of the mark's car. Another variation: Seal the mark's house or business while he's on vacation. Use *really sticky,* thin, paper, bumper-sticker material, so the mark will have more trouble on his hands when he finally gets around to removing the labels.

Landlords

Once upon a terrible time, a leaky landlord troubled our Captain Kill. The Captain is a veteran trickster, so he took his trusty roadkill patrol out on a specimen hunt just before final inspection to vacate the premises.

"The guy was a real jerk, and I wanted to get back at him a few days after I had cleared the state with my deposit refund cash in hand. I found the perfect resting spot for that roadkill.

"I took the grate off the heat register in the apartment and pushed the dead 'possum back as far as it would go. Then, I replaced the grill. An hour later I had my refund and was gone. It was winter and the heat ran a lot. I suspect my ex-landlord got quite a surprise a couple of days later when he showed the place to the new tenant. The place was a rat trap when I lived there, so I turned it into a odor trap when I left."

more

Landlords

A thoughtful gift for an errant landlord comes from the Lord God of Vengeance, who says an ant farm makes a fine going-away present, especially if it's left in some obscure location where only a dedicated and/or expensive exterminator can find it.

Another friendly fan, an old, toss-back hippie named Joe Donolay, is truly a relic from another era. But, he has a message for nasty landlords who do mean things to innocent tenants. Joe suggests that you "call the landlord's mother if there are gross, disgusting sex 'n drug parties in your building. Invite her to the party and tell her that her son is the prime sponsor . . . hey, he owns the building. Naturally, you don't tell her in advance what kind of party she's getting involved with."

Joe says this has worked well for him three or four times.

Landpersons

Being basically gentle folks, Americans would generally respect the rights of others. That's probably what M. Sgt. Ranger Rick, USA, thought during his days in 'Nam as a Ranger.

Despite this, M. Sgt. Rick was once sharing a basement apartment with a young lady friend. He says his upstairs neighbors belonged in a zoo. These are probably the sort from gene pools who have bruises on their knuckles from walking.

"We were had. The upstairs wife was the landlady's sister, and the landlady was shacking up with a local cop. Half the time, the cops and these broads were the ones raising hell. We had no recourse through the law, and trying gentlemanly moral persuasion didn't help either," Rick relates.

"The situation was untenable. We buried the VC in better holes than this dump. So, my friend and I had to leave at great personal inconvenience and financial loss. But, my friend and I pooled our thoughts and figured we ought to leave the place clean."

In their basement apartment stood a big water pipe that was sealed with lead rope at the joint. Rick applied hydrochloric acid just prior to their final departure from this awful abode. He says that three days later, four feet of water stood in the basement apartment. Much damage resulted, including electrical problems and structural cracking.

Obviously, this is a case of changing whine into water!

Law Enforcement

Sometimes people who give assholes a bad name get into the law-enforcement business, a growth industry that has more than its share of hypocrites. Perhaps you have real, honest reason to get back at a cop, sheriff, district attorney, constable, or whatever. Here is one way to doing it, thanks to my inside source, Edwin Mouse.

According to Edwin, many of these hypocrites break more laws than they enforce and are living proof that there are at least two or three systems of justice in our world. One of their universal traits is that they like to party.

"I recall one time when there was a truly hated man serving as DA, sheriff, chief, or whatever, and a lot of people had it in for him for really good reasons. These were not crooks or slimes bitter about being caught. These were straight people with legit gripes about this arrogant jackass. Here is what someone did," Edwin told me.

"The guy had a big party with lots of booze and food. A lot of his criminal justice buddies and their women showed up, of course. And, like most of these

(Continued...)

bashes, a lot of people got really tuned up. Our trickster had told some news people to crash the party quietly 'for a scoop.' Our trickster also made certain that 'someone' had stashed a goodly amount of coke in the house.

"Then, 'someone' made certain that some of the tuned folks who might like coke ('someone' really did homework) got into the stash, in a room where the host had no idea what was happening. About three minutes later, some on-duty officers who were straight and honest and had been quietly tipped about this whole operation by 'someone' came to the door and were easily admitted. They went right to the coke room, as did the news people."

The rest of the story is a study in confusion, embarrassment, news frenzy, political gossip, sexual gossip, and a lot of real ethical questions. The majority of the mark's political mentors — older men not at the party — took a very, very dim view of the entire situation, regardless of what was said in the mark's defense.

Actually, as Edwin Mouse told me, there was more damage done to the mark by what was not published or prosecuted than by what was made public. See, there really is justice, if you're willing to go out and get it for yourself.

Lawns

Our intrepid landscape demolisher, Mr. Heffer from Missouri, had a nasty, nosy neighbor who used to scold Mr. Heffer for not taking care of his lawn like the neighbor did her prized lawn. Mr. Heffer decided to attract more attention for her lawn.

"I waited until June, when the local K-Mart was selling garden plant seeds for about a nickel a bag and I bought all of their leaf lettuce seeds . . . I went over to that old biddy's lawn and tossed those seeds all over the place one night when we were due to get a day or two of rain. No need to scratch that stuff in . . . just toss it amid the grass. It grows great and soon she had the damnedest-looking lawn you ever saw."

Added to that idea, The Lord God of Vengeance says that he uses either clover or dandelion seeds to get the same effect from a crabby, bluegrass freak who refuses to have any impure strains in his putter-perfect lawn.

When Bill Murray played Karl, the gifted assistant greenskeeper in that wonderful film *Caddyshack,* I knew genius had arrived. If ever there is a Hayduke movie, we gotta get that Karl character in there. Darren

(Continued...)

from Arizona isn't the same character, but, he has a wonderful landscape suggestion if your mark loves his lawn as much as Ted Knight loved his golf greens in *Caddyshack*.

Darren says, "You pour lots of liquid Dawn detergent all over the mark's lawn. When it rains or is watered, it bubbles all over the place, like green champagne."

Several readers have asked me for less esoteric and expensive weed-killers to use in having fun with marks' lawns. Try this: Mix one part laundry bleach with three or four parts of water. Sprinkle it at random on plants or lawn, use it to make fun designs, or to write funny and/or foul words.

more

Lawns

Here's one to help your mark harvest some wild oats. According to Sal Barclay, your local farm store sells a product known as Ortho Bugetta TM as a snail bait. Actually, this product is a hybrid oat strain that grows super fast. Some night, sprinkle it all over your mark's prize lawn. He will soon be dealing with an unusual botanical eruption.

Kilroy is obviously a lawn-lover. He suggests that some rainy night you visit your mark's lawn and spread the contents of many large boxes of corn flakes on the lawn. By morning, the mark will encounter a lawn that's full of soggy, highly unpleasant-smelling oatmeal that is very difficult to remove. If the weather stays awful, the stuff will rot the grass. If the sun comes out hot enough, it will bake it hard. Either way you have achieved serial revenge!

more

Lawns

Colorado's Bill Basque is a great friend, but a badass if you're his enemy. He likes to lay lengths of thin wire in his mark's lawn so that when mowing occurs, the wire may bind up the mower. Or if the wire's very thin, it will rip and fly off like shrapnel, scarring the mower blade and the mark. If it is too thick to cut and binds the blades, hopefully it will also burn out the motor.

I'm sure you've all seen the wonderful ceramic statues that adorn the lawns of many mold-minded middle Americans in towns like Polyester, Ohio. Why not create a formerly living version of the same for your mark's lawn? The idea here is to help with the landscaping some evening or while the mark is away for a period of time by propping up large roadkill in the mark's lawn. Dead deer, dogs, even groundhogs will work well, especially if rigor mortis has already set in.

Leprosy

I became interested in this disease many years ago when Lenny Bruce was masquerading as a Catholic priest and hustling rich, guilt-ridden Jewish folks in Miami to contribute to a leper colony he had founded. It was very quasi-legal even if he did get busted. Later, when Jerry Lewis passed over leprosy, hangnails, and psoriasis, settling on Jerry's Kids as his telethon disease, I knew the day of our truth would come.

That day hasn't come yet. But, in the meantime, you could go to your favorite printer and create some letterhead from a law firm or some state government agency that would be hard to trace. On this letterhead you could create a letter to be sent to all folks in the neighborhood, condo, apartment complex, or whatever saying that Mr. or Ms. Mark, the owner, is selling the property for use as a leprosarium. You may embellish the remainder of the letter, then imagine the response.

Letters

Despite the frothy-mouthed ravings of the old pharts who run the Reaganista Party, the Soviets do have a sense of humor. There is an old Soviet practice known as *anonimka,* in which someone writes an anonymous letter to a superior or party official falsely accusing a colleague of misconduct at the office, factory, school, or institute. Soviet officials are, believe it or not, far more paranoid than Reaganistas, although we are closing the frump gap quickly, and tend to overreact in the zeal to investigate.

Anonimka has created more than one major flap in the Party and among what passes for industry in the USSR. Recently, *Izvestia* editorialized against the practice, tirading against "false, cowardly attacks." The Soviet press tries to discourage people from using anonimka to get back at their enemies by slandering them.

I checked with my publisher and so far we haven't sold the Soviet Union rights to my books, so they can't blame anonimka on me. Otherwise, it's a pretty doggone good stunt. It was Sir Edward Bulwer-Lytton who said, "The pen is mightier than the sword," but as I'll add, that's only if you're willing to push it.

Library

This trick is very simple, as outlined by Doug Hummell of Jacksontown, Pennsylvania. Go to your local library and take out a card in your mark's name. At most, all you will have to do is fill out a card with his/her name, address, etc.

The rest is simple. Take out expensive and/or rare books, and don't return them on time, or place them in your mark's home if you have access. She or he will get calls. Discovery will cause bewilderment, costly confusion and maybe court problems.

Light Bulbs

Only someone with a wild sense of humor like my buddy Bob has could come up with this one Rube Goldberg device to break light bulbs. It's a nasty metal device with two arms tipped with sharp points. These two arms are loaded by a heavy spring. The device is attached to a light bulb, with the pincer arms held back by a cocking lever. The unit is armed by that lever, which is attached to a pull-cord. This cord is substituted for the standard pull-cord of a light fixture. When the mark goes into the darkened room and pulls the cord, *whoommmm,* all sorts of fun happens when that heavy spring that's holding back those terrible pincers is released and they explode and obliterate bulbs in less than 1/500th of a second. This stunt is very dangerous and must have originated in some strange mind at some U.S. government installation.

Linoleum Floors

Have a mark whose place is furnished in classic lino? Pour a bit of methyl ethyl ketone (MEK) on the floor—instant destruction. According to Killroy, the stuff will also scar and craze plexiglass.

Lipstick

Here's a refinement of the shoe-polish-on-the-telephone-receiver trick for marks with jealous lovers. Place a small amount of lipstick in the phone receiver. It takes such a tiny amount to do the job that the mark probably won't notice it, even if his phone is some color other than red. His or her sweetie will notice it, I guarantee that. I used this myself, and it's effective.

Lockers

Once a bitchy little preppyette made life nasty for our Masked Revenger. It had to do with high school lockers. So he made two trips to the school office: One was to boost a couple memo sheets, while the later visit was to place a forged order to change the lock on the girl's locker in the custodian's box. You can imagine the fun—unofficial and later, official.

Locking Gas Caps

Have a cap to spare? One of our good buddies down in Columbia, South Carolina, Andy Weiner, suggested on WIS radio that you put someone else's locking gas cap on your mark's car. It's easier for you to get a new cap for your car than it is for him to get yours off his.

Machismo

A lot of guys think with their zippers, which soon becomes a pain in the ego to normal people. That very splendid lady, Paulette Cooper, has a fun idea to get a mite of revenge. She uses a picture of a gorgeous lady and a handwritten note about how wonderful she heard the mark is in bed, and how very good she is, and that they ought to get together. She leaves a telephone number. That's the kicker.

"You use one of your local telephone company's line test numbers because it's always busy — the phone that rings forever," Paulette says.

She suggests a variant where you've actually been out with the mark. Here you get a photo of some beautiful lady who looks like you — never use your own photo. It's okay to be romantically explicit in the note, by the way. Either way, the guy ends up frustrated, physically or mentally.

Mafia

Every so often the feds or state police bust a Mafia chieftain, sometimes on pretty serious charges. You can use this criminal to aid your cause. As anyone who knows the Crime Corporation's operations will tell you, these powerful bosses retain their control even while in the slam. Thus, it would be fun if your mark wrote a vile, nasty, threatening, mocking, or other not-nice letter to this Mob boss. You could include some "doing the dozens" about the guy's family, his parish priest, his momma, too.

Shortly after this letter is received I bet your mark will be visited by some large gentlemen who don't have necks. What happens next is of amusement to you, no doubt.

Dick Smegma adds some refinement to my basic idea by noting that you should send a copy of the letter to the guy's attorney. He also cautions that you wear gloves to type the letter,use a typewriter other than your own, use totally sanitized paper, and wet the stamp with a sponge and not your tongue. If the Mob guy is from another city, either have the letter mailed from there or from the mark's own town.

Magazines

You'll have to wait until the statute of limitations expires before I identify the magazine in question here, but, let me tell you how I got nasty with one that had rudely and crudely allowed its computers to do me in. I won't bore you with details, but it managed to screw up my initial subscription, extension of same, and an address change. All of this within two years, and I was eventually getting dunned by a collection agency on three separate bills for which I was getting no magazines. It cost me a $20 trip to small claims court to get them off my back and the matter settled. *Phew!*

Here's what I did next. By this time, I also had five other people to whom I owed some hassle of varying degrees. I got a new subscriber card for each mark to this, my least favorite magazine. No, it's not funny nor especially clever, but I know it cost my main magazine mark some serious money and I know it cost my other marks some time, energy, and letter hassle.

As I've said before, to be effective, you don't always have to be clever or funny.

On the other hand, there is Schizoid Sam who knows a way to obtain magazines more inexpensively than you are now, unless you're stealing them. He

(Continued...)

points out, quite correctly, that college student rates are the absolute lowest in the business, the idea being to hook those potential consumers early. Sam suggests you become a "student" to take advantage of these low subscription rates. Here's how.

"Go to the bookstore at the nearest college or university and pick up those subscription fliers that are on counters, bulletin boards, etc. You an also find them in all classrooms, as companies pay kids to post them.

"These fliers list hundreds and hundreds of magazines at special student rates. You simply fill out your name and address, and send them a check for whatever you want. They will ask you for your year of graduation . . . so let's make you a junior. That means you write in next year's date there. When you renew or subscribe again, just add a year. So many of these come in to them each year that nobody checks anyway," Sam relates.

By now, everyone knows how to order thousands of magazines for hundreds of marks or how to get your own subscriptions more cheaply. Here's a new twist from the Idaho Wildman, who says you can order a select few magazines especially chosen to hit the mark where it hurts hardest. For example, he says, "Suppose your mark is some evil woman whose husband escaped by running off with a nurse. Subscribe to a few nursing journals in her name, using a gift card to Bitch, from The Happy Couple." The neat thing about this is every hobby and every occupation has at least one special interest journal or magazine of its own.

Mail

If your mark has a rural mail box, go over at night and remove the entire box. Leave a printed, official-looking notice on the support or on the house door that reads something like:

> Your mail box has been removed by order of the Postmaster General because of failure to comply with Federal Regulation 86R-#1, subparagraph F-785-GH. Contact your local Postmaster for further instructions.

Do this after the mail has been delivered on a Saturday. The phone calls the mark makes will be wonderful, as will the confusion at the post office. For this special delivery item, we owe a parcel of thanks to David Kirkpatrick.

As reported before, for years I have either routinely tossed out junk mail or returned the postage-paid envelopes affixed to a package of heavy rocks. You can also gross out selected junk mailers by returning the envelopes stuffed with hardcore porno pictures. James Q. Carter takes it one step further. He learns the name of the company's CEO, then sends the porno addressed to the boss's executive secretary.

more

Mail

Mr. Death is both funny and useful. He suggests you simply steal your mark's rural letterbox in the evening. The postal people will obviously not deliver mail if there is no rural box. Mr. Death says that the mark will put up a new one. You wait a day and then steal it. Do this several times, after you are sure the mark and/or the postal inspectors are not looking for you. Here's the kicker: after a year or so has passed, drive by the mark's place and toss out all of the purloined postal boxes onto his lawn.

Or, if your mark lives in an unincorporated suburb, township or rural area, the mail comes to a large, post-mounted mailbox. You could change the name and/or number of your mark's box. This will confuse the carrier for a day or two, which may be enough to pull a short scam.

I love cooked eggs, dripping with butter, a great habit I picked up in Mexico. I later learned from Major General K. Oss that he loves cooked eggs also, but, in this case, the yoke is on the mark. The general says that lightly cracked eggs placed in your mark's mailbox on a hot summer's day quickly cook into a very odorous

(Continued...)

mess. Perhaps if they are placed there after the mail service on Saturday, they will have all day Sunday to strengthen.

I checked this out with my postal consultant, Paco Pendeja, who told me that the postal carrier is likely to be as upset by this mess as the mark himself. Also, the carrier is in a position to add further to the mark's woes about the mess, according to Paco.

more

Mail

The Indiana Cave Man has a good idea with a cautionary notice.

"As a refinement to your trick of the change of address card for a mark, let's get a secondary mark with the same name. Reroute the primary mark's mail to that other person. The post office will get blamed for the mess, of course."

The Caver went on to wonder what would happen if we also filed a card sending the secondary mark's mail to the primary mark's address? Then, I wondered what would happen if you started looking for various marks with the same names in different cities?

Cave Man passes along the warning, though, that "tampering with the mails is a big crime, and postal cops are very efficient."

Mail Forwarding

My goodness, Steve has terrible handwriting, but what a wonderful mind. Here's his ample idea for helping the U.S. Postal Service deliver all their mail.

"Peel-off labels are useful. You can remove them and replace them with custom-made labels of your choice, if you follow the proper computer-looking formats. You can also remove your mark's labels if you swipe his mail. Then simply put those labels on nasty porno, religious, or other obnoxious material and mail that."

more

Mail Forwarding

I get a lot of requests for outfits that do mail forwarding. To find them, scan the classifieds in such magazines as *Rolling Stone, Mother Jones,* and *Moneysworth,* or look through some of the counterculture publications. But, because mail forwarding and drop boxes are always so important to Haydukers, I am listing some here which are very professional in operation. If you have others which you've used and wish to add to my list, please let me know.

- Abell
  520 Isabel Dr.
  Santa Cruz, CA 95060
- Mail Forwarding
  Box 125
  Wynnewood, PA 19096
- Morris & Morris
  P.O. Box 80767
  Los Angeles, CA 90008
- Zebra Mail Center
  P.O. Box 11028
  Houston, TX 77391

Mailboxes

Millie Kemrer shares an idea that I hope doesn't get her caught in the rain, sleet, snow, or hell that falls on our U.S. mailpersons. She has a friend who displaced her mark's mailbox identity.

"A friend of mine owns a small apartment building with one really obnoxious tenant who used to get drunk and raise hell on the first and fifteenth of each month when his government checks came in. She spent hours talking to the main man without any positive results. So she simply, and illegally, removed his name from the apartment's mailbox complex. He didn't get his checks . . . or anything else. She told me he moved out."

Managers

RT is an extreme example of the Peter Principle gone berserk. Actually, he is a high-management type in a large institution which has several branch offices around the region in which the company operates. He is also a hardcore jerk, a man who gives Kafka-like meaning to the term incompetence. You could count his friends on one hand and still have four fingers and a thumb left over. Get the picture?

Because he was exceptionally nasty and snotty to his subordinates, they chose to get back at him. They targeted his office because the man was a victim of executive trappings. As RT's old nemesis, the IFC Poster Child, tells it, "If the man had half a brain, we'd have immediately driven him bonkers. As it was, we had to work harder."

For starters, they doctored the photos in his office for several weeks, e.g., slipping new photos in the existing frames. On his own wall-mounted portrait (yeah, he had that in his own office), they burned out the eyes. Then they pasted a fake moustache on the new print he had mounted.

After a month, he ranted and raved to both his staff and to security about this office vandalism. The breaking point came when someone put a bunch of helium-filled condoms in his small adjoining conference room just prior to his marching in a group of important clients for a meeting.

As a finale, the revenge seekers waited until he left for a three-day conference. Then with the help of a forged work order and a couple of cooperative maintenance workers, they had his entire office moved to a branch plant forty-five miles away. RT returned to a bare office. All the staff feigned total ignorance, showing him the work order with his own perfectly forged signature on it. It took him the entire day just to locate his office contents and ten more days to get the move straightened out. He got no sympathy from his fellow executives. It was wonderful, and according to Poster Child, the campaign continues. He adds, "Going to work is fun again."

Marks

After studying George Hayduke's books and those of his paled imitators, I figure there are five categories of mark. Knowing these differences is more than just academic; consider them to be psycho-intelligence that you can use to make your revenge either more bitter, more sweet, more fitting—or all of the above. Here are my five categories of mark.

1. ***The loser.*** This mark is dumb or innocent and rarely realizes that a zap has taken place. Your scams and stunts here call for high creativity and imagination. The potential is here, too, for long-running and continuing revenge efforts. The Loser will likely blame bad luck or his/her own personality for the misfortune(s).

2. ***Someone else, not me!*** This one is also known as the secondary mark. This secondary target is often innocent and is used only as a catalyst to wreak more revenge on the primary mark. A good example of this is to inflict an "accident" on the innocent bystander (secondary mark) in a restaurant (primary mark) when the bystander's meal, clothing, family, or property is assaulted and he/she blames the primary mark and takes action. If you're a truly cruel person, this mark is worth a lot of laughs.

3. ***Why me?*** This mark knows he or she is a victim, but the blame or evidence always points elsewhere: the dog, a stupid repairperson, a bumbling waitress, clerk, etc. Like the Loser, this type of mark rarely catches on to what's happening.

4. ***Common paranoid.*** This mark knows he or she has been the victim of some dirty trick and usually has an idea as to why. The great part is that the mark rarely knows who to blame. As the anguish intensifies, mental blocks prevent logical thought processes, creating repressive paranoid emotion. The mark's own actions at this point often cause more problems for him/her.

5. ***The game.*** This classification is based on the crude, but effective, "Godfather Syndrome," as the Indiana Cave Man terms it. The mark knows who did "it" to him or her and, usually, why it was done. Sometimes, the mark will attempt retribution. The idea is to discourage this by being awesomely awful in your choice of scams. The mark should fear trying to retaliate.

Mass Transit

Filthy McNasty has been to the pet shop and bought several populations of ant farms. Filthy's ant farming is more than a hobby; it's shared with the public.

"I'm going to populate my least favorite bus with thousands of the little critters. Scratch, scratch," chortles Filthy, with no picnic in mind.

Sometimes Filthy takes a whooppee cushion on board the bus or trolley, adding, "I drop some calcium carbide on the floor, then sit on this cushion. The combination really moves people."

Here's another. You get on a bus or jitney carrying a small, closed, cottage cheese container with some fork holes punched in the lid. Hopefully, it's on a nonstop freeway line. You suddenly yell, "Oh shit!!" Wait the few seconds while all attention swings and focuses on you, then look back at your fellow travelers and say with controlled-panic gravity, "Dear God, all of my Brown Recluse Spiders got loose on this bus. Please, please be careful. They're extremely dangerous; one bite is agony. Oh, my God." Sniggle and sniffle and *act*. Filthy says this will cause an exit stampede even if the bus has not yet stopped.

Spiders or not, I feel the bite of potential lawsuits against a busline which has been bad to you.

Mealtime Guests

Davenport's Thelma wants to share a great thought that works each time. If you have guests who drop in for dinner at odd times without invitation, here's a helpful tip: Pick out the dinner plates you want to use, and smear a bit of fat on them. Just before handing the uninvited guest a plate, let your tired, old dog with the ill mouth actually lick the plates. Explain that your dishwasher is broken, and the dog is one of the family.

Meat Loaf

Thanks to Mot Rot, I know how important meat loaf is. According to Mr. Rot, meat loaf starts out semisquishy but gets harder and harder as it sits in the leftover section of your refrigerator. Even Mr. Rot agrees that meat loaf can't be traced through ballistics, although it hurtles through the air in hardened states at great speed. Used as a blunt instrument, it can cause trauma.

Meat Shoppes

I love custom butcher shops, always have. I've never been to a bad one. But, Macho has, and he really beat their meat in response. He got a bad steak — tough. He returned the unused portion and was told to "forget it" when asking for some adjustment.

"I was really reasonable about it, too," Macho says. "I showed the guy the meat and my receipt. He said I bought some cheap beef somewhere else, pulled a switch, and was trying to cheat him. We argued and argued; then he threatened to call the cops. I left. But had he screwed up!"

Macho knew of a real putz who also shopped there, a guy he wanted to nail for another reason. It looked like combined revenge time. Macho called the market in the other mark's name and ordered over a hundred dollars' worth of fine meat. He adds, "Don't go whole hog and run up a big bill. Keep it believable."

He had a girlfriend from outside the neighborhood pick up the other mark's order and charge it to that mark's account. Macho says, "Man, we ate well for a long time on that scam. It never would have happened if old Mr. Butcher hadn't been dishonest with me."

Media

I despise the misuse of this word in reference to people who work for magazines, newspapers, radio, and television because it is almost always used incorrectly, plus it has become a buzz word.

Here's your language lesson. Media is the plural form of medium. Radio, for example, is a medium. Radio, newspapers, TV, etc. are media. They are mass communication media. Reporters, commentators, writers, journalists, and anchortwinkies are *not* media. They are people who work for media, even if many of them don't know the difference. Now, here's the rest of it.

This section is devoted to Joey Skaggs, a very well-known scam artist who preys on "Media" much like the roadrunner destroys Wile E. Coyote. In my opinion, he has proved himself worth his weight in disloyalty to the system and in showing how easily it is manipulated.

Skaggs' forte is to plant phony stories and appear on interviews to spread sillymation. Some of his classics that made ocean-to-ocean news across the U.S. included sperm banks for the stars (celebrities), a bordello for dogs, fish condos, etc. He's been at it since 1966. Even

(Continued...)

in the summer of 1986, he nailed *Good Morning America* with his Fat Squad, in which he claimed dieters hired strong people to physically restrain them from eating. No, I'm not kidding. Ask the very embarrassed David Hartman, GMA's host.

An artist and visual arts professor in New York City, Skaggs has used his own name and pen names, and has appeared under different funny names for more than twenty years now. He has fooled the Establishment media, and his scams have appeared in all major newspapers, wire services, and networks. Sometimes he gets calls *weeks* after his hoaxes are broken. Some of his other stories include:

- A coalition of ethnic descendants going to court to protest the name "gypsy" in gypsy moth.
- Development of cockroach hormones into a medicine that cures acne and menstrual cramps.
- "Crazed" U.S. Special Forces detachment "attacked" a Nativity scene in New York's Central Park (he partially staged this).

Why does all of this work? Mostly because a lot of news people are lazy, and a lot more are gullible, and many just "want to believe" so they can share it with the public. Finally, don't ever forget the most widely read newspaper in America is *National Enquirer* and remember that more Americans read *TV Guide* than any other publication. I rest my case.

Medical

I'm not sure if this is for or against us, but one doctor in every fifty is operating with bogus credentials, according to a 1985 study by a U.S. Congressional subcommittee on national health care. Perhaps a study is in order to see which group gives the better care: 49 of 50, or 1 of 50. In any case, if you should happen to find out, please let me know. I am always happy to get stories of and from the medical industry for the next book.

For this volume, the only funny medical story I heard was from The Intestine Internist who says that someone got really upset at a local doctor in the Boston area who spent more time on the golf course than on his practice or family.

On one rare night when Dr. Mark had to stay at one of the hospitals in that city, his unhappy assailant used some 2 by 4 boards to build forms around the back tires of the Doc's Porsche. He then poured a bit of premixed, quick-dry cement into the forms. Within the hour, the doctor's $52,000 auto and, I guess, its owner, were sentenced to the area for awhile. Some guys get away with mortar!

Mercenary

Given the mood of the middle-mind American mentality, this one will work well. It feeds on the Soldier of Glory image that too many Ameridiots adopt. The basic idea is as simple as the marks: you buy an ad in one of the *Soldier of Fantasy* glossy-color comic books that run Mercwork ads, using your mark's name. Be sure to include real heavy active duty service in Vietnam, the Middle East, or Central America, and that the mark's Military Occupational Speciality (MOS) is one of the combat/intelligence number groups.

What's the scam? Various elements of the U.S. government are not happy about private soldiers making and carrying out deadly foreign policy. Thus, *big* trouble with the U.S. authorities can come to your unsuspecting mark. In addition, in the past few years there have been some rather well-publicized cases in which "mercenaries" have been recruited from such ads to do some highly illegal things, e.g., bust dopers out of prison, murder spouses, smuggle explosives to some Middle East baddies.

Microwave Ovens

If you have access to your mark's kitchen, remove a dozen or so raw eggs from his refrigerator and place them in the microwave oven. Set for about two minutes and quickly depart from the area.

Sometimes it pays to be nasty, not funny. According to Akron Annie, who quick-dried her ill-fated pet poodle in a microwave, you can quickly nuke one of these marvelous appliances out of order in easy fashion.

"Slide a piece of aluminum foil underneath the drip pan inside of the oven," she says. "The miracle waves do the rest. Blitzo . . . one destroyed microwave."

Military

Going from merc to military is often no more than a jump out of the old sheepdip pen. Anyway, when Lt.C. Mac was a lot younger, he spent some time in Vietnam. He once had a rare chance to get a bit of R 'n' R, but had to get bumped on a very brass-crowded flight. As a junior officer at the time, he had little chance to be on that flight until he met the flight manifest sergeant with the Circle F Brand.

"I was dumbfounded when this smiling NCO told me I had made the flight; he'd gotten me aboard," Lt.C. Mac recalls. "He told me he had bumped some people because of official priorities. Nobody questioned it; there was a war on. But, I was hardly official. I must have looked like a lost dummy, so he explained it to me."

The flight manifest sergeant told our hero, "Well, sir, your driver sergeant told me you are an OK man and a good officer. That counts for you. Now, sir, look on this flight list. See some of these names with a little 'F' penciled next to them? That little 'F' is our code to fuck over those people because they deserve it."

Lt.C. Mac stared, then said, "What about the big

(Continued...)

'F' with the circle around it?"

"Well sir, that means to *really* fuck that guy over, like bump him, yet send his luggage to Alaska or have a crewman dump it overboard, or to lose his papers at the other end if we don't bump him. We have quite an unofficial officer evaluation network, sir."

The point of Lt.C. Mac's nice little story is that if you or a friend are in a position to put circled 'F' marks next to people's names on passenger or other duty lists, please keep that power in mind. Also, this stunt will work well when you leave the military and are reborn a civilian. It also can tell you something about the *real* Golden Rule.

I got this next idea after reading some really horrifying letters a former GI in Vietnam wrote to his pal just before he deserted and went over to the other side. A friend of mind, an investigative reporter who did an article on "Turncoats in Action for the VC," based much of his work on government documents and intelligence reports about these Americans who not only deserted, but also took up arms against their countrymen. The notes, copies of reports, letters, and his story gave me this idea.

You write a very subversive letter from your mark to one of that mark's best friends, a sweetheart, a family member, a hometown newspaper editor, the unit chaplain, a former teacher, coach, or whatever. You really fill it with a lot of anti-American, pro-Commie stuff. Make it really radical and theme it so it reads like the mark is about to go over and/or do serious damage to (sound of bugles) *National Security.*

Also make certain that a rough draft or other copy of this letter is left lying around an office, dayroom, barracks, rec center, or somewhere that a *right*-thinking GI troop will find it. By now, I am sure you have guessed the rest.

Considering the normal paranoia of the military and adding on today's super-heated anti-Communist propaganda, your mark is going to be in a whole lot of trouble, even if he eventually beats this rap. The term "military justice" is just as nonsensical a contradiction as "military intelligence," but with a much longer arm and memory.

When my demented mind flashes back to those fun 'n gory days, I always trip over George Orwell's famous quote which is lying around with my mental blocks: "Those who take the sword perish by the sword. Those who don't take the sword perish by smelly diseases."

Orwell was a military man; also British, you know.

more

Military

Ever had a cook you hated when you did KP? Here's what one "Old GI" from Florida, as he signed himself, did about it.

"This red-neck was just pure poison on KPs, pure nasty with no cause. Since it was almost always wet in the kitchen in Asia, I came up with an idea. I had seen him sprinkle a lot of foot powder in his shoes, so one day I substituted lye powder for the foot powder. In about five weeks, he was carried off that base on a stretcher and put on a plane home."

Milk

Speaking of stuff that won't come out or off, according to the Lyndora Moore, condensed milk is a great addition if you want something that (1) won't come off anything, (2) is very messy, slippery and sticky, (3) smells megabad after a few days.

Likewise, Anon writes, "Use Eagle Brand condensed milk as a smelly glue or worse. If this stuff gets a chance to dry, nothing short of sand-blasting will remove it."

Sometimes, bad things happen to truly nice people. For instance, Orrie Baysinger wrote to tell me, "My kid spilled some milk in the car. It got into the carpet, under the floormat, molding etc. After one week, we had fermentation and impossible stench. No way to clean it up. It was awful and lasted more than a month. Think about it."

We didn't have to think too long. So thanks, and a tip of the mighty milk mug to you, Orrie.

Milk Carton Kids

I learned about one of the nastier pieces of sabotage during a telephone talk show in New Orleans, when a delightful chap told how he used the media-creation hysteria of "missing kids" to do in his mark. I refer to the missing kids thing as Milk Carton Kids, but, please, don't get me wrong, I love milk. Anyway, here's his scam.

"I created a missing kid with the help of a printer and a friend who was a retired cop and also hated this mark of ours. We created just enough cover to make the kid seem real to someone with more than casual interest.

"Then we created a small investigation and carefully created enough media interest to get some modest coverage. After a week or so, we created 'witnesses' who had seen the abduction, all in the form of another public announcement. We circulated a description and 'police artist' sketch.

"Guess who the description and sketch, which we had an artist friend do from a picture, looked like? Right you are — our mark. Our next step was to have these run off and posted all over town. It wasn't long until real police interest was generated, which brought

(Continued...)

heavier media attention.

"The guy got really hyper and denied everything, in a panic. You know, the 'Oh God, yes, I quit beating my wife' kind of thing. Eventually, he was cleared, but it took much more expense and energy on his part than it did on the police's part. They just dropped the thing, after giving him hell for looking like the suspect and acting guilty."

Mobile Homes

This came in from Jimmy Carter, but he isn't the one with peanut hulls stuck to his boots by pig poop. He says if someone who lives in a mobile home, camper, or recreational vehicle gives you trouble and won't listen to reason, it's time to deflate someone's tire, although not literally.

According to Mr. Carter, using a hose clamp, attach a section of inner tube to the drain pipe on the sewage holding tank on the mark's mobile home or camper. Attach the other end, again with a hose clamp, to a device leading to the vehicle's tire or one of those emergency inflator units. When the mark flushes the potty, a great deal of pressurized sewage will literally blow up in someone's face.

Model Aircraft

Filthy McNasty and Vera from Los Angeles have a grand air-raid number. Buy and fly a radio-controlled model airplane, or "borrow" a unit from a secondary mark. This number goes great with attacks on participants and spectators at ball games, concerts, parades, etc.

"Buzz the crowd, dive on the players, attack and ignite smoke devices or small bombs, using remote control," Vera adds.

Molesters

Serious child molestation is far too serious for Hayduking. It calls for radical surgery, e.g., meatball circumcision with a rusted chain saw. But, as Dick Smegma points out, the concept of molestation may be used as the basis of a revenge stunt against some deserved jerk. It works like this. Acting as an outraged parent, you write a nasty letter to the mark in which you imply that he or she has molested your child. The trick is not to make direct accusation, but to rely on innuendo and the ability of neighbors' imaginations to fill in the worst. Copies of the letter are sent to all of the neighbors, co-workers or whomever, as well as local law-enforcement people, child welfare officials, etc.

A sample of Dick's letter follows:

Mr. Mark Nasty
1234 5th Street
Anytown, USA

Dear Mr. Nasty:

This is to inform you that, in the future, you will refrain from approaching and/or ad-

(Continued...)

dressing my eight-year-old daughter.

You will *not* touch her in any way, shape, or form.

You will *not* refer to her as "Honey," "Darling," "Sugar Pie," "Sweetie," "Baby-doll," "Baby-Cakes," "Sugar Lips," or "Lovey-Poo."

You will *not* offer her any candy or gifts of jewelry, regardless of the time of year, or her own birthday.

You will *not* offer her transportation in any vehicle for any reason, whatsoever.

In short, you are to stay ten (10) feet away from my daughter at all times.

A copy of this letter is being simultaneously sent to every resident of your apartment building, and every resident within 1,000 feet of your apartment building, plus the Chief of Police, and the Office of the District Attorney.

If *any* of the above prohibitions is perpetrated by you against my daughter, appropriate criminal and civil legal action against you will follow.

Sincerely,

The Mother of a Terrified Little Girl

Motels

Larry is a businessman who must travel. When budgets are tight, he stays in smaller motels not quite as ostentatious as the deluxe, gilt-rated places or the Holiday Clone-American Inns. He usually gets clean lodgings. But, not always . . .

"It was kind of late. I had to get off the road to prepare for a sales presentation in the morning. The place was horrible. The maid from Motel Hell haunted me there. The service was horrible and my bed buddies had four legs and crawled. Yuk," Larry said with a shudder.

When he complained in the morning, both the clerk and the maid gave *him* verbal hell — turned out they were married (brother and sister, I'd bet). Anyway, Larry had a pal who sold medical supplies, and he saw him before going back there.

"It took some doing and a couple of bucks, but I was able to get an old lab cadaver. 'We' checked in with me using a fake name and ID. I had my 'friend' in the car. But, I brought him in the room, put the stiff in bed, and with a show of going out on the town, left — never to return."

(Continued...)

Larry said he often wondered about the maid's reaction when she found the cadaver the next morning. "I wonder if she thought she'd crawl in with him and get a little action — they were pretty evenly matched. Or, maybe she just ate him. She was quite a ghoul; that place sure was old Motel Hell."

In another instance, Larry checked into a much more expensive motel and found dirt, cigarette stubs, and other evidence of the previous guests — the room had been dusted by a wisk, whisper, and promise but, never cleaned. Again, his complaint to the night clerk brought a bored yawn as the guy barely looked up from his paperback. He assigned Larry another room.

The next morning, Larry waited until the maid had made up the room, and did a good job. He left just as she did. He carefully did not lock the door as he closed it.

"I checked out, handed in the key, left the building, and then quickly doubled up the back stairs, entered the room, and carefully slipped that sanitary seal band from the toilet cover. I next had a very pleasing and full-morning sit-down, shut the lid, replaced the band, locked the room, and left the area."

Did you notice in there anywhere that Larry said he flushed the thing? Hmm, neither did I.

Music

Here is one of the most ambitious and hilarious ideas yet: how to turn a deserving mark's home into a booming speaker cabinet. Bob the Computer Kid needed to get back at some nasty neighbors who lived in a wood-siding exterior/plaster interior house. Here's what he did.

"You drive a 10 or 20 penny nail with a very broad head into the side of the mark's house, choosing the side with the fewest windows, obviously.

"Then, you attach a violin, viola, bass fiddle or piano wire to the nail. I found that lower frequency wires work best. Apply as much tension as possible on the wire, even stake it. Then stroke it with a music wand—cat gut works best."

Bob says the results are tremendous. "Vibrations amplify through the entire house. The structure is just like a speaker cabinet. The windows will rattle, and the wood will hum. My work made enough eerie, low frequency noise to wake up the mark and his family that night. They were terrified.

"What I did was to paint the nail the color of the house, so I got away with it for two weeks before they found the nail. It was great to sneak out and 'play' their house at two or four in the morning, then disappear and observe the panic and, once, even the police."

Bob says these folks moved after that summer. Evil spirits? Nah, Bob's a nice guy.

Neighbors

Thanks to Chris Schaefer's diligent reporting, we know of a wonderful success story in which Mike Waldrop of Oak Grove, Oregon, got even with a land rapist who ruined Mike's lovely view by building an ugly multi-story building butted against Mike's property. As usual, the coven of big $$$ attorneys had everything greased against him, so Mike had only one way to get even.

He painted the back of his house in multi-colored checkered patterns, put bright red wavy lines on his roof, then painted a seven-foot mural of a chunky man exposing his posterior toward the new building. Mike cast the old "moonglow" at the land rapist. Thanks, too, Chris, for sharing this with us.

Because Margaret Mead had died and she didn't know to whom else to turn, Sandy in Châteauguay reported to me that the Missing Link and his brood were living next to her in that quaint village in Quebec.

"I can't speak to them, as all they do is grunt and root. Their horrible offspring come into my yard and frighten my animals and plants. I fear they may try to copulate with my animals. They stand outside my house

(Continued...)

to watch me eat meals. The adults from this den next door throw trash into my yard and wander around filthy and frightening. You, George, gave me the inspiration to rise above the usual banal attempts with police, animal control officers, public welfare officials, etc."

What the wonderful Sandy conjured up involved the use of journalists, always a wonderful secondary mark because of their blind junkie's need for a fix of the sensational and bizarre. She came up with ideas to "tip" reporters to a great story involving the Bumpus Neighbors and their address:

- A crazy cult holed up there with guns and hostages.
- A terrorist cell planning to recapture Quebec for the Queen.
- A home robbery in progress.
- A teenage prostitution center.

I'm sure you get the idea. A little bit of scam, a bit of paranoia, some quarters dropped on those neighbors to the press and police and an instant "situation" is created — never mind the made-up stuff from Sandy.

Did she do it? Is the fact that Sandy moved just before the "event" went down any indication? Did it work? Would you be reading it here if it hadn't?

Divorce doesn't have to be all bad, or, as Mr. Justice points out, it doesn't even have to happen. He likes to run an ad in a local newspaper saying something like: "Moving out of town (or to small apartment) due to divorce. Free patio and lawn furniture, yours for hauling away." Mr. Justice says to do this when the mark is away for the day or weekend. But, why wait? It could be just as much fun to have the mark there to deal with the problem, considering how rude human vultures can be when they think they're getting something for nothing.

Hint: Use a public pay phone to place the ad, give the ad-taker at the paper that number, and then hang around a few moments since most newspapers require a call-back to check on the ad.

The same skit will work for firewood, too. This time the ad says: "Wife allergic to woodsmoke. Free firewood to be hauled away."

more

Neighbors

The spearhead of the Grumpy Neighbor Patrol, the redoubtable Stoney Dale, is back with another report. Stoney says you can have some innocent fun with the mark by repeatedly putting "For Sale" signs in his yard, on trees, on the porch, etc. Always advertise "Assumable 9% Mortgage" to get extra attention. If the grumpy neighbor rips down the signs, keep putting up new ones.

Here's another idea Stoney called up from his twilight zone. It works well with pseudomacho types or the Nervous Nellie person.

"In the dark of night, take a length of black fishing line and attach it to a nail or piece of the gutter support of the mark's home. Tie it low to the ground where it will be even harder to spot," Stoney advises.

"Go back and hide behind some sizable object a hundred feet or so away. Pull the line really taut. Wet your fingers and rub the line slowly, or flip the line briskly with your fingers."

Stoney says the slow rubbing produces an eerie, screeching, low-howling sound back at the house, while the line flip gives off a "boing/twang" noise.

"The person inside hears the noise and thinks it's within the walls of the house itself. If the mark comes out to look, relax the tension and let the line fall to the grass, making it invisible. When the mark retreats, repeat the devilment, as it were," Stoney adds.

A few accompanying telephone calls and other bizarre cult and mind-game stuff will contribute greatly to this screeching sound.

Newspapers

Late in 1985, fake copies of the *San Francisco Examiner* with a banner headline, "Peaceniks Seize Pentagon," were placed in about 100 newsracks in the city's financial and Civic Center districts.

A phony front page wrapped around old *Examiner* copies was similar to the real thing. The page carried teaser headlines for non-existent stories on the non-existent inside pages. Among them were "TV-Cancer Link Discovered" and "Missouri Loves Company — Nimitz Coming Too," a reference to the city's fight over stationing the battleship Missouri in San Francisco. There also was reference to the fortieth anniversary of the atom bombing of Nagasaki.

The pranksters, who have remained unidentified, also jammed the coin slots so readers could get a free paper.

Obscene Telephone Calls

Personally, I love 'em, but never seem to get any — obscene phone calls, that is. Is it my personality or that women never make any obscene calls? Yes, I know, a lot of ladies do get them and don't like that and want to know what to do. Here's the Largo Bum to the rescue.

"This works best with the guy who wants to meet you somewhere. I refer to him as the Purpose Caller. It's risky, but I advise you to encourage him a little, and then tell him you'll meet him in two hours. Give him the address of the nearest biker bar or police station — and then have the place staked out by the inhabitants therein."

Office Nastiness

We can thank local real estate czar Frank Domo for this plan. When your mark has to go to a funeral, is ill, or has some legitimate reason for being away from the office, he or she is vulnerable. That's when you call the boss and/or the boss's secretary and say something like, "Hey, where's old (Mark's Name)? I'm here at the ball park, football stadium, hunting camp, topless bar or whatever, and he has the passes. Where is the old devil?"

It would be great if the square person on the other end of the line piously tried to explain the nature of the true problem. You could chortle and launch into the line, "Oh sure, old (Mark) sure knows how to make 'em up. He said his boss was stupid, but even a terminal idiot wouldn't buy a line like that."

Then you say, after a pause, "Ooops, you aren't the boss, are you? Oh, oh," and hang up.

Officer of the Law

Harry Callahan, who used to be a real law enforcement officer, says it's actually very easy to pass yourself off as a cop. He says that fake IDs and badges may easily be bought and displayed.

"Nobody, but nobody, reads anything on these IDs," says Harry. "Thanks to TV, if you look, talk and act like what people think a cop is, they'll believe you are one. It's really easier than it sounds.

"I've used this scam to scare the living hell out of some dubious people who were acting in a very unsuitable manner. It always worked."

I must add that this is also highly illegal, despite it being unlikely you will be unbadged. Go for it.

Oil

If you have a mark whose machinery or vehicular workings need to be lubricated, Bob the Computer Kid suggests you add carborundom powder to the petroleum at the rate of about three ounces per gallon. This will turn the oil mixture into a liquid sandpaper, which is fabulous for destroying engines. It's quite a nasty trick. The powder is available at hobby stores selling supplies for rock collectors; it's used in polishing.

Outdoor Signs

This is elaborate, but funny. Just ask Killroy. Remove the offending highway directional sign and bring it to a place where you can work on it safely. Paint over the existing letters with the same color of paint as the sign's background. Then spell an annoying message about your mark using retro-reflective tape on the original sign. Do it neatly, cautions Killroy. Replace the sign. Your insult of the mark will reflect to hundreds of folks.

Glad to hear from a whole passle of folks who hail from Chainsaw, Pennsylvania. Included in this randy crew are Little D. Flapper, Cranki, Bullette, Taf, Nancy, Mamie, Jewells, Ike, Muffy and Chuckles. Their MO is messing up the advertising signs at drive-in theaters, restaurants, shops and malls. They reword those types of signs which use movable letters.

They turned the ad for the film *RAIDERS OF THE LOST ARK* into "LOAD OF RAT SHIT REEKS," while *TAKE THIS JOB AND SHOVE IT* became "BAKED JIVE SHIT ON TOAST." They raided a deli sign after hours and created a message about the owner's daughter's lack of virtue with certain farm animals. Another drive-

in sorty turned *THE FOUR SEASONS* into "FART ON SUES SHOES," while the other feature, *THE EMPIRE STRIKES BACK,* became "SEMI PRICK TEASER."

PA Systems

It's right out of *Porky's* or *Animal House,* but this gag from CW is funny, and I know it will work because I've used it, too. You have a store, bar or office as your mark. This outfit must have a PA system for it to work to maximum effect. But sometimes in the right setting, plain voice power will suffice.

Anyway, you call the mark-place and tell whomever answers that this is an emergency. You plead with them to page Edward Meoff. Obviously, nobody responds to the page. You sound more emergency stricken, and exasperated in saying, "Oh! OK, I know his brother Jack is there, please page him, quickly."

Success depends largely on your histrionic ability.

Packages

Maybe your mark is a lonely sort of person because of the severe personality defect that caused him or her to become your mark. With that neat reasoning, Jay from Illinois has a kind suggestion on how your mark can meet many new friends. In humane fashion, Jay suggests, "Call fifty different people and tell each one of them that there is a special package waiting for him at the mark's house. Give the address. Try for odd-hour pickups, if you can. Or, if the mark is not without friends, schedule parcel pickup for a day he is having a party."

What's this? You say there's been a real death in the mark's family? You really hate this mark? If I may add a Hayduke refinement, *that* is the day to have the "packages" picked up — funeral day.

Paint

It's yet another landlord beef. This time, the owner told the tenant his rental place wouldn't be painted "this year because there's only enough money to paint one house, and it's going to be my own home." The tenant offered to do the painting if the landlord would buy the product. The landlord laughed and said: (1) wait until next year, (2) buy the paint yourself and do it yourself, (3) live with it, (4) move. The tenant, who calls herself Scorpion, had a fifth option.

"I remember my high-school chemistry teacher telling us about compounds which do nasty things to paint. I quickly found after a bit of label reading and experimenting that most shaving creams will bleach paint.

"Guess whose house got a bleach job a day or so after being painted? He blamed it on the paint and got into a ruckus with the store owner. It got to small claims court and the landlord lost. No proof. In the meantime I had moved."

more

Paint

Ed Akni, one of our fine scouts, has found a splendid product that removes paint easily, quickly and chemically. It's called Peel Away, and you just brush it on whatever surface you wish to treat, let it dry, then peel away the paint. It lifts up to eighteen coats! The stuff is patented and has been used all over the world. It first became available in the States in 1983. Ask for it at a hardware or paint store. I just bet you can think of dozens of nasty paybacks you can uncover with this stuff.

Paranoia

As many readers know, folks who are into even semiserious paranoia make great marks. Put another way, markdom feeds on paranoia better than a gaggle of nursery-school kids turned loose to feed in at Mickey D's with free food coupons. But, as the Indiana Cave Man notes, a true paranoid is very dangerous because he may act first. There is some professional basis for this caution, too.

When I was in graduate school, taking a course in abnormal psychology taught by the famed professor of psychology, Dr. Kurt T. Bazz, I recall he told us that "the truly dedicated paranoid can switch from victim to aggressor very quickly if he or she strikes out first to prevent some persecution or other hostile action. . . . It is quite debatable as to whether paranoia is a cause or an effect."

I guess that means that if you really are a jerk, then someone is out to get you. If you're a bully, some people will naturally fight back. As the veteran trickster Dick Tuck relates, "Almost all deserving marks are at least slightly paranoid. And, if not, they soon will be." For example, if your mark has a paranoia about utility companies, shut down and padlock his gas or electric meter. If he or she is paranoid about trusting a spouse, twist that paranoia slowly.

One way to feed and flourish these mental hassles is to send your mark some reinforcement. I find it useful to subscribe to the U.S. Government Printing Office lists, many of which offer booklets on various personal and medical services. Catch the drift? They have publications on acne, herpes, abortions, balding, canker sores, bad breath, fat people, mental health, drug reactions, alcoholism, stress, heart attack, marital infidelity, etc. See the Sources section for the easy way to get these grand weapons.

That cheerful trickster Filthy McNasty has brought a lady friend to our merry band. Readers, say hello to Vera. However, Vera does not love a parade, and it has more to do with reality than the obnoxiousness of America's Parade Master, Ed McMahon.

"Wait until the horn and tuba section approach you," Vera relates. "Then, produce a big, juicy lemon and step out where all of the horn players can see you.

"Bite into the succulent lemon with gusto. Suck on it. Chew it wetly. Make sure they see you. This causes a universal and involuntary puckering reaction and a spinal sensation akin to nails down a blackboard. It will help rain on their parade."

Kudos to dear Vera for helping us create a sour note for the band.

Vera says this next parade-buster is really rough and should be used with discretion and thought. She suggests you toss a big, rubber snake up in front of the mark's horse. Horses react to snakes by rearing and bucking upward, tossing the rider flat on the keister.

Next on Vera's passing parade is what she calls her Smoke Screen Goody. From a chemical supply house, purchase a pint of titanium tetrachloride. Place the bottle in a paper bag. When you want to unleash mountains of smoke, place the bottle down, break it, and depart.

In a minute or so, the titanium tetrachloride will react to the air and spew tons of smoke. As Vera relates, this is the exact stuff skywriters use.

Parking Lots

College administrators have to be among the dumb beasts in our fields. Of course, it figures. The weakest students in college today are the education majors; then later, those who flunk out of teaching become the administrators. Or at least, that's what my pal Professor Pudenda McCavitt told me.

Anyway, once while he was in college, Captain Kill found that some ego-stained administrators had proclaimed a major part of prime public parking lot as theirs and instructed workers to put up chains to keep out lesser folks, i.e., teachers and students.

But let him tell it. "Each administrator had been given a duplicate key to open the lock. One evening, I simply slipped another lock on the gate adding to the security, as it were. I had to do this only three times before the idea was dropped, along with the chain.

"I figured if the lazy bastards wanted a prime parking spot, let them get here earlier than anyone else!"

Parking Tickets

Carl Cologne hasn't paid a parking ticket in years. When he finds one on his car, he simply drives or walks around searching for an unticketed car sitting in an expired meter spot. You got it. Carl places his ticket on the other car's windscreen, ala an officer. The other guy, not reading the ticket and feeling guilty anyway, puts his check in the envelope and, voila, the ticket gets paid.

Parties

Block parties, an old favorite, are gaining new favor among the affluent suburbs and the singles housing areas. While block parties can be fun, they can also be damned annoying. Filthy McNasty says that most of those parties have to have a municipal permit. You might want to call and cancel the permit the day of the party, or you could cancel the live music, the caterer, etc.

Quick to cover all avenues, Filthy suggests going the other way by being certain that *lots* of supplies arrive. Call every caterer and booze supply house in town and make sure that each delivers tons of refreshments for the folks. If your block is older folks, rent a punk or new wave band for them.

Here's another grand idea. Go to a remote location and call the police. Have a friend in the background either fire several shots or set off a string of five or six firecrackers. Scream hysterically into the phone about shots being fired. Scream the mark's address, fire some more shots, then hang up. Caution: police record all calls.

Pear Trees

Although this is categorized as pear, it will work well with any fruit tree. It just happened that Raymond F. had first fruition with this gag on a pear tree. Years ago, he had this cranky old phart neighbor who terrorized the neighborhood kids if they picked pears from his tree. However, the kids learned that the old duffer did not really own the land the trees were on. He pretended to own the fruit trees, but, in reality, they belonged to the city.

The plot ripens . . .

Raymond explains, "We told our parents we wouldn't pick the pears anyway. For some reason, the parents didn't want to irritate this old turd, but I can't imagine why not.

"We didn't pick the pears. We ate them while they were on the tree — it was a dwarf tree. We simply ate all the fruit and left the stem part hanging on the tree."

Pennies

We all know about gluing a penny to the back of a circuit breaker and how dangerous a stunt that is. But do you remember the chap who fried his mark's fish? Here's an easier way to turn your mark's home aquarium into a fish morgue, if the environment is salt water. Simply drop a copper penny into the tank, and within a couple of days, all those expensive fish will be belly up.

Personal Products

Go through those mail-order catalogs and find personal products to gift-order for your mark. Always order COD, of course. Send your mark a gift card before the product arrives telling the mark that his or her friends suggested this personal gift or are getting it for "his or her own good." Make it one of those "your friends don't know how to tell you, but . . ." cards.

The COD "gift" will be something like nose hair clippers, vacuum blackhead/pimple remover, Accu-Jac masturbator, body hair remover, bust enhancers, cellulite cream, etc. Even if the parcel is COD, the curiosity of 95 percent of all marks will demand they pick up the package because of the card you sent. It works.

Pets

Fred Rogers said on TV that everyone needs a pet. If one pet is nice, think how wonderful 312 of them would be. You could easily make arrangements to have a steady supply of pets delivered to your mark each week. These can range from the exotic at various pet stores to the irregular mongrel models at animal shelters to ???? whatever.

Obviously, this requires a lot of research and lots of hype. You will have to comb the classifieds in several newspapers as well as the Yellow Pages in several directories. Not to worry about the well-being of the animals. The mark will never accept or keep any of them after the initial deliveries. After that, it is pure harassment value time.

Phone Phreaks

The guileless guru of the phone phreak is TAP, and in one of their recent numbers they included a list of ten rather irreverent suggestions for folks just like you. Here, then, is the TAP version of "The Phone Phreak's Ten Commandments."

1. Box thou not over thine home telephone wires, for those who doest must surely bring the full wrath of the Chief Special Agent down upon thy heads.
2. Speakest thou not of important matters over thine home telephone wires, for to do so is to risk thine right of freedom.
3. Use not thine own name when speaking to other Phreaks, for that every third Phreak is an FBI agent is well known.
4. Let not overly many people know that thou be a Phreak, as to do so is to use thine own self as a sacrificial lamb.
5. If thou be in school, strive to get thine self good grades, for the Authorities well know that scholars never break the law.
6. If thou workest, try to be a goodly employee, and impressest thine boss with thine enthusiasm, for important employees are often saved by their own bosses.

7. Storest thou not thine stolen goods in thine own home, for those who do are surely nonbelievers in the Bell System Security forces, and are not long for this world.
8. Attractest thou not the attention of the Authorities, as the less noticeable thou art, the better.
9. Makest sure thine friends are instant amnesiacs and will not remember that thou have called illegally, for their co-operation with the Authorities will surely lessen thine time of freedom on this Earth.
10. Supportest thou *TAP*, as it is *thine* newsletter, and without it, thy works will be far more limited.

Photofinishing

Look through those X-rated magazines and mailers. Some of them offer wonderful ideas. For example, there is the "Adam & Eve X-Rated Photo Service" that develops those "special" pictures for you. Look for their address in my Source section. In the meantime, can you think of some ideas using these "special" pictures?

There are other outfits that sell you exposed film showing all sorts of bizarre and hardcore sexy stuff. You get it processed and it's yours. How about sending to one or more of those outfits with an order in your mark's name, including a postal money order? Switch films with your mark, and he or she will take the nasty film into some local lab. Even with mail order, it could be fun to explain to the kiddies or spouse where these graphically lustful photos came from.

Of course, you could just address the finished product to the mark's spouse or lover. I leave the rest to your imagination.

more

Photofinishing

Way back in *Up Yours!*, Jimi the Z suggested loading bulk Kodak Kodalith film into 35mm cassettes and shipping them off to some photo finisher who has done you wrong. Several people have written in happily to tell me how well it works in screwing up the C-41 chemicals used by these derelict photo finishers.

Captain Video has been using empty Scotch 35mm film cassettes, also a C-41 process. He switches the film and sends the Kodalith in the Scotch container to any lab that has screwed him.

I can give it my own seal of approval. A lab not only ruined some film I had taken during a trip south of several borders, but told me it was my fault for not exposing my film properly and allowing customs people to x-ray, and thereby ruin the film. Nonsense. I have worked as a professional photographer and I do not allow my film supply to pass through X-ray. It is hand-inspected. The lab manager and I argued. He told me to buzz off.

Instead, I sent in four rolls of Kodalith in other cassettes, using the names of four other semi-marks. I had no intention of ever going back there and had

(Continued...)

friends take in the film. I bet they have had a lot of annoyed customers recently.

Photography

Some nasty feelings were developing between John Houston and an amateur photographer over some embarrassing personal photos. After all his gentle persuasion turned negative, John moved to fix the mark's darkroom for relief. He filed the edge off a penny and put these metallic shavings into the errant photographer's developer solution for color prints. It made mysterious green spots all over the bad guy's pictures, ruining some vacation photos. As John puns, "Lens be friends."

One of my pals from South Africa relates a special use for the family camera. It seems his younger sister was being a real pain in the arse to everyone at a beach party. He borrowed her little Kodak camera and plotted with a pal. They left the party area, and he took a frontal tight medium shot of his friend peeing. Next he took a close up of his friend's member after the guy had done a little fantasizing. Then he put the camera back in his sister's beach bag. The best part is that little sister had borrowed her mommy's camera.

Pinball Machines

Any of you video-arcade freaks ever see an old-fashioned pinball machine? Just kidding. Seriously, if you've ever been ripped off by the very "professional management" at one of these subhuman hangouts, thank Ray from Kansas City for his drill on getting even with them. Here's the idea.

Take a heavy rubber band and a piece of buckshot. Place the rubber band and buckshot over the payoff hole on the board. Pull the rubber band back and shoot the buckshot at the glass. You can place the rubber band right down flush on the glass and let it strike.

It will make a funnel-shaped nick in the glass with a small hole at the top. A bicycle spoke or a straight piece of wire may be inserted into the hole in the glass and on down to the copper contact in the payoff hole. Merely press on the wire and the score will begin to register. There is no hazard with electrical shock since the voltage at the contact point is only 3.6 volts, less than an ordinary flashlight. This can be worked even in busy locations using several people to stand around the machine while this is being performed.

Pious Bigots

Tim, the young scholar from the University of Texas, shares some ways to stick it to the hypocritical red-necks so common to most college towns. These cretins pray to God against students on Sunday and prey on the wallets of those same students for the rest of the week.

One particular rip-off store proprietor was also a fundamentalist preacher, according to Tim. By the way, isn't having the word "mental" in fundamental religion a contradiction in terms? Whatever, Tim said that this man's antistudent behavior became totally outrageous, and nothing logical, moral, curricular, or even secular would work to get even. So. . . .

"We got some bumper stickers printed by the brother of one of my friends who owns a print shop in another city. We placed them up high on the preacher/bigot's store and on his church, using a ladder, of course. If they (the stickers) came down, we put new ones back up again."

Tim adds that if you use a good strong glue, the stickers do not come off as easily as they otherwise might.

Plants

A lot of fussy marks have fussy houseplants, the same as certain species of people have cats or small rat-like dogs. Tony from Illinois has a fun way of fertilizing some mirth into his life. He adds an Alka Seltzer tablet or so to each of the mark's houseplants, being careful to push each tablet under the soil. When the mark waters the plant, all sorts of hissing and bubbling will break the surface of the soil as the Alka Seltzer activates.

Tony adds, "I did this to a neighbor whose dog had totally dug up my bulb beds. She freaked out when the soil bubbled over in her plants that I had hit with the tablets. I was actually there and acting very concerned. Then I did it a couple of more times. She never caught on. She finally did tie up the dog, though. I still hit her plants a few more times just to piss her off. I didn't like her at all."

Plastic Money

At last, new games you can perform on your mark's credit cards. You owe the Lord God of Vengeance for these two ideas. He says that a large magnet placed near the mark's wallet or purse can zap, i.e., render useless, the magnetic strip on most credit cards. It erases the necessary codes. The LGV says this works best with cards for Automated Teller Machines (ATM).

Agreeing, Boston's Bart Phart says he once clamped a large block magnet just above the slot where people put their ATM cards. People thought it was just part of the equipment. He says it took thirty minutes for the bank to clear the complaints, figure out what was wrong, start to make amends, and order new cards — a one- to two-week wait.

Back to the LGV, he says that if you can get hold of your mark's plastic card, you can use a small screwdriver to alter numbers by pushing up or down on the raised plastic. He says you can turn 8 to 0, 7 to 1, etc. It makes shopping and banking less dull for the mark, of course.

Playing Cards

It was my army colleagues who taught me, finally, that I am a very poor card player. So, do you have problems winning, too? Have your "friends" cheated you? Captain Video has the answer — marked cards. He got nailed by some "buddies" who were dealing seconds to him. He later switched to this special deck I am mentioning here and cleaned out his cheating pal for 173 well-deserved dollars.

Poison Ivy

In the spring. when a young mark's fancy thoughts turn to plants and gardening, you can help the rash soul by substituting the usual flats of nice flower plants with some duplicates filled with seedlings of poison ivy.

I saw this work best on the public relations mouthpiece for a major coal corporation that was raping the land and destroying rural water supplies in western Pennsylvania. I was on a holiday visit with friends there in 1985 and again in 1986. The coal baron's paid liar's hobby was tending his own little flower garden far away from the embattled citizens who had no water because his company didn't give a damn where or how they deep-mined.

A friend of mine "somehow" added some poison ivy seedlings to the man's flats. The mark soon suffered one week of doctor-cared-for agony. I joined my friends and their neighbors in laughter. I urged them to send him a poison ivy bouquet as a "Get Worse" gift. As I was leaving that day, I'm not sure they actually did it. I hope so.

more

Poison Ivy

Poor Bob from Panorama City! He was being sexually harassed by a female co-worker, and all sorts of nice requests to stop didn't seem to help. She was literally poisoning his own social life. He got very blunt about her leaving him alone. No luck. He decided to get even.

"I drove to the nearby hills and collected some poison ivy. I ran some stems and leaves through my food processor and collected about a cup of juice, which I placed in a plastic spray bottle. I took this to work the next morning and gave the driver's side-door handle of her car a really good shot.

"She was out of work a few days with some splotchy outbreaks in various locations. Unhappily, as soon as she got back, she was up to her old tricks again. Well, so will I, hopefully, with a less subtle message this time."

Police

A trickster with access to his state's statewide police computer plugged in the license number of his mark's car along with a warning about the occupants of this stolen vehicle being armed and extremely dangerous escaped felons. Imagine the fun when two nasty and nervous cops jacked the mark, his stuffy wife, and his mother-in-law out of their car at shotgun point right outside the doors of a ritzy country club. It actually happened.

Estiercol Scaife is the kind of fun guy who will listen to the police band on his scanner until he finds something really tasteless and awful—sort of the crimeland version of seeing Daddy and Mommy Reagan in the nude doing weird things with the Tidy Bowl man. Scaife pulls up to the crime scene with a great show of making enemies and memories by asking all the wrong questions, trying to take Instamatic pictures and seeking gross, personal details. He grins a lot, drools and if appropriate, vomits or flashes money, makes gross jokes and insults people.

I forgot to add, Scaife is doing all of this under the frequently mentioned name of the mark. Tip: Use public transportation for this scam and push just enough so as not to get arrested.

Police Reports

Let's help our law enforcement officials make our communities better places in which to live. Find, borrow, or otherwise obtain a blank or an already-used police report form. They are fairly easy to obtain if you just think for a few moments. But, let's put one to good use. Using new Liquid Paper or some other whiting-out method, eliminate the portions already filled in if it's an old report. Type a new report, charging your mark with some horrible social crime: selling his mother-in-law into white slavery, bestiality, pimping, making bomb threats on the White House, etc. Get a very clean copy of this report and disseminate it where it will do the most good. If you can get blank report forms, you don't need any Liquid Paper.

Politicians

I was sitting at a lemonade stand at an airport in Washington listening to some politician argue with a newspaper guy about why there should always be limits on press freedom. No lie, here's what the politico claimed: "Neither the substance of America's favorite sport, politics, or its favorite food, the hot dog, can stand close analysis. If the innards of either politics or the hot dog were fully revealed to the public, they'd vomit from reflex."

That's why Richard Nixon probably did say, "I never lied to you, I just economized with the facts."

From his bumper crop of brilliancy, Dick Smegma brings us another winner for dealing with political losers. This time he's getting you involved in a Hate a Candidate Campaign. Want to pay back a pol? You get hundreds of bumper stickers printed which favor this candidate or else steal his own stickers from a campaign headquarters. Make sure these are the superstick type that guarantee not to come loose. For that reason you may wish to have these custom-printed at a place using that type of sticker stock.

Next, you, or you and your crew, want to canvass

(Continued...)

the town, placing as many of these stickers as possible on the trunk lids — never the bumpers — of every car you can locate. Or, you can place two on each car. The end result is beyond the obvious of losing votes for the candidate "whose" sticker you are disseminating. Some angry folks will threaten to sue. Also, the hoax will attract media attention.

Porn

In view of the controversy of the TV miniseries "The Thorn Birds" in 1983, a lesson should be learned. A lot of intensely religious people really take this stuff seriously. Perhaps that belief will add to the impact of the pornography you can use to attack your mark, according to LeRoy Zimmer, one of trickery's real fans.

"I'm an amateur photographer and find it very easy to make composite photos, using the faces of very well-known religious leaders on the bodies of sexually active men engaged in very perverted activities with prostitutes, animals, and kids. I also make female religious figures unwilling participants," Zimmer says.

Following Zimmer's lead, you could create the same genre of porn by using composites featuring TV stars, top sports stars, local politicians, etc.

Porno

Who says I don't include something for everybody? Here's one the Moral Majority and those other Old Poops from the Right can use to gross out local porno shops. Smear Vaseline or liquid soap on the covers of their nasty magazines. The effect is startling. Use a squeeze bottle to squirt white liquid soap on their doors and windows. This may demoralize the patrons from coming in the shop. Don't thank me, you owe this one to Filthy McNasty. If you still don't get it, think about it.

Pornography

Again, leave it to Dick Smegma to come up with the most elaborate, long-range scheme I've ever encountered. Dick tells of a friend whose family is very open sexually as well as being nudists. The father used his two children (boy of ten, girl of twelve) to pose nude in softcore porno pictures. Being very sophisticated and experienced kids, they were hardly harmed by the experience. The father had a calendar page for the year 1996 printed for the photo session and made certain it was seen in all of the shots.

Dick says the father is saving the photos until 1996, when he is going to burn his mark with them. He will plant them on his mark, who is a very rotten hypocrite and a very powerful man in his region. Victims? All the police will find is the "current" photos, with calendar approval, and no realization that the young kids are actually now young adults.

Dick calls the guy a creative and patient genius. I agree. Dick also stresses that the family unit is very healthy, very happy, very mentally alert and in no way harmed by this. As I grow older, I find that most sexually repressed, and repressive, people tend to be certified

(Continued...)

mental cases. That's too bad . . . right, Edwin Meese?

That reminds me of one of Macho's school chiefs. As this headmaster at his NYC school was an obvious jerk-off, Macho sought and obtained secret access to the man's office. After sabotaging the liquor cabinet with additives, including ipecac, Macho next unpacked very explicit photos of naked people having a good time and taped them very securely to the *outside* of the window shades of the headmaster's bedroom, facing the neighbors' apartment side. Macho left. Needless to say . . .

During the investigation that followed the embarrassing incidents and situation involving the headmaster's room and booze supply, Macho and others were asked about their involvement. Macho reported to me, "I do declare, I can tell a lie."

Postal Service

Nobody should make his or her mail delivery person angry, but you could make one angry with a mark. Herb Bobwander says you can forge a few really nasty notes to the person who delivers the mark's mail, signing the mark's name, of course. Complain about petty, untrue things and always insult the postal employee personally and nastily. Send another letter to the postal employee's boss. Be really mean, and always sign the mark's name. It will be fun when the employee finally confronts the mark.

Johnny Zip, our mole in the Postal Service, has this tip: He lightly puts Elmer's white glue over the outside of the stamps on outgoing mail. He tells his friends to whom he's written that all they need to do to remove the cancellation marks on the stamp on their letter is to soak it in water.

Johnny can also turn this tip nasty, saying, "If you're sending mail to some mark, use lacquer, paraffin or transparent spray instead of Elmer's. This way, the cancellation marks will never adhere to the stamp at all, authorities will be suspicious, and someone will be visited by a postal inspector. Be sure to use your mark's name and another mark's return address."

If you have a mark other than the U.S. Postal Service, you might try Watergating his or her mailbox, removing personal subscription magazines, or writing insulting personal messages to the mark from "A Postal Official." Always use "official" and not "worker." Trust me, it means more fun when someone starts to investigate the complaint.

For example, if your mark gets hunting or gun magazines, you can use a Magic Marker to scrawl "KILL HUNTERS" or "SHOOT SPORTSMEN" in bold letters across the cover and on some inside pages. If your mark reads *Playboy* or a similar magazine, your message could read "YOU SEXIST PIG." If it's *Forbes,* write "WE'LL SLIT YOUR THROAT DURING THE REVOLUTION!" Maybe your mark subscribes to *High Times?* If so, he or she will probably be semiparanoid. Try a message like "WE'RE WATCHING YOU, SUCKER" or "WE'RE POISONING YOUR DOPE." It's all very nasty, dangerous, and highly illegal. Does it surprise you, therefore, that these ideas came from Padre Patriot in Secacus, New Jersey?

If you're angry with the postal authorities for any reason, here's what Continental Paul did to get his sense of fun back. He suggests you mail a dead fish to some unknown person at some unknown address in the dead-letter office of your local post office. Eventually, reason may overrule postal regulations, and common sense might dictate that they deep-six your fishy time bomb. By then, your point will have been made.

Postal Stuff

Our consultant on cleaning up your postal budget by washing stamps has a new solution to cut costs. Buffy Bill says Mr. Clean, available in your supermarket, easily removes the cancellation inks used by the U.S. Postal Service. Bill also says that this is no lick in the wind, adding, "postal officials told Congress in 1985 that they had recovered a total of 13 million scrubbed stamps from big-time operators who were doing this stuff commercially. That has a value of $2.6 million."

Bill says that Mr. Clean works well to defeat the new inks the USPS uses to defeat the earlier washings. He also said it is highly unlikely their postal inspectors will ever go after the individual use of "sanitized" stamps.

Potassium Permanganate

Potassium permanganate ($KMnO_4$) is a multipurpose dirty-trick chemical. Available in granular form at many drugstores, it's used as a disinfectant and for recharging water-softeners. It colors water an intense purple and later decomposes into hard-to-remove brown scum. A strong solution of this chemical will color the skin a rich chocolate brown, which lasts for days. Like fluorescein, it's great for zapping the mark's pool, aquarium, or fountain.

Potassium permanganate is also a powerful oxidizer, much like potassium nitrate, and can be used to make pyrotechnics. When the crystals are mixed with an equal volume of glycerin, it starts a fire within a few minutes. Delay time depends on temperature, mixture, purity, grain size, etc.

A friend of mine used to use permanganate/glycerin bombs in plastic pill bottles to flame trash cans at a shopping center. Another friend put one in a chemistry set in the toy department of a store that had done him wrong. Store employees thought that the chemistry set blew up all by itself, because everyone knows that chemistry sets are supposed to do that.

This same friend also sprinkled some on her friend's bath towel, and he began to dry himself off very vigorously, rubbing the little granules into his skin where they created great splotches of a hideous brown color. She said it was very funny—to her. Her friend had no sense of humor about being variegated.

Potatoes

Stored improperly and left to rot, few things smell as awful as a potato. A retired farmer friend of mine, Mike O'Murphy, had a running feud with a coal company over their threatened ruination of his homestead water supply. Actually, his trick was more of a harassing operation at this point. Because he was being pestered by coal company lawyers, he decided that one rotten crop (the lawyers) deserved another (potatoes).

"I started to replant part of my potato harvest, one tuber at a time. I used to secrete the rotting potatoes under the lawyers' car seats when they'd drive out to the house. If I would go to their offices, I would plant a few spoiled spuds there, too. There are a few potato pranks I won't tell you about, either. Actually, it was a good use for the few spoiled spuds I had in my harvest," Mike says.

Pretty Boys

Everyone knows a chap who likes to shampoo and blow dry his hair every day in imitation of Plastic Man of TV anchorman fame, Mr. Cool Incarnate. Stoney Dale relates that these pains can be had, with a lot of fun.

"Most of these dudes use a certain thick, yellow shampoo which resembles honey. You can pour out some of the shampoo and replace it with thinned-down honey," Stoney writes. "Then your mark will *really* be stuck up."

I bet a lot of you lovely ladies would dearly enjoy doing that to some Mr. Beautiful you know all too well. If so, thank Stoney.

Prey TV

I was a bit misty-eyed when I read that some wonderful electronics/computer expert named Edward Johnson had programmed his computer to make thousands of repeat calls to Jerry Falwell's 800 telephone number because this fund-grubbing electronic Bible-banger had taken large sums of money from the guy's mother. He ran up Falwell's bill to the pulsating amount of about $500,000.

It's wonderful, using that pious pride-in-the-pulpit's own 800 number to bill him for calls. Bells are ringing . . . hee, hee, dial 1-800-Revenge.

Little Tommie Titmouse really gets burned when he turns on his TV set to see something worthwhile and instead finds some rich, electronic frenzied preacher begging for more money to use to ruin our lives. Tommie has a neat stunt to bug these vidiots as well as a secondary mark. Here's how he does it.

"I go to a pay phone and call the toll-free number for each of these holier-than-thou types and pledge $50 to $100 in my secondary mark's name. I also give them his address. If they ask for the mark's phone number (as some do) to verify the call, I give them the pay phone. I

(Continued...)

stick around ten minutes or so, and about half the time they call back. I simply answer and identify myself by saying, 'Hello, Mr. Mark speaking,' and we talk awhile to verify I am who I say I am."

Tommie says that in the end, the mark might pay to avoid looking like a fool or to avoid confrontation with these right-wing frauds. Or if he doesn't pay, the vidiots send out their field reps to harass the mark. Either way, both deserved marks lose. Sometimes, Tommie says, they sue and countersue each other — more fun.

Pricks

The first time I'd ever heard of Aruba was when a bunch of the Soldiers of Misfortune had some sort of cockamamy operation planned to conquer this gorgeous island off the coast of Florida. I next heard about it from a very gorgeous lady known as the Aruba Palm Tree Lover who wishes she did own the place.

When Aruba Palm Tree Lover was very young, she dated this jerk who insulted her, abused her, used her, and cheated on her. Her response was chilling, in a manner of speaking. She warmed to her tale as she recalled the incident. "At that age and dating situation, handjobs were the most frequent type of casual sexual relationships for guys. Usually, a couple would use Vaseline, K-Y or baby oil.

"After I wised up to this jerk and found out what a real prick he was, I came to grip with things and came up with a new solution to the problem. I mixed in a good bit of odorless-type Ben Gay with the other lubricants. After a minute, he began to really get uncomfortable. Inside of two minutes, he was dashing for the bathroom and some soap and water. He never blamed me, but he never called back, either."

(Continued...)

The very beautiful Aruba Palm Tree Lover also told me that she originally came from Newark, New Jersey, which would explain her nasty twist of mind. I have another friend who originally came from Newark, so I understood, right Pat?

more

Pricks

No, this is not scatological . . . it refers to a guy who is truly rotten to people.

Steve had a former employer who canned him for no good reason except that the boss wanted to replace him with a girlfriend he wanted on the payroll. Steve says it's a good idea to always obtain a supply of official letterhead and envelopes before you leave a company. Here's what Steve did.

"I bought an ultra sexy bra and put it into one of my old company's envelopes. I included a handwritten note to this chick about finding her bra in my car, and we were both so drunk and so horny I guess 'we' both missed it." He signed his ex-boss's name. He then addressed the letter in an incomplete fashion to a nonexistent lady at a nonexistent address. Steve mailed it.

"Naturally, it couldn't be delivered, so the postal folks returned it to the sender, the company return address with my former boss's name on the envelope. I knew his secretary, a prim, cold witch who was a snitch for his wife, would open the letter and find the bra and note. It was hilarious, or so some other employees told me later."

Buffalo's own wonderful Wayne says you should have an official-voiced caller tell the mark's lady friend that she is only one of several other women on the mark's self-confessed infection list.

"I did this, and the girl screamed and yelled to know who else was on the list," Wayne confesses. "After a while, 'the official' says that off the record he'd tell her, but she can't ever say who, how, or where, etc., to anyone. Then give her the names of a couple of close girlfriends, co-workers and/or sister, etc. If appropriate, you could even use her mother's name."

Pubic Hair

As this series of books and I grow older, we're creating a family of friends. They progress and grow older, also. Remember our pal Tyra E. Pierce from rotten roommates fame in past books? Tyra has graduated now and is out in the unreal world, and still as creative as ever at getting back at the people who aren't nice to others. This time, Tyra suggests an ally common to most of us — pubic hair.

"One year I roomed with a neatness freak who was overly clean with everything but my stuff. He tossed my towels on the floor so he could hang up his. Sometimes he refused to flush my toilet, which he would fill with biological sculptures, so he wouldn't have to dirty his.

"That's when I found how much power common pubic hair has to gross out people, especially a neatness freak. Pubic hair is abundant, free, and easy to gather and use. I found that placing a lot of it on his toothbrush, soap, plates, pillow, etc., caused him to move out, soon. The secret, of course, is to use a different color and texture than that of the mark, or you can even use your own.

"Today, away from the college atmosphere, out

(Continued...)

here working, I still find that our free friend, pubic hair, is quite useful in teaching manners to nasty people. My ultimate aim is for some secondary mark to stand up in a crowded mark-restaurant of my choice and scream, "*My God, there's a pubic hair in my soup!*"

Don't get lost, Tyra, you're our poet!

Meanwhile, beyond providing hirsute framing for Mr. and Ms. Johnson, pubic hair is a wonderful weapon for tasteless Haydukery that will, ahh, curl your mark's hair. Following are a few suggestions for the use of the short 'n curlies:

- If an old girlfriend or wife has some expensive facial creme, a handful of pubes mixed throughout the jar will toss that container, not to mention her cookies if you're truly blessed.
- A couple dark pubic hairs sticking out of the toothpaste tube when the lid is removed will cause your mark's teeth to chatter.
- Float 'em in someone's drink, soup, or cheese or any sort of icing, cookies, or other appropriate food.
- Stick pieces of pubic hair in your teeth and smile at someone you want to unnerve. This is fun to do if you want to make someone laugh, faint, or chunder at an inopportune time for them.
- Mail public hairs to your mark, either with or sans letter.

Quotes

Why quotes in a book like this? Sometimes, they make great graffiti. Or they are delightful to drop into conversation. As always, quotes I select make a pungent point. Also the folks who uttered these quotes are very special people. Whatever your reason, don't question mine, just enjoy reading this section. You can use these for any purpose you wish.

"Whenever I see the politicians on TV, I think someone has removed the diving board from the gene pool."

—William Escobar

"If you're the suspect, it's important that you project the blame elsewhere—immediately, forcefully and effectively. When in doubt, accuse."

—Jeff Salzman

"He opens his mouth to eject one obscenity after another. It's endlessly and totally uncouth."

—Vanessa

"Where God hath got it together, let no man put it achunder (sic)."

—Duckbutt Hatcher

"When the birds fly at night, the bone marrow is so good to suck out and chew."

—Mr. D from Austin

"Up against the transformers, muthahertz. All hail the power pirates."

—Jimi the Z

"Youth looks ahead. Old age looks back. Middle age looks worried."

—Sandy Kruckvich

"I'm learning to laugh again, but I'm not sure why."

—Mary V. Benson

"Eat my shorts!"

—Kranki Kathy

"When you resign yourself to fate, your resignation is instantly accepted."

—Paul Wilson

"A broken reputation is tougher to piece back together than a shattered mirror or scattered puzzle."

—Doug Ortman

more

Quotes

"What's the meanest thing you've ever done to someone, George, then laughed about it?"

—David Fowler
WPLP Radio
Tampa Bay, Florida

"Age and treachery will always overcome youth and skill."

—Ronald Reagan
Mt. Sphincter, West Virginia

"Do you know how to really get even, George? Live long enough to become a problem to your own kids."

—A mother
Radio talk show
Chicago, Illinois

"Cut off the head of the leading concubine and the rest will behave."

—Sun Tzu
Whenever

(Continued...)

"*Suo sibi gladio hunc jugulo* (I will cut this man's throat with his own sword.)"

—Terence
The Brothers
V, viii, 35

"The trouble with supping with the devil is that you must use a spoon twice as long as you need. In the end, it grows so long you cannot see the pot from which the food comes."

—Pope Something or other
The Vatican

Radio Station

Thank God there are radio stations whose DJs never answer the telephones. It makes it easier to nail naive marks. Here's how.

Find one of those stations within forty to fifty miles from the mark's home. Using press-on letters or Kroy type, create the station's call letters on stationery. Run it through a really good copy machine to create a professional forgery of the station's letterhead. On the other hand, you could borrow some real letterhead from them.

Type the mark a letter indicating that he or she has won some fabulous prize from a lottery drawing. The ticket was bought by ________________ (use the name of some friend who is on vacation or otherwise unavailable). The letter must indicate that the prize is substantial—$1,000 in cash, a TV, VCR, stereo, whatever. Also be sure to note that the prize must be *personally* claimed within two days.

Here's why you selected a station whose DJs never answer the phone: Instruct the mark to call between the hours of 7 P.M. and 11 P.M. because those are the only hours the "promotion" lines are open.

Getting no answer, the mark will either (1) worry about it, (2) drive the forty or fifty miles to personally collect, or (3) call during the day and make a fool of himself or herself. You could also claim that personal claim must be made within twenty-four hours, and there is no need to confirm.

Relatives

Brian G. is a heavy-hitting jokester. Once he had a family with whom he had to get nastily even. During the course of his planning, one of the family's relatives died. As he knew the family, he readily recognized their voices. With a bit of practice, he was able to recall and imitate the voice of the deceased, at which point he began calling the family at odd hours, playing weird music and sound effects in the background, claiming to be calling from the beyond. Acting like their dead relative, he started haranguing them for their evil ways.

Almost everyone has rotten relatives, folks who become an unwanted part of the family through the curse of birth or marriage, accidents over which we have little control. How then do you grind the ID and EGO of these humanoid hairballs into the dirt, as they deserve? CW to the rescue.

"It's simple. When they send cards, letters or other missives, you just send them back," CW suggests. "Mark their mail 'Refused,' 'Addressee Dead,' 'Moved, left no forwarding address,' or something like that. Then drop it back in a mailbox to be returned. You might even get a few rubber stamps printed with those quasi-official notices like the post office uses.

"When and if they anxiously call you, insist they have the wrong number, talk in a foreign dialect, shout obscenities, or just hang up. Refuse to answer the telephone if it rings again."

Religion

There are a lot of people out there who don't believe in God, which is fine as long as they don't make asses of themselves or pests to you about it. In many respects, they are as bad as the Jesus Junkies. Here's one way of paying back these Godless Goons. Go to some church and fill out a guest card in your mark's name. When you hand in the card, mention a large tithe and pleasantly ask the minister and his family to come calling to the mark's house, say next Sunday afternoon. Make sure your mark will be home for lunch and/or dinner.

According to Shelli of Goroncy, West Virginia, this trick will turn around on the Jesus Junkies. If your mark is a deserving one and is a very religious person, use the same scenario, only attend some truly off-beat cult or goofo-religion. Perform the same stunt in your mark's name.

Perhaps this idea should go in the "Political" category, but because Discordia Dea sent it to me in good faith, I shall abide by the "Religion" section. Basically, she wanted to get back at a blue-nosed Bible Banger who was running for office on a God 'n Morality ticket and plastering the city with horrible signs—true pollution. Polite complaints and requests to his headquarters brought scorn, then the candidate really started to attack his critics by invoking heaven's wrath on them in public. It was time to get even.

Dea got the candidate's home telephone number and put it on some printed election stickers she had made on behalf of the candidate. The stickers took the candidate's basic premise a good bit further to the Fruitcake Right than he wanted. Dea also ran Help Wanted ads on his behalf advertising for "paid staffers" and included the home telephone. "Call anytime, I'm always glad to do the Lord's work," the ad said.

The stickers went up not only on public property, but all over private store windows, church and synagogue doors, etc. They were placed in washrooms, lavatory stalls, on condom machines, etc. You can picture the result, I'm sure.

Here's some happy raps from Tor and Snow Dog for use when the Bible Thumpers come hammering on your door. First, tell them to wait a moment, then close and lock your door. See how long they wait. You can come back every five minutes or so and ask them to wait a little longer. Repeat as needed.

If they want to give you a brochure or pamphlet, accept it with grace. Then give them a pamphlet or brochure in return. This is why I keep telling you to save all that horribly gross direct mail porno you usually toss away. Trade it with your callers.

Finally, pretend you are a member of a weird cult and try to convert them. You can allude to animal sacrifice, Bible eating and removal of clothing, which you should do quickly. Invite them to join you.

more

Religion

Are you the victim of door-to-door Bible sellers? Our own Trab from Houston has a fabulous bit of theater that is a devastating example of overcope.

"Answer the door wearing a deep-black mask with red streaks. Open the door slowly, and peer out at the person around the door. Listen to the pitch, which will probably be nervous at best. Interrupt and say, 'Yes, my dear, I have a contribution, a very fresh one.' At that point, introduce what is in your other hand, hidden behind the door—a freshly obtained animal heart, beef tongue, or something equally gross from the meat market which you had all set up," advises Trab.

"As an alternative, you can answer the door in your underwear and have blood and animal slick all over your chest, face, and belly (as if you were eating some fresh sacrifice). Invite the mark to join you," chortles Trab.

According to the wonderful Sister Carla of the Order of St. Hedon, there are some special ways to produce counterproductive activities at an establishment religious service. I have known Sister Carla for some time, and she is a wonderful, sweet person with some delightful ideas, which she radiates from her Southern California retreat. Her suggestions for activity follow:

1. You and a friend can walk into a cathedral as a couple wearing clerical robes. Remove them, and do a streak during the ceremony.
2. Enter the church with a joint in your hand and tell the preacher that it's not sinful to smoke grass because the Bible says, "Let there be grass!"
3. Plant marijuana in the churchyard.
4. Pie the preacher while he is giving his boring sermon.
5. Open a large, noisy bag of potato chips or Nachos and make a lot of noise while eating them during the ceremony.
6. Pull a false fire alarm during a church service, thereby disrupting the service.
7. Buy an ad in the local smut paper advertising the church's phone number as being that of an out-call massage parlor.
8. Enter a synagogue with a pig on a leash.
9. Enter a church disguised as the devil.
10. Hand the preacher a hypodermic needle and a bag of white powder, telling him that "religion is the opiate of the masses."

more

Religion

Ilka Chase may not have known William Denton, but she called his shot when she said that "it is usually when men are at their most religious that they behave with the least sense and the greatest cruelty." While one church in particular has given Mr. Denton and his family a lot of grief, some of his get-back ideas will work with any religion. And, as I don't want to irritate His Popeness with William Denton's complaints, I will simply make this non-denominational.

The pay-back starts with rumors of a bootleg abortion clinic in the church neighborhood. This works best where the usual anti-abortion froth is at the mouther's nest. You compound the rumors by having some female friends with *big* tummy padding show up, spend an hour or two inside, then leave minus the padding. Refuse to let nosy neighbors near the house. Admit only your co-conspirators.

Finally, according to William Denton, you will start to attract pickets, police, and agitators. At this point, have the female friends come out with water balloons and attack the pious piglets who're picketing the "clinic."

(Continued...)

Here's a somewhat less combative idea. Go to one of the church-related meetings and when the wimps and wimpesses start to glorify motherhood, you might ask why nuns can't be mothers and why some members of the clergy are not allowed to be biological fathers.

Remail Service

You don't have to pay a fortune to remail letters from other cities. Having a mail-drop service is a great tool, but you don't need it for remailing. The cost of first-class postage, two envelopes and a short note will do the job. Write what you want to whomever you want. Address the envelope as you wish and seal the letter. Put the postage on it and a straight-looking return address. Write a brief note to the Postmaster in the city or town you've selected to remail this letter. Ask him to please *forward* this for you (don't ask for remail; ask for it to be *forwarded*). Slip the note and letter into a second envelope addressed to the Postmaster in that city. Use the same return address. Put postage on that outside envelope, mail it, and await the results. There is nothing illegal or immoral in this.

Restaurants

I actually saw this next trick performed by my friend, Ortega Beale. You need to have two slices of bread or toast handy. Spread some gooey jam on one slice very lightly and set it close by. Then lift the other slice to your nose as if it were a hanky. Blow your nose onto that slice, loudly and wetly. Make a demonstration of it. Spread the nasal contents around on the slice. Quickly switch slices and eat the one with the jam on it.

It happened one night that Lisa had simply had it with the teeny bopper waitri, plural of waitress, and their pimply paramours who stacked more hungry traffic behind the drive-up windows of the local Greaseburger fanchise store than O'Hare does in a whole day of flight delay. Pushing chuckles of a runamuck chainsaw from her thoughts, Lisa brought her petite nail clippers from her purse and eyed the order-circuit speaker wire next to the large, illustrated display board next to her.

Snip.

"If you think the kiddy-cretins and their kissy-face held up business traffic, you should have seen my silencing of the whole system," Lisa said proudly, gently trim-

(Continued...)

ming her lovely, long red nails with the very same criminal clippers of a few hours earlier.

more

Restaurants

Bob Grain always carries a collection of newly dead waterbugs and cockroaches with him for inclusion in his plans to get back at eateries which gastrate him. Bob says he tapes the little bodies to the menu or several bugs to several menus in his least favorite restaurants. At the very worst, you'll get some guy who will strip off the tape and eat the bug, figuring it was some free hors d'oeuvre sample.

Résumés

The following trick works well in a large company with a central copy or office services room. If you can get a copy of your mark's résumé (if not, make one up), leave a copy around the copy machine for the office gossips to find. If that's not enough, read on.

You can have a printer friend produce letterheads using some name and address to represent a professional employment agency. Type a cover letter on this letterhead to accompany a copy of your mark's résumé, both of which will be sent to his or her present boss. The cover letter should state that the mark is very unhappy working with unprofessional, cheap dolts and wants to escape his current enslavement. The mark's boss will get a big bang out of reading this letter, and so might the mark . . . later.

Ritual Madness

Many ethnic food markets cater to customers who like to eat goat and sheep heads, bull testicles, beef tongue, Bulgarian toe jam plus other exotic delights. Much of this stuff looks like central casting's idea of horror film gore. I thought I might catch your interest here, as these items are truly useful.

Heidi Marie says these culinary catastrophes make wonderful combinations with a devilish imagination to drive a mark wild with fear.

"Imagine how an occult sacrifice would look on the mark's doorstep—not only to the mark, but to the neighbors as well. You can use any of the animal heads, bushels of entrails, and blood, plus you should always include a doll or some other symbol for a baby in this ritual," Heidi advises.

Roadkill

Although George Hayduke institutionalized the concept of roadkill, some of his biker buddies went further when they created a cooked version called Furry Curry. I'm a genteel person, and I was moved.

According to Henry Zeybel, writing in *Easyriders,* Furry Curry is made from the "tiny roadside creatures which have paid the ultimate price of the machine age." He adds, "Any sharp-eyed rider can find roadside delicacies to supplement his dinner table."

Here's one of his excellent recipes that helps us use our deceased little forest friends to recycled advantage.

1. Scrape up whatever it was, and strip off any of the outer cover that's left.
2. Soak what remains in salt water for a couple days.
3. Whatever isn't already hamburger should be cut into half-inch cubes and sauteed until medium. What is semihamburger should be smashed with a hammer, molded into patties, and stored.
4. For the rest, melt butter and mix in onions, garlic cloves, lemon juice, curry powder, and brown sugar.

5. Stir until you have one big lumpy mass. At this point, dump in a pint of sour cream and stir until the sauce looks like bile.

If the sauce is not thick enough, add some gun grease and shortening. I'm told this will feed ten squeamish straights or one righteous biker.

Robbery

Let's turn your mark into an armed robber. For this we owe a debt to Chuckles the Cop. Find a convenience store where your mark likes to browse the paperback books, magazines, etc. or where he shops for the evening paper, milk, etc. Learn the inside, behind-the-counter telephone number of the store. As soon as your mark goes inside, rush to a very nearby pay telephone—which you've already staked out—and make a telephone call. Here's what you tell the clerk when he or she answers your call.

"This is a robbery. Don't hang up or look startled, just listen to me! My associate is in your store pretending to browse (describe your mark—appearance, clothes, etc.). He has a gun and will blow your head off if you don't give him all the money in your cash register. I'm telling you this so nobody gets hurt. When he comes to the counter, give him all your money or he'll kill you!"

Hopefully, there is a silent alarm in the place and the clerk has already activated it. The other options are equally amusing, according to Chuckles.

Rocketry

George Orr got really upset with some sorority pledges, calling them Nancy's kids after the wife of our Leader, because they were singing and chanting their nonsense at an hour when he was trying to sleep. George says that calls to the University of New Hampshire establishment to complain brought scorn from the fascists there. So, George acted on his own.

"The next night, when those chantresses started, I broke out my Wrist Rocket. Then I taped two pennies to each large M-60 I had, both for stability in distance and for shatter effect, and loaded one in my launcher. I had a friend light the explosive, then let fly with the missile toward the noisy women's large windows."

Crash! KARRBOOOOM!!!! This was followed by silence and George went back to sleep.

SOBs in General

Write an endorsement letter, make a phone call, or otherwise publicly support every nut, idiot, dictator, crook, jerk, killer, psychopath, etc., that you can think of—all in your mark's name. It's much better if you can use his/her official letterhead, or you can make up official-looking stationery. This is a great idea, thanks to wonderful M. K. of Long Beach. May I add some suggestions? Do this in newspapers, and write to government officials and others in the public eye. Be outspoken, obnoxious, and demanding—all in your mark's name, naturally.

You might wish to start a file on your mark with some government agency. Start writing threatening letters and/or writing "good citizen" letters to various state and federal government agencies for and about your mark. The more rotten your imagination, the better the letter, I bet.

Sail Frogs

People who live in areas where there are large numbers of toads constantly encounter specimens that have been run over and flattened out on the street. When they are so flat and dried-up that they can almost be tossed like Frisbees, they are called "sail frogs." They are also fit for mailing in a first-class envelope. One stamp should be all that's needed, but you might use two, just to be safe.

Salespeople

Want to get rid of pushy salespeople who sell with all the couth and subtlety of a high-pressure, crowd-control hose? Ron from Florida has the answer.

"I was seriously interested in a resort condo, but I really resented the unfair sales-pressure tactics, especially on older people who got a bit confused and fearful. I decided to get even.

"I acted like the perfect customer. I really took up the salesman's time, and this pushy creep had it all down. I asked questions for hours and then we got to the fine print and the terms. I was totally agreeable and talked about my banker, lawyer, etc.

"The pushy man went to his superior because I was buying three units, and they worked out the entire deal. We're talking several hours of their expensive time. Me? I was on vacation, and this was fun.

"At the last minute, after they'd signed and handed me the pen, I looked at them, smiled and said, 'Ah, heck, I was just kidding,' put down the pen, turned and walked away. I never looked back but I could feel the daggers of frustration and hate at my back."

Samaritan

There is some Good Samaritan in many of you. Let's put it to practice. There are a lot of unfortunate people in our world—ex cons, homosexuals with criminal records and alcoholic and druggie derelicts, for example. Wouldn't it be a fine Christian gesture for your mark to convert his nice suburban neighborhood home into a halfway house for these unfortunate creatures? Why don't you help him?

To start things off, you need to spend a few bucks on a legal ad to be placed in your local newspaper announcing your mark's proposal to open a halfway house for prostitutes, heroin addicts, perverts, etc. at your mark's home address. I guarantee this will stir up the neighbors.

As a corollary, you could also have a trusted associate make some selected stops within the mark's neighborhood, posing as a social worker making inquiries about the mark's reputation preparatory to his opening the halfway house.

Satellite Television

One of the mean stories of 1986 was the scrambling issue involving satellite dish owners and the money-greedy biggies at HBO (Time/Life), CBS, Showtime, The Movie Channel, and others who scrambled their signals to shut out millions of rural dish owners who cannot get cable TV or any signal otherwise. It was a sad situation in which the rich telecasting monopolies got moreso and the poor, rural folks got shut out. The government? Forget it — they're part of the rich.

All of this brings me to a really hilarious incident that happened in April of 1986, when someone calling himself Capt. Midnight actually cut in on and blocked out the HBO signal one Sunday night to make his own declaration of war on the avaricious scramblers. He vowed to strike again.

Now, here's what I'd like to know: Are there any satellite hackers out there reading this book who could come up with ideas for Hayduking these greedy telecasting biggies who scramble for *big* profits? I'd very much like to hear from you, and anything useful will go in my next volume of fun and infame. Speaking of those greedy jerks reminds me of the next topic.

School

Does your least favorite teacher put everyone into terminal boredom with slide show after slide show—often really an excuse not to teach? Perk up the action by sneaking a few hardcore porno slides in with the regular ones.

Likewise, Mr. D. has one that some folks from LBJ High School in Austin will remember. It's safe, but fun. Here's how he did it. Take a piece of chalk and carefully bore a hole in one end, making the hole large enough and deep enough to hold a strike-anywhere kitchen match head. Cut the head off a match and fit it into the hole so that only a tiny fraction of the tip protrudes. Glue some chalk powder around the tip to camouflage your work, but leave a tiny bit of match head exposed for striking. Plant it in a classroom.

When used on a chalkboard, the chalk will make a sizzling sound upon ignition of the hidden match head and will spew out a dark column of smoke for several seconds.

I was the epitome of the class clown when I was in high school several hundred years ago. That's no brag, just fact. Here are a few fun things you can do if you're still sentenced there and want to get back at some dictatorial administrators, bumbling bureaucrats or tenuous teachers:

• Draw or paste something very gross or very obscene on pull-down maps, movie screens, etc.

• Take down a roll-up map and screen, lay them flat, then load lime or other dusty substances in them. Carefully roll them back into the holder, then replace them, so that when the mark rolls them back down . . . cough, cough.

• If your school has gone back to the nineteenth century and instituted a dress code to please your own local version of the Rev. Pious Q. Preacher, get as many of your friends as possible to disrupt it without violating it. I bet, for example, it says nothing in there about dying your hair green, picking your nose at lunch, painting your face or vomiting in class.

• Institute massive searches for "lost" contact lenses during assemblies, at lunch, study halls or between classes. Clutter the room and halls.

• Free all the captured animals and insects being held prisoner in the biology labs.

• Send irregular streams of your associates to the office to have some bizarre rumor confirmed or denied.

• As a citizen, demand to see your own school records. Almost everyone else has access to them, so should you.

• If the student newspaper can't or won't do it, publish the salaries of all teachers and administrators. If they are paid with public funds, this information is in the public domain. Demand this data from some uptight bureaucrat in the central office.

- Add some very kinky personal items to selected teachers' mailboxes.
- Create some sort of revolutionary manifesto and leave it around so that it is sure to be discovered. Or have a mole plant it for the administration's gestapo. Then leave cryptic messages about Monday being "D-Day" or X-Day or whatever. The forces of tyranny will be all massed for the revolution that never arrives. It makes them look more like fools.
- Print false notices using official paper and format, then put them in mailboxes. Use your imagination.
- Need forms to copy, examples of the signatures of administrators and teachers? Check office wastebaskets; they are great sources for these bits of valuable raw materials.
- If your school doesn't have a teacher evaluation program by students, make your own. Create forms and pass them out to students. If the bad guys fight you, create nasty publicity and scream about your First Amendment rights.
- Use official channels to announce a going-away party for a teacher who isn't leaving, or a baby or wedding shower for a teacher who shouldn't be or isn't.

Security

So that no bad person will steal your mark's automobile, RV, bike or other vehicle, perhaps you had better secure it. Chain and lock the vehicle to something solid and immovable. If it's dark, the mark may not see the security chain and try to drive off. Can you hear the sound of your security damaging the vehicle? What sweet music.

Septic Tanks

Von Henry had (note use of past tense) a lot of hassle with a person who dumped refuse on his property. The usual complaint and cheek-turning failed to stop the dumping, so Von turned a new leaf, rather than his cheek. "I located the mark's own home and noted he had a septic tank system with a clean-out opening between the house and the tank itself," Von recalls. "I found that a couple of spray cans of that foam insulation worked really well once it hardened and plugged the pipe."

That immediately reminded me of something the very wonderful Linda Ellerbee, who outgrew NBC-mentality, once said about septic tanks that very much relates to the principles that sometimes guide my actions in revenge. Linda said, "In a septic tank the really big chunks always rise to the top, while it's usually the smaller pieces that clog the system." I wonder if that was her metaphor for the networks, too?

Sex Toys

Because so much of sexual matters involve the ego, libido, and a person's other mental parts, sex toys can be used to your advantage when messing up someone's mind. I learned a lot about this while sharing a radio talk show with the sex therapist Donna Muller, who is a gorgeous, Double C version of Dr. Ruth. This lady's Made in the U.S.A., though. Anyway, she says if you have an ex-sweetie, ex-luster, or someone to whom you owe a mind-screwing (the editor made me change the original word), sexual paraphernalia — fun toys for inventive girls and boys — can be a good weapon.

"You can mail-order him a dildo along with a Get Well or Sorry about Your Illness card. You can sign your or someone else's name. Or, sign no name. Sign it 'Frustrated with Limp Wimp,' something like that.

"Or, send him an Accu Jac, a penis enlarger, or Stay Hard pills. You can do this to her, too, Peruse some of the personal ads in the more explicit sex magazines and you'll find just the ticket," Muller advised.

One of her favorites involved one of her slutty friends who was making her husband's life miserable by

(Continued...)

openly shacking around. Muller dummied up a very realistic-looking letterhead from a local motel and created a Frequent Customer Club for her mark/friend to belong to. She sent it to her lady mark at the office where she was an executive, knowing full well the secretaries would have the gossip around in no time.

Included with the letter was a very explicit catalog of very kinky sex toys from the famed Postal Palace of Porno, owned by Hulk McCutcheon, one-time pro-wrestling villain.

Sexual Insecurity

Once upon a time, according to Boy Jorges, there was this teacher who was very insecure about his own sexuality. Sometimes, he took this out on his students by being an especially nasty prick. A couple of bright young guys noted this and decided to have some phone phun.

"We called him anonymously and started telling him just how very, very much we thought of him," Jorges related. "Then my pal started getting clinically personal with his compliments. The poor mark got really upset and stuttered all over the place."

According to friends, the mark stewed and worried about this for days, dreading that he was unknowingly sending out gay signals. The two straight tricksters then started putting gay literature into his mailbox and sending him mash notes. After a couple weeks, they tired of all the fun, while the mark continued to worry.

Shampoo

Some popular shampoo products resemble a thick, white milky solution. There are many interesting additives that will blend with and hold in these shampoos without being easily detected (Elmer's glue, Nair, and Resin).

Shaving Cream

Durango Bob used to belong to a fraternity, I bet. Or at least, he was in a swinging dormitory. Here's his idea of big fun. Take a manila envelope and fill it with shaving cream. Slit open one end, and shove it under the mark's door. Knock on the door and get down low so you can see the mark's shoes approaching. Quickly line up the envelope, stand up, and stomp down on your end of the cream-filled bag, squirting all the glop on the mark's shoes. Run like hell. You could also substitute other squishy things for the shaving cream.

Shell Casings

Our Jimmy Carter was ripped off by a scumbag merchant in his city and did all the nice, polite things to get the deal righted. The creep just laughed at Jimmy. Jimmy went to a nearby rifle range and borrowed a dozen or so empty rifle cartridge casings of various calibers. He wired a little message tag to each one and began having them mailed to the salesman/mark from different parts of the country. Some of the tags read:

- My loaded brother has your name on it.
- Next time, you get my bullet . . . in your ass.
- Just the right size for a crooked cheater.
- I'm way above your caliber . . . but you'll still be dead.

You probably get the idea. Jimmy cautions you that the authorities would probably take almost as dim a view of this as will the mark. He suggests you be very careful with prints, handwriting/typing, etc.

Shoplifting

If you know one or more of the stores that your mark frequently patronizes, you can add his/her name to that store's list of known shoplifters. It's easy if you work there or know someone who does. It's also a rotten trick that will cause much unhappiness to fly back and forth between accused and accuser when the confrontation finally happens.

In another variation of this, Ronnie Lenguin says to create some local police department letterhead using a photocopying machine and some purloined originals. Create a warning letter from the local police naming your mark as a major shoplifter. Send this letter to various local shops or leave them lying around your mark's office.

Shut-ins

In honor of Rosey Rosewell, I'd like to dedicate this to people who should never leave home. If you have a mark you hate and wish to isolate at home, fill up your caulking gun with a tube of Liquid Nail. When you know the mark-family is in the house for the evening, loiter outside until all is quiet, then simply place a bead of Liquid Nail to the cracks between door and frame, plus windows and frame.

Ever hear of anyone being locked *in* at home? This stunt is an absolute surprise to the mark. It's also a lot of fun.

Sinks

This scam is known as the Fishbein Effect, as it is named for Dr. Chunder H. Fishbein, a noted rhetorician at the Wanker Institute of Anti-Semantic Behavior in Fulco-on-the-Hudson, New York.

"Use black electrical tape to close down the handle on the spray hose at your mark's kitchen sink. Make sure the hose nozzle is pointing out toward the middle of the sink, and then ask your mark for a glass of water. If that is not appropriate, just wait for the action to take place."

Interestingly, according to his notes, this same idea came during a radio talk show from a young lady named Jenny in Orlando, Florida.

Slime

Not only is this a wonderful name to call people, it is a commercial product available in toy and variety stories. It's sort of a runny variation of Silly Putty, as one wag put it. The potential of this stuff is awesome. It can be used to gross out and sabotage marks, and to play messy mind games.

For example, you can put some Slime in the coin return of a pay telephone or in earphones. It is also an unwelcome addition to stereo headphones. It makes a nice complement to a salad bar. When combined with butyric acid, it goes on meat as a sauce. Perhaps a drool of it could come off your nose, ear, mouth, or some other orifice, which you could direct at your mark, especially if same has a queasy stomach. The uses of Slime are bountiful, indeed, and we should all thank its maker by buying and spreading Slime around.

Slippery Stuff

Yes, you, the ordinary citizen, can order "Instant Banana Peel" from police supply houses. It's a chemical which is dusted on the road and wetted with water. It then becomes slippery as the dickens, so much so that nobody can walk on it. Police use it for skid pans and riot control. You can use it for parades, street games, classes, dances, etc.

Smoke

"Smokey the Bare" says that where there's smoke, there might just be Liquid Smoke, the stuff you use when you cook hamburgers, steaks, etc., and want that outdoor, hickory-smoke flavor.

"Just think how your mark's car would smell if you doused a good shot of Wright's (Liquid Smoke) all over the inside. How would that seem to a prospective buyer if the mark were a car dealer? It could easily work in an office, home, or apartment, too," Smokey informs us. "The best part is that this liquid contribution to your trickster's revenge kit is universally available in any supermarket, and it is innocent looking, yet so easy to use."

Smokers

One of my worst enemies is someone who violates my privacy with his or her smoking in a location or under circumstance where my rights overshadow theirs. Sorry, smokers, I abhor the noxious odor of tobacco smoke. It's too bad your olefactory senses are so far gone you can't smell your own hair, clothes, skin, breath, home, etc. But, I digress.

CW offers a very good trick I have used and used and used. Here's all you do to help a smoker quit—at least in your territory. Add three or four horsehairs to her/his cigarette or cigar. Some disturbed smokers I tried this trick on noticed the smell, others noticed the taste, and happily, two got physically sick.

more

Smokers

Smokers are as out of place in my life as George Bush's clip-on bowties would be at a Paris fashion show. So, here is an easy get-back. Prick a number of very small holes in the fag (the cigarette, you klutz) near the filter area. When the smoker/mark inhales, he will pull in mostly air from those undetected holes and wonder what's wrong with his smoke. If this doesn't work, douse the mark with a gallon of gasoline from a very safe distance once he or she lights up. Whoa, just kidding . . .

Barney Vinceletti has a charming elevator story about another non-smoker who tired of ingesting the stale poisons that these lung killers leave around. Barney says the friend targeted this sand-filled ashtray in the elevator in his apartment building by replacing the sand with a mixture of potassium nitrate and sugar.

As Barney added, "You could experiment with the mixture, but my pal left just enough there to scare the hell out of the smokers on board next time. If you want to be more conservative, you can leave used condoms in those ashtrays . . . fill 'em with milk or whatever. Personally, I prefer the nastier approach."

Sneezing and Coughing

Pat Buchanan is a fourth-grade-level class clown who never got out of high school, even after he graduated. You know the type . . . if the world were a bottle of Dom Perignon he would be an aluminum screw top. Well, I was almost embarrassed to pass this along, until a friend, whom I respect as a real trickster, suggested the same thing. That lets me off the hook.

Sometimes, an obscene sneeze is in order, but don't ask *me* when or where. When you feel a real sneeze coming on, go in your usual loud voice, "*Fah . . . fah . . . fah . . . fah . . . fah . . . faw . . . KEW!*" Or, when you have to cough, you simply cough the word *Kotex* very loudly.

Please don't ask me to go over that again.

Snot

This reminds me of those ball players or old farmers who always blew their noses out in the field. According to Mr. Charlie, the method is to stuff one nostril shut with an index finger and then clear the other nostril with a mighty blow of air. Switch to the other nostril and then tidy up with your shirt sleeve.

A bartenderess I know, Bonnie Woodland, uses this old tactic to deal with obnoxious customers she cannot otherwise insult. "I uncap the jerk's beer, and while bent over the cooler unobserved I clear my nose into his open beer. I then pour it for him, and he never notices my additives because of the foam."

Soap

Drill a hollow area out of a soap bar, saving the shavings as you go. Fill this hole with the horrible ingredients of your choice. Blood-red ink is an excellent filling. So are smelly substances such as "liver of sulfur" (ammonium sulfide), tuna fish, roaches, beetles and excrement, to name a few.

After filling the cavity, plug the hole with a paste made by mixing the leftover shavings with water. This plug may take a few days to dry. Finally, plant this special bar of soap in your mark's bathroom.

Did you ever try putting a small sliver of soap about the size of your thumbnail into a coffee machine? You will produce an epidemic of Hershey Squirts the likes of which can empty an office in no short amount of time. According to our expert, liquid hand soap will work as well. Oh, boy, where have you gone, Joe DiMaggio?

Speakers

Speakers, and often amplifiers as well, can be destroyed by connecting their terminals to the 117-volt power line. The Indiana Cave Man adds that if you can't get at the wiring of the mark's loud stereo or PA/background music system, use a razor blade or sharp knife to sever the wire between the voice coil in the middle of the speaker and the spots on the back of the cone where heavier wires are attached.

Also, speakers and some types of microphones can be ruined by iron filings placed in the magnet gap. In some models, you must pierce the flexible barrier covering the gap to introduce the filings. Cut-up fibers of fine steel wool work best and are also effective for shorting out amplifiers, TV sets, computers, and other electronic equipment. Put the fibers in a flexible plastic tube, insert one end into the appliance, and blow.

Sperm Bank

I bet you know some righteous hypocrite who spouts Biblical stuff and criticizes others for nasty things, but who also leads a secret life that's kinky and lewd. Ask any honest hooker who her worst johns are, and she'll always finger some publicly righteous prude who turns into Mr. Hyde for his sexual repression. Let Saucy Sybil suggest some fun for this jerk.

Send a registered letter in the mark's name to the nearest local sperm bank "applying for a loan." Make the letter as straight and naive sounding as possible. Ask that the reply be sent to the home address in strict confidence as the mark admits to an embarrassing sexual dysfunction. It's not as important that you ever discover how or what they responded to the mark. Be happy in knowing that his letter and admission will create all sorts of jokes and silly gossip among the sperm bank's employees. Fun, ain't it?

Spooks

Here's some real inside stuff from Spookland. The CIA is still paranoid about Shasha, the best-yet ID of the KGB mole who is inside. It might be fun suggests our company conner, Laser Davidovich, to make up a stencil which proclaims that Bill Colby (or Dick Helms, Bill Casey, George Bush, or even Ronald Reagan) is Shasha and spray that message all over Washington and environs, including greater downtown Langley.

Here's another idea for spearing the spooks. An accomplice might monitor the employee car traffic from Langley HQ someday, noting where some of the folks go. As most of these people are clerks and analysts without Farm training, this should be easy. You can use your stencil device (above), or use the old bumper-sticker trick. The main thing is that the mark will have to report this matter to CIA security, which will open an investigation and a file.

This idea is universal, i.e., you can do the same thing for embassy employees of your least favorite countries. Of course, the messages will differ, but the results will be the same. Professional paranoia is such a wonderfully universal language.

Spoons

Want to have some harmless fun harassing your mark at the airport? Bob the Computer Kid leads the way. You slip an ordinary teaspoon into the pocket of his three-piece suit while he's at the airport lounge or cafeteria. Imagine the fun on his or her second or third time through the metal detector then having to empty his pockets.

A spoon? People will look and chortle.

Caution, warns Bob. Don't use a knife or fork. They are "weapons" to the humorless people in airport security; a spoon is just clean fun.

Spouses

Maria Mollusk called one of my talk shows with a grand scheme for your mark on the occasion of a party in honor of the happy couple's anniversary. I'll share it with you.

"You go to a selected bar, restaurant or gas station bathroom and remove the seedy, old, cruddy toilet seat from its moorings. Wrap it in a very fancy fashion with a big bow and nice card. The card is, of course, signed in your best forgery of the mark's handwriting or that of his secretary, if appropriate.

"The card says something sweet like 'To my wife (husband) on this special day in honor and loving recognition of the years of . . . (and so on and on,'" Maria explains, chuckling through her beard.

In all probability, denial will be fairly useless in this situation, and the other guests will be either amused or mortified. It will probably end the celebration party, too.

You have an unfaithful spouse or you have a friend who's being cheated on. Sharon the Dismemberment Queen has a civilized way to let lots of folks in on the fun, especially if the cheaters are already married to others.

"I obtain a typical portrait of the mark, which isn't very hard to do, then I write a brief wedding or engagement announcement in the style of the local newspaper for that area," Sharon explains.

"My hook is that I use the name, vital stats, etc. of the mark's lover as the other person in the story. True's true, right?

"Which hurts more, the pain or the fun?" Sharon asks, "happy co-respondent."

more

Spouses

One of my good friends in Pennsylvania caught a guy messing around with his girl. Know what he did to get even? He let the guy marry her!

Spray Paint

If you think gun laws make no sense, you need to meet Artha Woods, a councilwoman from Cleveland, Ohio, who proposed local legislation which would require the registration of people who buy cans of spray paint. The lady said she was tired of seeing graffiti sprayed all over Cleveland and thought police could easily track down the authors of new graffiti by tracing their spray paint cans.

The *Spokesman-Review* of Spokane, Washington, reported that officials in Los Angeles and in Spokane were considering the same legislation. The Spokane newspaper commented in its editorial, "People don't cause graffiti, spray paint does."

In 1986, the Los Angeles city council proposed a ten-cent-per-can tax on spray paint to pay for graffiti removal. Would it be cheaper to remove inept and incompetent politicians? I guess so, the 10¢ tax measure failed.

It's obvious that when paint is outlawed, only outlaws will have paint. Or, when lawful painters have to register their cans, only criminals will paint graffiti. Or, will painters spray outlaws or become outlaws?

(Continued...)

Whadaya think, Artha? I'm kind of confused, which puts me in your league, I suspect. Have you registered your can, Artha?

Stench

Perhaps this should be filed under fish, but, in honor of the out-of-work jokesters who fished Mellon Bank, here goes. Get the largest fish possible, and after you've removed the hubcap from your mark's car, stuff the fish into the cavity, then replace the cap.

Later, if you can gain access to the mark's air conditioner, remove that cover and place the fish into the impeller while the unit is off. When the unit is turned on, the result is usually spectacular, especially if the fish is aged for a day or so.

Harry Callahan adds, "I once saw a luncheonette closed for a month after this stunt was pulled there. This would also work well in an office or a motel."

If you've ever been gassed you'll enjoy this. After all, there's nothing like military gas training, being Maced or nailed by one of Uncle Gerald's missiles of flatulence. Why not pick your favorite scent, e.g., Mace, CS, etc., and spray a massive load of it into your mark's air conditioning unit intake? Perhaps you could rig such a surprise for the central air conditioning unit intake of a large building that you wish to evacuate, e.g., a club, bar, restaurant, school, etc.

Thanks to Foulbowels Anderson, we now have a splendid payback for someone who is forced to work in a laboratory or other space in which there is not a lot of fresh air, yet there is a commode. Actually, it will work effectively in any sort of closed area where your mark is trapped by work or other circumstance. Let Foulbowels tell his story.

"I had this idiot lab tech I needed to bother. So I came into work early after two straight evenings of drinking beer—lots of it—and eating hardboiled eggs, cheese and blind robins. My flatulence alone was melting structural steel that day.

"I let myself into the tech's small lab about an hour before anyone else was due in the building and turned off the water supply to his commode. Then, I Loctited the water supply handle at the base. I flushed the thing, so now there's no water in the tank. Next, I took one of my most world-class, obnoxious dumps of all time in the tech's commode. That thing was against all the laws of man, nature and civilized warfare. Finally, I cleaned me up, shut the lid down and walked out, closing his door behind me."

Foulbowels says a plumber spent three hours getting things back together—after a one hour wait for him to arrive. In the meantime, the lab tech had no choice but to work in the stench as important tests were due, and the company could not afford for the lab to be shut down. The lab tech had to be sent home in the early afternoon suffering from blurred vision and headache.

Stencils

This idea is especially useful if you want to get back at someone who's spreading nasty lies and rumors about you or a friend. It's brought to you through the courtesy of Dick Smegma. You obtain a stencil with a message something like this:

JOHN JERKOFF
555-1212
1234 Anystreet
Histown
MOLESTS KIDDIES

Or, you can accuse him or her of having sexual relations with dead animals, with desecrating churches, bombing synagogues, torching an orphanage, or some other vile act. Hold your stencil up against any smooth-surfaced wall and let go with a blast of spray paint, peeling away the stencil. Instant smear campaign.

Stereos

Have an enemy whose stereo, TV or radio bothers you? Pack some steel wool in the electronic circuits of the offending machine. When the power goes on, the entire board shorts off. Poooofff. Thanks, Killroy.

Here is yet another idea to discourage inconsiderate louts who play loud stereo music when you need peace and quiet. Much as I like Rock music, I sometimes think New Wave was invented to encourage the practice of audiophonic revenge. In this instance, CW has a grand suggestion if you have ready access to your mark's stereo.

"Replace his good needle with an awful one, an old one, one with a tip like a square nail," CW writes from his redoubt. "Your sabotage-needle will screech, scratch and make all sorts of nasty noise and damage on the records."

How many of you have had to share automobile space with some spaced out cuckoo who plays his in-car system loud enough to shake the moon? Our old pal Col. R. Micheals finally tired of this cacophonous car pooling and created a fireworks display to end all displays.

He literally had come down with migraine headaches from traveling in this vehicular stereophonic sonic boom, but he needed his job so he had no choice, but to Get Even.

"I purchased fifteen feet of dual filament speaker wire and borrowed a couple of Instamatic flash bars. I carefuly spliced the bulbs into the speaker wire in parallel. Since I had access to the guy's car I was able to splice my loaded wire right into his speaker wire system and placed the bulbs all around the inside of his car.

"As they went off in sequence, I was literally able to blow his mind in any direction I chose. As the bulbs exploded, it was like being in an indoor fireworks display. I pretended to be screaming and kicking in panic, too, as part of my cover.

"It cured the problem for as long as I had to ride with the guy. He was so shaken he never did get anything checked or repaired. Nor did he ever turn on the damn machine again."

Stickers

If you want to slow customer traffic to a particular store for some justified reason, have your printer prepare some fairly large stickers for you. The backing should be as permanent-stick as possible. Keep placing your sticker near the stickers at store entrances which explain shoplifting policies, business hours, etc. Your sticker will say "WARNING. ANYONE WEARING A PACEMAKER IS PROHIBITED FROM USING THIS ELECTRONIC ENTRANCE."

WARNING
TRESPASSERS
WILL BE SHOT
SURVIVORS
WILL BE SHOT AGAIN

NEVER MIND
THE DOG.
BEWARE OF
OWNER!

IS THERE LIFE
AFTER DEATH?
TRESPASS HERE
AND FIND OUT

NOTICE
ANYONE FOUND HERE
AT NIGHT
WILL BE FOUND HERE
IN THE MORNING

"Stopper"

This wonderful invention comes to us courtesy of The Tennessean, who suggests many marvelous uses for it. Essentially, "The Stopper" is a two- or three-inch square of wall panel through which five to eight large roofing nails are pushed. The Stopper is then laid on a road or path, sharp end up, and covered with loose gravel, dirt, or leaves. Our patron says they make wonderful welcoming mats for trail bikers, motorized hunters, and others who trespass on your property.

Use several at a time, and spread them out. As The Tennessean says, "Most cars carry one spare, but that doesn't help three flats. Bikers rarely have a spare tire."

Store Mannequins

As noted in the Bathroom section, these plaster models make great pseudo victims to entrap real victims. You can use fake blood and your ax-murderer's imagination to create a real mess, e.g., a mutilated "corpse" for someone to find. I once did in a drunken friend who needed to be taught a lesson, i.e., stop hitting on everyone else's ladies. After one of his especially comatose drunkathons, I fixed him up in a sexually compromising position with a store mannequin and took some photos. Then, a friend and I arranged the same scene—live—in his livingroom for the benefit of his family and guests as they came downstairs much later that morning. It's a good thing I'm a nice guy or I would have used a small boy mannequin.

Strobes 'n Stereos

Does your mark enjoy the old disco bit with strobes or are there strobes in ye old markhome? If so, Dr. Deviant says you can use this strobe to drive your mark into near seizure if you can guarantee captive response.

The Doctor advises, "Any strobe light set between ten and twenty-five flashes per second will induce a temporary seizure in most people. The affected nerves just can't keep up and they shut down, causing a bad-appearing seizure situation."

Again, I checked this with my medical consultant, Dr. Chris Doyle, director of the Dr. George Holiday Sanitarium, who confirmed the ten to twenty-five flashes dose. While on the subject, Dr. Doyle had a related suggestion.

"If your disco-mark also has a mind-boggling stereo system — most do — and it annoys the hell out of you, use it to pay back. If the mark is a heavy sleeper, put the headset over his ears. Otherwise, move the big speakers right up to the bed and surround the mark if you can.

"Then, hook that monster system up to the alarm and set it for some horrible hour that will cause max-

(Continued...)

imum unhappiness to the mark, not to mention ear damage. Crank up the volume, set the alarm to ON, and leave with a smile on your face."

Students

If you've ever starred in the role of college student, you know the act of hiring someone to write a term paper for you. You might even know someone you hate who always writes wonderful papers, even when hung over, or you hate the class snob for being so proper and getting As without making any effort, so here's how to get back.

One suggestion is to wait until the mark has placed his or her paper on the pile on the teacher's desk, when you can then go to the stack of papers and remove the mark's original paper. Use common sense on your approach to this.

Then, we have the scam. Replace the mark's own paper with a specially written new one. This new one contains all the elements guaranteed to garner an "F" grade. You should also be sure to include several personal references to the professor or some unjustified ethnic and racial charges, too.

Stump Rot

You see this miracle product advertised everywhere from Sunday newspapers to backyard gardener magazines. Simply pour it onto the stump or into holes you've drilled into the stump, and the stump just sort of shrivels away. A product with that potential is just too good to pass up in a book of this sort.

Stupid "Success" Story

The most stupid success story since the last book came to me from a reader in Harrisburg, Pennsylvania, who sent me a clip about some dunderhead who dressed up in an ape costume and was going around scaring people in a rural area near that state's capital city.

Local police were quoted as saying, "Citizens who've seen it say it isn't human . . . a six-and-a-half-foot hairy creature with long arms and big fangs. Personally, we think this creature came out of costume shop, rather than a deep swamp."

Seems they were right. Checks with Harrisburg costume-shop records turned up leads that led to an arrest on various charges. Why was this a stupid stunt? First, the buyer shopped locally and used his own name and address on sales records. But, the most absolutely stupid thing the guy did was to pull off this stunt in a rural area of Pennsylvania, a state which has more licensed hunters and gun owners than any other in the nation.

Boom! Boom! Potential end of prank.

The guy was lucky to end up being tried by twelve rather than carried by six.

Stupid "Success" Story, Pt. II

A lot of times radio show hosts ask me about such words as illegal, guilty, law, and other such terms as once faced one of history's master dirty tricksters, Richard "I am not a crook" Nixon. I always tell them that you can't be guilty unless you're caught and proved to have done something illegal, as so many distinguished citizens prove in and out of our courts every day. So, I am not sure we can call this a success story; I guess that is up to the principals involved. Perhaps, it was best identified by San Francisco's RB who first sent me the newspaper clip. RB called it "Haydukery at work."

In the small town of San Carlos, about 30 miles south of San Francisco, an ex-police officer and his son were charged with criminal libel early in 1986 for forging the police chief's signature to a racist political campaign letter in a local election the year before.

According to local officials, the letter was a lie and the defendants had a history of holding grudges against people with whom they'd had a dispute. In addition to the letter, the son was also charged with dumping "an odorous mixture of blue cheese and ammonia" in the city hall-police department ventilation system, and with

(Continued...)

spray-painting nasty anti-police graffiti on downtown buildings.

According to local officials, the two men may have been getting scenarios for their vendettas from a how-to book found in their home by investigators. That book is titled *Get Even,* according to the newspaper account.

After studying that newspaper clipping, I found all kinds of stupid decisions made by these two losers. But, maybe it was all just in fun.

Stupid Drivers

One of our grossest forms of stupid driver is the lazy numbnuts who parks in zones marked Fire Zone, No Parking/Parcel Pickup, Handicapped Parking or something like that at your mall or supermarket. Selwyn Miles has a very gentle reminder for those mindless jellybrains. After unloading his own shopping cart, he returns the empty cart and places it against the offender's right rear fender. Or if he knows this is a repeat offender or someone who is equally obnoxious, i.e., a jerk or jerkette who refuses to move when asked nicely, Selwyn lays his cart on its side behind the fender. That way, the dumb driver either has to move that cart or, hopefully, won't see it and will ruin some finish on the car when pulling out.

Do you have problems with tailgating by land-bound versions of The Blue Angels? Jimi the Z has pumped up a wonderful response, using his fabled smoke generator. He ran a line into the headers from the electric pump and plastic reservoir from an old windshield washer unit. Jimi wired same to a panel switch. His special "Jimi's Mix" for smoke includes one part WD40, one part drain oil, two parts mineral spirits and a dash of D76 film developer. Not only does the smoke effect work well, according to Jimi, but the stink factor is through-the-roof bad.

If you're not as mechanical as Jimi, a great fan in Tampa suggests you merely load a combination of WD 40 and 40 wt. motor oil in one of those squeeze catsup bottles, open your window and fire the stuff out into the slipstream so it will rush back all over the tailgater's windscreen.

But, don't pull up behind Ed Sasquatch and hit him with the high beams of your Detroit monster. Ed mounted a high-powered spotlight in his ride's rear deck aimed right back at the inconsiderate tailgater. Plugged into his car's cigarette lighter, this 300,000 cp baby gives it right back.

Subscriptions

Here's a switch on the monkey warfare of magazines that use those annoying little advertising inserts. You can use the "Give-A-Gift Subscription" cards that are inserted during the holidays to zap two marks, according to Captain Kill.

Write in one mark's name as the recipient and the other mark's name as the giver. Naturally, you check the "Bill Me Later" box. I like sophisticated, literary humor like this.

Subversives

Ahahah, now there is a term from the McCarthy era! But, as I write this, we are in a neo-McCarthy era, so, what the hell? Here is a refinement for the crank letter idea of *Make 'Em Pay!* You "have" your mark write letters of praise, wish-to-join and to pledge money to all of the Communist, crank church, neo-Nazi, etc, groups. These efforts will also draw the attention of various snoopy governmental agencies.

Success Stories

There's a disciple of chicanery living in Pittsburgh, who was written up in the local newspaper. According to the newspaper, Jude Pohl is a "true patron of lost consumer causes. He does not rant and rave. He does not slink off. He is the soul of quiet persistence . . . Invariably, he gets justice."

That's our kind of person!

The feature article told how Pohl took on supermarkets, film companies, loan companies, and other giant corporations that usually stomp all over us little folks.

Do we have a fan in San Jose also? Early in 1983, wonderfully uptight San Jose experienced a scam that not only destroyed some mark's home, but also cheated seventy-five men out of a payday. It seems someone called the California State Employment Development Department, the out-of-work-helpers, in January to "hire" seventy-five men to tear down a vacant house in East San Jose. The work had to be fast.

It was.

It was also cheap. And, the man who owned the house wasn't the man who made the call. The owner showed up in shock when his place was down to its foundation.

The call was a hoax. The owner was out one house, and those seventy-five workers were out some thirty dollars. Meantime, someone else was having a real laugh.

In Gibraltar, Michigan, hundreds of pictures depicting a Brownstown Township school secretary in sexual acts were mailed to schools and businesses and scattered along a street, police told Associated Press.

Children reported finding the pictures on their way to a suburban Detroit elementary school, according to the AP report. The pictures were inscribed with the woman's name and address.

"It is likely that a picture of the woman's face had been superimposed on the photos," said local police Sgt. Dan Grant.

During WWII, the OSS found that sugar in the gas tank is not a reliable way to sabotage motor vehicles. The myth is universally believed, however, which is good mind-bender news. Instead, save your empty sugar sacks. Drop one on the ground near the mark's vehicle and sprinkle a handful of sugar on the ground under the gas-tank filler. The mark will be afraid to start the engine until the fuel system is purged. It's cheaper and faster than actually sweetening the fuel, and it causes almost as much grief.

It must. According to the Indiana Cave Man, he once incapacitated an entire herd of earthmovers belonging to the U.S. Army Corps of Engineers, which was working at a land-raping site.

"All I used was half a dozen, empty five-pound sugar sacks with a bit of residue scattered around the machines and the ground under the fuel tanks," he notes.

more

Success Stories

I cannot go into detail because of both the newness and the nearness, but I can tell you that our old veteran contributor, The Skull, has used Haydukery to the utmost to create a demolishing hell for a woman who totally messed him up personally and financially on a rental deal. You will have to take my word for the fact that he did her in with a classic combination of techniques. Perhaps in some issue down the publication line I can provide details. Otherwise, The Skull holds a High Five for 100 percent success in a *big* win.

Dr. Barry Lebetkin is director of the Institute for Behavior Therapy in New York City, an upright place, and not some CIA shrink front for illegal assassination stuff like it sounds. Dr. Lubetkin says, "There are certain situations where people feel justifiably vengeful and no amount of talking to them about forgetting about getting even works. It's probably healthy to some degree."

Later, the good Doctor mentioned a patient who told him that he once put liquid cement in the door locks of twenty new cars at a dealership where he'd been way overcharged for repairs, then given no satisfaction with

(Continued...)

his complaint. Dr. Lubetkin added, "The patient said he got the idea from some funny book on getting even with enemies."

Is that flattery, or what, folks?

It's nice to know people do have a sense of humor in South Carolina. In February 1986, a South Carolina couple offered a $5,000 reward for the person who swiped a personal photo showing the lady topless and then printed it in a brochure inviting hundreds of people to a "sex orgy" at the couple's home.

The two-page brochure, which was professionally done, also showed four other photos, out of focus, but clearly of explicit sex acts. They were mailed to 200 people, including friends of the couple, their pastor, and business acquaintances. The copy in the brochure invited recipients to come have a swinging sexual time with the couple and their guests.

And, speaking of publications, here's grand news. Barney Vinceletti got his first novel published and "it offends almost every icon of society" as Barney puts it. I read it, he's right. It's called *The Bird of Paradise.*

Suitmen

Suitmen are the three-piece corporate types who are the lounge lizards who stalk and prey during Happy Hour. Our friend Kilroy has a rather involved and potentially destructive sting for these flesh-feasting marks.

Check in your local library for the Thomas Register, and find the name of two of the major competitors of your mark's company. Next, get letterhead and envelopes from the mark's company, or create them by using some of the more sophisticated versions of PressType. Let's say he works for the Worthen Widget Company of Bumjump, Georgia. The two competitors are Mighty Manufacturing Inc., of Chicago, and Widget Master of Broomfield, Colorado. Address a letter to Widget Master, using the Chicago address of the second competitor. Also, find and use the name of an actual executive at Widget Master to whom you should address your letter.

Obviously, the post office in Chicago will not be able to locate any such company as Widget Master, and they will return the letter to the sender. It will no doubt be opened by some company secretary, unless you specifically direct the return address to a certain office, which may prove advantageous.

Why is all of this nasty? When the person at Worthen Widgets opens the returned letter, to see where to direct it, here is what it will say:

WORTHEN WIDGET
COMPANY LOGO
ADDRESS

Mr. John E. Presser
Widget Master Company
Chicago, Illinois

Dear John,

Please forward the $15,000 payment we agreed upon last month for the manufacturing data and new product specs I furnished you. Come on, man, we had a deal, remember?

Sincerely,

I. M. Mark

Naturally, an incendiary letter like this will make the rounds of corporate powerdom very quickly, especially if Mr. Mark is an unpopular chap. Also, the mix-up of two companies and towns will cause some suspicion that Mr. Mark was dealing double. All in all, he's on his way down the corporate crapper. This stunt has about a seventy-percent kill(roy) ratio.

Super Glue

A sharing reader from Huntsville, Alabama, shared a takeoff (no pun) on the old super-glue/male member stunt. A lady caught her husband cheating again after repeated warnings. After a few nights of nonfighting, she let him sleep peacefully. After gently arousing him sexually in his sleep, she quietly and carefully coated his fingers with super glue, handed him his penis, and then intertwined his fingers around it. According to our Huntsville agent, the chap had to go into surgery for corrective action.

Super Glue Bombs

Here's a truly funny idea from Kilroy. We're all aware of what the mail-order trade calls bubble packing. You can make messy bombs with that stuff, something that could stick with your mark for days.

The idea is to cut out one individual bubble from the sheet and puncture a hole, one sixteenth of an inch, in the bubble. Inject Eastman 910 into that hole and fill the bubble. The hole will seal itself, and you have a tiny glue bomb. Place these little nasties in people's shoes, clothes, bedding, pants pockets, seats, etc.

If you tire of sticking it to your mark, you could use other additives to fill the little bombs.

Super Glues

By now, everyone in the nation claims to actually know some guy who had his Mr. Happy super-glued to his leg, a phenomenon which reminds me of the veracity of the Westmoreland Bodycount System in Vietnam. Back in the world of reality, though, the fabulous La Croix Bothers muse on a new method of getting folks to stick around after a robbery, Haydukery, or whatever. Their idea is simple: "You put a dab of a super glue on each fingertip of each mark, then make certain each mark presses those fingertips hard against a flat wall for thirty seconds. Then it's bye-bye time for you."

In this case, parting really will be such sweet sorrow for the mark(s), which is why you have to hand it to the Brothers LaCroix for this stunt.

Supermarket

California's Mot Rot puts some practical ideas to work. Do they work? According to Mot, one very deserving rip-off supermarket in a "nearby" town got sued for selling dead cats (packaged in store wrapping), in their meat section.

"I wonder who the stockperson was who put the fataled felines in there?" Mot says with a wild laugh.

Supermarkets

If your local supermarket has been rotten to you and just happens to have an in-store security TV camera, Filthy McNasty has some suggestions. Filthy says, "You can suspend a truly gross centerfold from a porno magazine in front of the lens or get some fat woman to moon the thing. I also pretend to steal, then when I'm confronted, I raise royal hell and threaten lawsuits. Sometimes I get free food as a pacifier."

There are rude shoppers who persist in blocking the aisles while they gab with cronies or let their kids run rampant thorugh the market. They obviously need help, so why not give it to them? Add some small, yet very expensive items to their cart, perhaps burying them among the regular purchases. Some caviar would do well, for example. On the other paw, you could remove staples that look necessary, like diapers, aspirin, Tampax, etc. from their carts.

Tor and Snow Dog have a stunt that sounds like fun. Engineer the total disappearance of your mark's shopping cart very near to checkout time. The best dumping ground is to move the offending vehicle to the preparation area that adjoins the produce department in most chain stores. According to our dynamic duo, this stunt has a grand aggravation factor.

more

Supermarkets

Dick Smegma liked our food fight scam from *Make 'Em Pay!* but also has one of his own that works everytime. It's simple. When you need to extract revenge upon a market, grab an unused PA microphone or telephone in a quiet area of the store and use your own version of this generic script:

> "Attention Food Circus Shoppers. To make room for incoming stock and for the next ten minutes only, we have a *Super Special* on fresh, whole milk — only 25¢ per gallon. That's right. Only 25¢ per gallon — buy all you want for the next ten minutes."

Instant chaos everytime, Dick adds.

Our supersnooper, Captain Video, has been prowling the revenge section of his least favorite market again and has come up with another Black Light Special.

"Did you know that the 6½-ounce cans of cat food and of chunk light tuna are exactly the same container?" the good Captain asks rhetorically. "A bit of water applied to the glue sections of the label easily remove same without tearing. From there it is just an instant to switch the labels, re-attach, and resupply the

(Continued...)

supermarket shelves. Nobody is the wiser until Mark II opens whichever can."

Sweeties

Upon meeting Consuela, his brother's four-legged consort from Colon, Panama, Dr. David McGeary shuddered and said, "Lips that touch swine shall never touch mine." It's a nice sentiment, but old-fashioned. Now, let's see how others handled this old problem.

Being a good chap, Andrea knows some ladies. He told me a story about a friend of his who found his sweetie had hot pants for another guy — any guy. He decided to help. He placed a Tabasco-type sauce mixture in her liquid vaginal soap. A mysterious burning rash curtained her sexual adventures for a while. Funny thing, it would reoccur. Maybe, it was the guys she was shacked up with?

This next mark is one of the major hypocrites of our century. A staff member of the Meese Commission on Pornography, this doofuss was *also* a secret chaser of young skirts and knickers, an AC/DC slime. Mr. Justice saw a way to get even with this pious pillar of his fundamental church and head of his very proper household. Mr. Justice had a trusted female associate call this dork's unlisted home telephone number on a day they knew he was away and that Mrs. Wonderful was home.

(Continued...)

The female friend identified herself as a doctor from a local, exclusive health clinic and asked to speak to the mark. Informed he was not at home, the "doctor" hemmed and hmmmed a bit, then came right out with it.

"You are Mrs. Mark? Well, I am sorry to be the one to tell you this, but as it concerns you, too, I guess you need to know." She went on to explain that the mark's AIDS and genital herpes tests were "generally negative," but that she (our "doctor") still wanted to talk to him about identifying the woman with whom he was involved because they had reason to believe she was a carrier.

Now that probably gave the old fun couple a few grists for conversation upon his arrival to the old hearthside, eh?

Not nearly as mean, but a sure barb at the other half's suspicion quotient, is the mistaken identity gambit. Tommy Tolar from Little Rock suggested it and here's how it unrolls. When your mark introduces Sweetie to you, look very puzzled, then say, slowly, "Ahhh, this isn't the same lady/man you introduced me to last __________?" (*Pause, then smile, punch mark playfully in the arm, and say,)* You old hot pants, you. Wow, you sure know how to pick 'em." Then proceed with embarrassing, personal comments of a generally sexist nature.

Paulette Cooper has a nice touch for an errant spouse whom you wish to make your mark in a support case. It's easy. You simply make sure the mark's correct name, but wrong address, are recorded for the support notices. That way, the mark never really hears about the money due, the hearings, all the rest. The next item may be an arrest notice, and that always gets through personally.

Paulette has another thought which is devastating in its simplicity. Your mark has a wife, live-in, or very close girlfriend. You send flowers to her in the man's name. He'll always wonder.

All of this probably caused my newlywed friend from New Orleans to remark, "It used to be wine, women, and song. Now, it's beer, the old lady, and TV." His marriage ought to go swimmingly, which reminds me . . .

more

Sweeties

There still seem to be nasty folks doing rotten things to more innocent folks. Sometimes, though, a few of the nice folks win. Steve 10-89G from Racine is a fine example.

His ex-fiance was one of those cheating, flirt-bitches so common on TV soaps and, I guess, in real life also. After their break-up, she had some problems with nasty prank calls which Steve had nothing to do with—just as he wanted nothing to do with her anymore. The calls came from new boyfriends and randy nuts whom she had teased.

Yet her family blamed Steve, and her friends threatened him. Her parents even threatened legal action. Our innocent Steve took action. He made a tape recording in his own voice, saying, "There's a bomb in your house set to go off at 1 A.M. Get everyone out, or I'll blow you all to kingdom come in one hour."

He gave the tape to a very trusted friend and instructed him to call her house that night at midnight. At 10:00 that same night, in front of witnesses, Steve boarded a four-hour flight to Las Vegas to visit his sister, who met him at the airport with witnesses. When Steve's pal played the tape, Steve was over Wyoming talking to some witnesses—a perfect alibi.

Naturally, the police were called and a great and grand furor arose. Steve and his family were indignant—his parents more so because they knew nothing of this scam. Steve and his family threatened legal action against her folks and the police. They refused to even discuss this matter with the ex-fiance or her parents, even when the other folks tried to eat crow, and she called him crying for forgiveness. Great job, Steve!

You probably bought nice, pretty flowers for your sweetie when the going was great. With things as dead as they usually are with ex-sweeties, why not send some bouquets of dead flowers or one with horrible odors, poisons, etc. It's the thought that counts. We thank the IFC Poster Child for this thought.

K. Williams used the mail and some interesting postcards to get revenge on a cad who'd done some nasty things to nice folks. Here's how. "Get a postcard or two from a motel or hotel in a nearby city. Send it to the mark at his home address, or at work if you think it would do more good. Hopefully, his wife, boss or secretary will see it first. You know the mail delivery person will also see it, which can add to the gossip if it's a small town. You can be certain that the wife, boss or secretary will want to discuss this secret life with the mark." Here's a suggested message for the card.

> I had a wonderful time the other afternoon (evening), darling. Wow, I had no idea you were such a lover, considering that frump you said you had at home. I just love your tongue and those kinky

toys, the video tapes and, well, your, ahh, you know. Sweetheart, I can't wait until the next time. I'll call soon and tell you some things I want you to do with me. See you next week.

Love,

Diane (or whomever)

Of course, with some modification this will easily work on a female mark, as well.

When the Labor Lady from Denver decided to get back at her ex-husband for his myriad extramarital meanderings, she scammed the names and addresses of his many ex-girlfriends—mostly one-week or one-night stands. On Father's Day, she had her teenage kids, with great senses of humor themselves, send mushy cards to Dad in care of each of the girls. In all cases, she noted, the girls dutifully forwarded the cards to dear old Dad. Dad was not amused, she reported.

Let's say your lady has decided to "bed 'em and spread 'em" with another guy, which is her gendered prerogative, of course. You have many options, one of which involves a dildo. You take an especially large, gross model and wire it to hang from the rear license plate holder of her car. Or instead of dangling it down, you can wire it upright or horizontally like a trophy. You might consider different colored dildos, too.

According to A. H. Sylvester, the designer of this devilish dildo delight, it will be days, even a week if you're lucky, before the ex-sweetie discovers why all sorts of folks are staring and laughing at her. Then, she'll know she's been had yet one other way. In addition to women, I bet this could also be used with comically devastating results upon the ego and/or reputation of a gay sweetie.

It's Cara Savage again, back with some devious devilment from our darling damsel. In this scenario, your mark is one or both members of a couple loving, but not living together. Go to your local free clinic and pick up a pamphlet on facts about gonorrhea or some other such social horror story. The bigger the type the better. Carla says to buy some little bitty white envelopes, the same type the clinic uses to dispense pills. Or boost a few of theirs.

"Fill out the front of the envelope with the name of the mark whose apartment or house will be planted," Carla instructs. "When you include the date, back date for five or six days so you imply that the partner is not only infectious, but also cretinous. Then, scrawl in doctorlike writing 1 cap 4x daily, Ampicillan 350."

Carla says to fill the envelope with large, opaque placebo pills and plant it and the literature where a guest is likely to spot them before the host or hostess does. Paranoia and tempers will rage as you have pricked the two biggest social biggies—disease and infidelity.

I first picked this next one up during a telephone talk show in Ohio, but later I saw it in *Playboy*. Basically, a man wanted to end his relationship with his live-in lady. He was leaving on a business trip and told her he would be back in two days and wanted her and her things out when he returned home.

When he got back, he saw that the apartment was in good order and that the girl and her goods were gone. He did notice the telephone was off its cradle, though. Picking it up, he heard a strange language on the line. It turns out the girl had dialed the time and temperature number in Bangkok, Thailand, then left the apartment with the phone off the hook. In *Playboy,* the girl had called Tokyo, and the man's bill was $8,000. Just imagine the hassle with the telephone company, as in "Sorry, but somebody's got to pay." Guess who?

Swimming Pools

More refinements keep pouring into the Hayduke pool of pustule. Carl called from Champaign, Illinois, to suggest putting several pounds of a product known as Mr. Bubble into a mark's swimming pool. It will feed through the filter and foam everything. It's tough to defoam, too, Carl claims.

Or, would you like to fill up a mark's pool with urine, but just can't make enough of the product? Try the almost next best thing — urine color and stench. I'd like to thank Hacer Polvo for this idea. Combine three parts yellow food coloring with one part green and two parts fox urine lure. Ye mark will think that the Jolly Peeing Giant just whizzen full the pool. It looks and smells just like an unflushed commode, Hacer says.

According to Missouri's Mr. Heffer, a nasty scavenger fish known as the carp will live in even heavily chlorinated water. It will also crap up a pool really well. Mr. Heffer says to toss some carp into the mark's pool when the mark is away for a weekend. Include some roadkill and other food for the fish. "Guaranteed, the mark will have to drain and totally clean that pool; it will be that bad," says Heffer. That's good.

(Continued...)

Mr. Justice is a neat guy to invite to a pool party, especially one being hosted by your rude neighbor who likes *loud* music, and *obnoxious* guests, and doesn't mind sharing them with you, never mind that you don't want to be shared with. Mr. Justice acts after the party has ended, and, using a sharp knife, makes a major slash in the pool's vinyl liner near the bottom of the deep end. He then inserts a large piece of broken branch taken from a nearby tree, hopefully as in overhanging nearby, and jams it into the rapidly draining slash. The mark thinks the rip happened accidentally. But, you'll know better.

Mr. Justice also has ways for you to help your nasty mark winterize his pool, saying, "When the mark covers up and buttons down the pool for the winter, but doesn't drain it, you can help out by slipping some insulation under the cover and into the water." For insulation, Mr. Justice recommends things like roadkill; a gallon of used motor oil; garden fertilizer; large piles of dog, horse or cow poop; etc. Our helpful hero adds, "The mark literally will be able to walk on that water when he uncovers the pool the next spring."

more

Swimming Pools

Our old friend Stoney Dale had a bad time at a very snotty country club when the elite made sport of his humble origins. Undaunted, he came back that night with a couple of chocolate candy bars and tossed them into the sacred swimming pool—after unwrapping them.

"The pool was drained the next day because officials were certain the pool had been used as an unauthorized commode," Stoney reports.

I bet if you laid some toilet paper around the pool area, as well as in the pool, it would add to the illusion.

Syringes

As mentioned before, these can be used to inject all sorts of additives into all sorts of products, foodstuffs, containers, etc. James Q. Carter once had an acquaintence in college who kept mooching food from him. After James Q. couldn't make the moocher understand in a civilized way, he injected dish soap into fruit-filled cookies and donuts. After a long stint in the can, the prolific pilferer persisted no more.

Tailgaters

Barney Vincelette, the wily conductor of our symphony of skullduggery, waves his baton at tailgaters, offering them a cacophonous coda. Barney says to hook a cheap, surplus cargo parachute to the rear deck of your car, the luggage rack, or the back of your station wagon or truck. The risers should be secured with rope having a break point of 100 pounds. When the tailgater offends you to your breaking point, inflate the chute so the risers break free and the unit wraps itself around the offending vehicle. Speaking of impaired vision. . . .

Talk Mongers

An Iowa lady who worked two shifts during the Depression of 1982-83, told me she had a friend who used to call her and chat at 7 A.M.

"She had to go to work at 8:30, so she called me at 7:30 to talk. I worked two shifts to keep my kids fed, clothed, and housed, and I had no time for this silly broad. I tried to explain this to her, but it never sunk in.

"My idea was simple. My sister was in college in California and worked the day shift, so I asked her to call my 'gabby friend' at 4 or 5 in the morning and repay the favor. It worked. I got an apology from her, and we became better friends."

Tampons

Yes, lovers of the nasty, there is even a Mrs. Skull out there in wonderful Warmland, USA. She passes along a fine idea if your mark is a woman, as opposed to a lady, and you want to really gross her out and disgust her. Mrs. Skull says to see that a couple of used tampons — used in any way you wish — are mailed, delivered, given, or whatever to Ms. Mark or to someone else in her name.

Make no bones about it, I would not want to cross Mrs. Skull!

Tape Recordings

If you have a tape recording of your mark's voice that contains enough words and you have a lot of editing time on your hands, you can splice together a delightfully rotten, obscene call featuring your mark. Dial a family member or a second mark. When the target answers, push the Play button on your machine and let Mark I say it all to Mark II. This friendly idea comes to you courtesy of Darrell W. Woffard.

You can also add your own lyrics to someone else's music. Jimi the Z says to borrow a "Vocal Zapper," a forty-dollar gadget which filters out the vocals on recordings, leaving all the instrumentals untouched. Next, use your own lyrics, using your imagination and mark's susceptibility in regard to content (crude, political, outlandish, gross, sexual, etc.). Zap the original vocals on a standard recorded tune, and dub your own, new vocals, or get someone who can sing to do it for you. You can then disseminate your new vocals for this standard tune over PA systems, Muzak, radio, etc.

Taverns

There was this really big rip-off bar called RandyPants, kind of a rowdy swingers' place. For reasons best left unexplained at this time, Annie Fellantori thought it would be a blast both to get even and to make some money.

"I got a friend to go in on a very crowded, very busy night. He sat right by the door, out of sight of the bar, and collected a buck 'cover charge' from everyone who entered.

"He had a little penlight to make a show of checking IDs, and he used a Magic Marker to make an X on the peoples' hands when they paid. In twenty minutes, he made $108. He split after twenty minutes before some employee got suspicious. I highly recommend this stunt to anyone."

Tea

Like many other druggies, tea drinkers have to get their daily fix of the narcotic caffeine. If your mark happens to be one of those unfortunate addicts, Gnarly Bumpo of Carlsbad Caverns is pleased to offer some very useful advice.

"What's so great about the new packaging of chewing tobacco is that it comes in containers that look just like tea bags. You can probably slip one into some old coot's teacup so he'll make 'baccy' tea. He'll take his first sip and keel over."

Straight shooting there, Gnarly. As a refinement to the idea, you could also switch substances inside those real tea bags or insert additives. Many such custom blends come easily to my twisted mind.

Tear Gas

Mr. Anon suggests that this stuff is, in his words, "dreadfully easy to make." All you have to do is to bubble chlorine gas through acetone in bright sunlight. The sun's ultraviolet light is the catalyst. According to Anon, the resulting chloroacetone is far more effective than commercial tear gas.

Telephones

Is it my imagination, or is it true that since her divorce, Ma Bell has become one of the cheapest, but most costly whores in town? After seeing the high-priced novel that passes as my phone bill, I swear that the Reaganistas and Ma Bell have ganged up to rape us poor folk.

Using a bit of American ingenuity and the reorganization of Ma Bell, you can defeat those locked telephones in offices and other places. Simply unplug the modular cord of the "locked" phone and plug in your own carry-along phone that you probably bought somewhere for ten bucks. Use your phone to make your call on someone else's line and bill. Thank Mike the Madman for this budget easer.

Telephone solicitors are reaching out and touching far too many people, if all the complaints reaching the PUC are an indication of this incursion into our privacy. As usual, most of our flak is directed at the frontline troops—the solicitors. It's true that many of the solicitors are folks just like us—simply trying to make ends meet in these rough times. Most of them will accept a simple "No, thank you." Then there are the rude ones, the others for whom we've reserved the following ideas:

• Ask a few questions about the product or service for sale, then start asking very strange personal questions about the solicitor. Get kinky.

• Listen to the pitch for awhile. Then if the solicitor indicates that he can take credit cards, agree to buy. About halfway through giving your credit card number abruptly hang up. When he calls right back, act totally surprised and pretend total ignorance of what the solicitor is talking about. Either say no and hang up, just hang up or, if you're really devious, start the whole thing over again with the agreement to buy, read half of the card number, etc.

• Blatantly proposition the caller. If he or she is of the same sex so much the better, as it will get him or her off your line quicker.

• Belch, fart or make odd noises into the telephone.

• Begin talking in tongues or start praying.

• Read Allen Ginsberg's poem *Howl* to the solicitor.

Need the name and address of someone and can't get it anywhere? Let Ma Bell help you. Despite the clever conspiracy by Ma and the Reaganistas to split Ma's responsibilities, thus raising her revenues, she still has a department known as CN/A, or Customer Name/Address. CN/A exists so authorized telephone company employees can get the name and address of any customer in any Bell system. All telephone numbers, including the unpublished ones, are maintained on file there.

You use CN/A by acting as a bored, casual employee and call in with a rap something like this: "Morning, this is Bill with Customer Service in Niwot. I've got an old guy on hold who's raising cain about not making a series of calls to area code (303) 555-1212. I need the customer's name for that number." You can also run this backwards, i.e., give the name, get the number. Just act cheery and natural. You can get a list of CN/A numbers in your area from TAP.

Back from his latest antihitchhiker sortie, Ray Domino is just about to head off for his other job as manager of a church league softball team in Outback, Ohio. But first he says, "This isn't clever, but it makes people sick, so that's good. Snort, sniffle and hawk up some really gross mucous, including greenies and other nasal mucilage, then blow your nose really thoroughly all over the handset of your mark's telephone. It works great in public places."

Want to drive your mark semiserious? According to Anon, many home computers have a telephone autodial capability. For example, the unit on a Commodore Vic 20 can be programmed to dial any number(s) you wish. Set the program in operation and it will go on forever without trace to you. That is, the unit will dial you mark's number, and if the mark answers, your computer will not be satisfied with contact, so, when your mark hangs up, the computer will do it again. Ring that number. Tote that barge. You can program this scam to work forever.

Did you ever want to be a bill collector? It can be a lot of fun, especially if you choose to ignore the 1978 federal law which forbids collection agents from browbeating debtors in a number of situations.

Call your mark late at night at home. Scream and shout, pretend you really hate the mark. Tell him or her you represent some legit company in your city. Be abusive, make strong-arm threats. If you get the spouse, be even more insulting. Call the mark at work. Switch names of collection companies. Spread confusion.

Next, get a trusted friend to do the same thing. Mention real stores that you know the mark frequents. You will soon have the real collection agencies and stores wondering about the mark, who will be calling them, too, trying to track down what's happening. This stunt just seems to snowball. Who knows, maybe you will actually destroy the mark's credit rating for a short while.

more

Telephones

Dr. Yaz has a great way of turning a simple, kiddy telephone stunt into a very creative revenge tactic. It's the old silent phone call bit. He calls the mark and says nothing while the mark says hello half a dozen times before hanging up. Dr. Yaz, of course, is recording all of this on a high-quality machine. A couple replications of this tactic soon brings on cursing and swearing from the mark. Several more calls drew even more explicit and scatalogical threats — all of this recorded, of course.

"With a bit of judicious editing and some pre-framed questions also recorded on the telephone, we put together a nice tape which made this mark sound like a real foul-mouthed psychopath. Naturally, we sent copies of the tapes to his parents, girlfriend, teachers, minister, and family doctor," Dr. Yaz says.

Unless you have a bizarre sense of humor — and I guess you must or you wouldn't have gotten this far in this book — harassing phone calls aren't much fun for most people to receive. Personally, I love 'em because it's another chance to abuse some sicko and turn his vindication in reverse. Or, you can do what John Nothankyou from Phoenix did and turn a neat reversal

(Continued...)

of the calls to his own advantage by playing a mark. Don't be confused, read what John did.

"Most phone companies are very community-mindedly uptight about their customers being abused by harassing calls and are quick to help you get relief," John explains. "I use this willingness to punish my mark. Here's how.

"I call the phone company and pretend to be my mark. Obviously, I have to know a good bit about the mark and his/her phone number. I tell the company I have been getting nasty, threatening, sexual calls, etc. I tell them I don't want the police and I don't want a hassle; I just want a new, unlisted number.

"Every single time I have done this to a mark, it has worked! The company is pleased to satisfy me so easily. They immediately switch the mark's number and usually tell me what it is on the spot. Bingo."

Now the mark's friends and associates cannot call him. The mark will not know his or her own number . . . and you will. Think about it.

Chinese Gordon managed to knock out a corporate telephone switchboard once with just a few moments of access to the front of the board. His trick was to insert fine sprays of heavy mercury into the works by means of a small pressure device nozzle he managed to get between the console boards and frame, much like you'd caulk between seams of a building. He thus knocked out an entire telephone communication network. The mercury shorted the wiring, which superheated, boiled, and exploded the guts of the system.

Dick Smegma says that if you hang around any large airport with a pocket telescope, which is inexpensive and fits easily into your shirt pocket, you can carefully observe, with practice, people placing long-distance calls at pay phones, "punching in" their telephone credit card numbers on the phone buttons.

You should always pick someone who deserves this sort of thing being done to him, of course. Or, you can simply follow your mark and do this to him or her as a primary pay-back, obtaining the telephone credit card number, and making dozens of business calls from another public phone, using a mark's name and address during the conversation. For example, you could order merchandise to be shipped C.O.D.

Eventually, the mark whose telephone credit card number you "borrowed," will demand that the phone company investigate, and they will. They'll call the companies listed on the credit cardholder's bill, and their investigation will point to your mark's name and address.

Should someone at an airport ask what you're doing with a telescope, explain that you are with a private detective agency, and you are trailing some guy who is cheating on his wife or, vice versa.

In another version of the same thing, where you don't need the telescope and you're not known to your mark, you can pretend to make your own call from the neighboring telephone and let your eyes do the wandering and recording while the mark does his button pushing.

Tenants

I believe in landlords. Well, some landlords, anyway, as I have been one myself. Anyway, this nice man, Jason, from St. Simons Island in Georgia, wrote to explain how he handled the other side of the landlord/tenant dispute.

"As a landlord, you get stuck with a lot of unsavory and deadbeat tenants. It seems that legal rights go against us landlords. But, if you want someone out, I found a perfectly legal way to do it. I've done it, and it works.

"Most laws say you cannot lock a tenant out. There are no laws about unlocking the tenant, though. I send my unsavory tenant, what you call a mark, a registered letter saying that new locks are to be installed for security purposes. I always make sure to appear personally and give the tenant the new keys before the operation takes place.

"I am a rotten carpenter, and you just can't get good help, so I personally remove the door to that tenant's apartment and take it away for lock-changing. I am such a bad worker that I might not get that door back for five or six days. Sometimes, really bad people could come into the tenant's apartment and steal things. Often these people are the tenant's friends. Nice folks. Great scheme. It works," Jason notes.

Things that Smell Bad

If your mark happens to be a business or organization with public bathrooms, here's something that will give you a few laughs. Locate the paper-towel machine, and note the names of the manufacturer and the model number. Later, write to them on some official letterhead and ask for a duplicate key. Say your janitor lost yours. Send them a couple dollars cash for it.

When you get the key, enter the mark's rest room, unlock the towel machine and remove it from the wall via the screws located inside. Chip a hole in the wall behind the unit. Insert a dead fish or piece of chicken in that hole, and replace the dispenser. Clean up all the mess on the floor and leave.

According to Kilroy, if you don't want to leave so permanent a smell, you can simply unlock the unit and place the offending odor-maker in there with the towels. In that case, happy, happy face-wiping, secondary marks!

Time Bombs

Doug Draut passes along the plans for a nifty time bomb that odorizes your mark's home, car, apartment, office, etc. Doug says to use empty cold capsules and fill them with baking soda. Put some vinegar in a plastic bag. Drop the capsules in, and fill the bag with air. Seal it. Break open the capsules inside the bag and quickly drop it in the mark's property. The gas causes the bag to rupture, causing the smelly vinegar to leak everywhere.

Tires

Blasting caps may be hard to get hold of these days. But, if you're as inventive as I am, you might want to really blow a big hole in the tires of your mark's car or whatever. Swab the tire tread with window-cleaner so it's dry and clean. Then use high-quality black electrical or duct tape to fasten two blasting caps side-by-side on the tread of the tire. If you do it right, about two or four revolutions down the road will blow the tire right off the rim. Tape well, sweetie.

Speaking of your mark's tires, always carry a valve wrench so you can remove the valves from his vehicle's tires. This great tool costs under a dollar and is so much safer than a knife or spike when it comes to deflating a tire.

Toasters

Once more, my friend Kilroy is the toast of the tome. He says that such a simple device as a kitchen toaster lends itself well to the deviant imagination.

"Look down inside your toaster," Kilroy says. "Notice the heating elements that turn bright red when the toaster is turned on. These elements can easily become a detonator for the fuses of firecrackers or smoke bombs. Or, you can hang rubber bands on these elements to cook up an especially obnoxious odor."

Toilet Paper

According to Stirling Sphincter, bathroom stationery is overlooked when it comes to having fun with people. There are many fine uses, including writing letters on toilet paper, plus this old high school classic.

All you need is a six- to ten-inch piece of toilet paper and some creamy-style peanut butter. Dab some of the peanut butter on the paper and gently pat it in place on the backside of the mark's trousers. It's easily done at parties, for instance, and it may be a lot of minutes before the fun when he discovers your poo poo plant. His protestions upon discovery will serve to make more of an ass of him.

Toilets

I don't know why so many people, especially little boys of all ages, find toilets so funny. But, bathroom humor is very big. C. W. from Hastings, Nebraska, has a trick we could label the "Heinz squirts." But, let's let C. W. tell the story.

"Take one of those little plastic ketchup or mustard containers, or one of each, that you get in fast food places. Lift the seat off the mark's toilet. Slice the top of each container and set it gently on the edge of the porcelain toilet below the seat. Orient it so the packages line up with the seat knobs. Gently—very gently—put the seat down.

"When the mark sits down, *splooey, spooley, spoooooly* . . . the packages will squirt their contents all over the mark's behind, legs, pants, jeans, or whatever. This trick works great with females, of course."

The mark in this case might just be a bar, restaurant, hotel, gas station, or public place. Or it could be a private residence.

According to Ann Nonymous and her friend, a toilet can be a great mind-bender, too. They advise you to call your mark on the telephone, pour a pitcher of water into the handy commode, holding the telephone so the mark will hear this. Flush the facility loudly so the mark will hear the flushing. Laugh softly into the phone, or tell the mark that's what will happen to him, etc. Now hang up. You may repeat this at random intervals if you feel the mark has not been flushed enough. It makes many paranoid marks very nervous.

Kilroy had this idea for a mark's porcelain throne. Locate the main water shut-off valve outside the mark's home (if the shutoff is inside, you'll have to sneak into the house). Torque it to the full open position with a wrench, and then run a bead of super glue around the shaft of the valve so it can't turn at all.

You need to get into the mark's home in order to carry out the next step in the commodious chicanery. Once there, do the exact same thing to the valve directly connected to the thunder jug itself. Remove the cover on the toilet tank and unscrew the float on the float valve. Be sure to leave the tank float in position, though. Touch a few beads of super glue around the edge of the tank—don't use a full bead as it might form a waterproof seal. Replace the cover.

Flushed with success, you can now await your mark's first operation of the tampered toilet. Within minutes, he or she will be doing a wild Moses, trying to part the overflowing effluvial sea.

more

Toilets

Although most of us never went to the University of Arizona, I bet we all know someone like Tom. Stay on his good side. Tom says when you owe someone a toilet-tinged pay-back, open up the top of his water tank and dump a half box of laundry detergent in there. When the mark flushes the toilet, he gets a foam flood of washday miracle foaming up and up and up — all over the bowl and the floor. And, it just keeps on foaming and flowing.

Meanwhile, Jed Wisebooger, a used toilet sludge collector, once had this next stunt pulled on him, according to Bullet Bill. Tricksters who were furious with Jed for his cheating them on several business deals got to work in the basement beneath his living area. They uncoupled "his" toilet drain below the trap and rerouted the pipe out and down into the backseat window of Jed's company car.

Bullet Bill reports, "Jed spent that weekend at home with his derelict family, all of them eating, drinking, pooping, and peeing.

"When he went down to get into that car to go to work Monday, he found a four-wheeled, mobile septic tank in his driveway, despite the modest leakage at the door joints."

Toll Roads

A man named Ron from Florida advises paying toll-road fees by check if your mark is the highway system, the state, the toll road, or the collector. It's all quite legal and a hell of a hassle, especially if it's for a small amount. It involves a lot of red tape, I.D. checking, and time wasted while other motorists get impatient. But it is legal, and you can explain that you have no cash with you. (PS: It's good to stash away fifty dollars in the glove compartment in the event the law comes down on you for retribution further on down the road.)

Toothpaste

Have a friend who's not very clean or nice about borrowing toilet articles? Or, want to pay back a mark who is super-clean about personal toilet articles? Lil' Tommy Toothpaste has a great revenge trick for you.

"Take your mark's partially empty toothpaste tube and carefully push small raisins up into the tube, mixed in with the paste. Do this about three or four times. The mark squeezes out toothpaste that night and these horrible, mangled gooshy things come splooping out too," Tom says with a straight, gleaming smile.

A female mark might be wont to squeal, "Euuuuhhhh, grooossssssss!"

Syd Thrip goes about it a mite differently. He pushes out all of the real toothpaste, screws back the top of the tube, and then inserts a syringe needle into the bottom of the tube. He says, "I have this syringe filled with various things at different times, depending upon the mark. I imagine your readers can create insert compounds of their own."

Pressed for details, Syd says he has refilled his marks' toothpaste tubes with library paste, hot sauce, diarrhea splashings, soap paste, etc.

Trappers

I grew up in the country and learned to despise trappers almost as much as land developers and strip miners. Ever see an animal in a trap, dying from trying to chew off its own leg to get loose? I have.

But, let's lighten this up. In fact, let's lighten his load. If you know where one of these cowards is trapping, go along his trap line with some bottles freshly filled (the last couple days) with human urine which you've kept refrigerated. Pour copious amounts on and near his traps. The animals will stay away. If the traps are in the water, spring them with a stick or smash them with a rock. Later, if you get the chance, piss on the trapper personally.

Travel

Ever have someone break your mind, heart, ego, or a business deal by planning a trip, vacation, or other fun travel and then suddenly call it off? If the conversations I have with people across this country are any indication, it seems to be a common nasty that insensitive friends, lovers, spouses, associates, etc., do a lot. There are many truly nasty ways to retaliate. Rather, here is a fun one.

Announce to your mark that you've won a trip for two to Paradise Island. (You fill in a location that will make the mark flood with droolish delight.) Make all sorts of neat plans, plan big fun, and really build up the all-expenses paid nature of this trip. Really heat up the anticipation. If appropriate, heat up that angle sexually, too. The anvil is in place; now it's time to trip the hammer. There are two basic ways to drop the hammer:

1. Leave with someone else, with whom you've planned to really go all along.
2. Leave by yourself, which was the nature of the contest, real or imagined, all along.

Whichever you choose, your actual departure day should precede the mark-planned one by a day or two.

(Continued...)

When the mark tries to contact you, have a friend, family member, or associate explain innocently that you are in (your so-called previously planned vacation spot), and then fill in with circumstance/details you provide before departure. Oh yeah, be sure to send the mark a nice postal card.

Travel Plans

If you've ever played airport roulette, you know how easy it is to cancel or alter your own flight plans. Did you ever consider doing it to or for someone else? You might sometimes need a lot of information for this, like names, dates, destinations, card numbers, etc., but if you do it during busy times, the airline people rarely check too much. Be sure to gather as much information on the mark as possible.

Trees

As a lover of trees, I almost didn't include this one. But, sometimes, you have to go out on a limb and oak for the best, especially ash a last measure. You have to have an ultimate nasty for a mark and this mark has to have a favorite tree — one he would easily trade off for the death of his grandchildren. See, I am a tree fan. Okay, so you have the mark who fits. You buy a can of chemical stump remover. You drill a two-inch hole halfway through the mark's pet tree, aiming downward at a 30 degree to 45 degree angle. Pour the stump remover in this hole, then plug the hole with the cutting you removed or a fabricated one if your drill dusted it. Repeat if necessary.

Turntables

Don't ask me why, but George Orr claims a major freak-out is for a mark to find a very dead horseshoe crab spinning away on the mark's turntable "the next morning." Somehow, I bet this works well in the Southwest desert, e.g., Phoenix. Katy McCutcheon says that any small, dead animal will substitute, e.g., voles, bats, or sparrows, or you can coil a small, dead snake around the unit.

That reminded me of Big Jawn Old who once experimented by flat-rolling a bit of feline roadkill with his D9 to see of the resultant object could be hardened, cut, holed, and shaped like a record. He reports success in his experiments. But, as he hadn't yet completed his pay-back as I was writing this, he asked me to withhold further details until the next writing.

Twist-off Bottle Lids

You can have a lot of fun with people who have to live with twist-off caps. Simply turn the bottle upside down, thinly bead some super glue or Eastman 910 around the rim, let it dry, and turn it upright.

The resultant damage is called Belted Biceps Biopsy.

Typewriters

If your mark has one of those typewriters that does not use a ball (the typefaces are on individual keys), Annie Fellantori says you can use needle nose pliers to pry the little typeface heads off the key strikers. Then you simply mix up the letter and replace them, the S on an L key striker, the R on an A, etc.

Universal Price Index

Yet another superhighway on the road to computer domination of our lives is the Universal Price Index, those ugly zebra-stripe lines that now appear on almost all consumer products. They can be had, though.

Mike the Madman points out, "Each pair of lines has a meaning to the encoding device. With the help of a Magic Marker or a black, felt-tip pen you can change that meaning. Just fill in the space between two or more lines, and you screw up the system. Let's show them how much we hate what they are doing to us."

So if a store or a clerk has caused you so much frustration that you want to get back, take a nail or small file and scratch across the magnetic strip or deface the metallic strip on unit pricing products. Your work will either jam the machine or glitch the system.

Useful Addresses

Here are some potentially useful addresses you might wish to use in your pay-back efforts. In future books, I would like to expand this list, either as a resource or as a target. I would be pleased to hear from you if you have any additions or corrections.

BUREAU OF ALCOHOL, TOBACCO & FIREARMS
Enforcement Branch
1200 Pennsylvania Avenue
Washington, DC 20004

CITIZENS COMMITTEE FOR THE RIGHT TO KEEP AND BEAR ARMS
Liberty Park
12500 N.E. Tenth Place
Bellevue, WA 98005

DRUG ENFORCEMENT ADMINISTRATION
1405 Eye Street NW
Washington, DC 20005

(Continued...)

FEDERAL BUREAU OF INVESTIGATION
Nine St. & Pennsylvania Avenue NW
Washington, DC 20535

FOOD AND DRUG ADMINISTRATION
5600 Fishers Lane
Rockville, MD 20852

GENERAL ACCOUNTING OFFICE
Fraud Division
441 G. Street
Washington, DC 20002

GUN WEEK
P.O. Box 488, Station C
Buffalo, NY 14209

INTERNAL REVENUE SERVICE
1111 Constitution Avenue NW
Washington, DC 20002

U.S. DEPARTMENT OF JUSTICE
Tenth Street and Constitution Avenue NW
Washington, DC 20530

U.S. DEPARTMENT OF LABOR
200 Constitution Avenue NW
Washington, DC 20002

Utilities

Of course, there is the ultimate. Instead of tampering with, defacing or destroying your mark's electric meter, you could simply steal it. Caution: *Know what you are doing first. Juice kills!* It also entertains. I like this idea because it causes all sorts of problems, both power and bureaucratic. Cut it and run with it. Maybe you could mail or deliver this meter with a ticking death threat to another mark.

Vending Machines

Yo, it's Ray from Kansas City, again, and this time he's got a gripe with vending machines that spill, don't pay off, or are never attended. He's tired of losing dimes and quarters and never getting a refund, so he declared his own dividend. He took a long piece of doweling with a razor blade stuck into the end and reached way up into the machine where the empty cups are stacked. He slashed the bottoms out of about ten of them before his reach gave out. This will make ten more people unhappy enough to do something, which will make ten more people unhappy, which will — eventually beget a great deal of hassle for the vending machine company.

Bill Webster from D.C. has one of the most astoundingly simple ways of dealing with certain outlaw vending machines I have yet encountered; turn them off. His plan applies to those which need electrical power to operate or to refrigerate the contents. Judge Bill adds, "If it's a machine peddling cold soda or one that has ice cream, and either of them has ripped you off without any response from the owners, geezus, it's simple. Pull the plug."

Hmmm, why didn't *you* think of that?

Video Games

Fred Steinbeck passes along some freak news about efforts to infiltrate video games.

This trick isn't exactly new, but in some video games a small flaw in the coin totalizer allows free games. Take a small but weighty object such as a "D" size battery or pocket knife, and give the machine a sharp rap between the coin-deposit and coin-return slots. If you have done it correctly, you will get one free credit. Do it more, and get more. There's no law of diminishing returns here! However, some machines have been fitted with a "tilt" switch, so, ya win some, ya lose some.

Agent NDS tells of a free-game trick on the Junior Donkey Kong machine. Take a flattened straw and insert it about three inches along the right-hand crack between the cash box and the machine, about two to three inches down from the top crack between the cash box and the machine, and wiggle the straw up and down. You will rack up some credits.

more

Video Games

Want to get even with one of the rip-off artists who manufacture those game cartridges or the shop selling them? According to Jimi the Z, our electronic expert, all they are is two dollars' worth of IC chip in a fifty-cent plastic box, so not much loss there. Jimi says to take a copper marking pen, the type used for PC Board touch ups and run it down the video game cartridge terminal. Blow on it to dry it, and it won't work anymore. You could also do this to your mark's personal cartridge library.

Welding Compound

This is basically a cold weld product that lets you make all sorts of "repairs" around the home and office. It "repairs, fills and bonds iron, brass, pewter, aluminum, steel, copper, and bronze." I'm not at all mechanical, but I can think of all sorts of things your mark might need to have "repaired." This product is available from U.S. General Supply Corp.

Whistle

I knew there was a reasonable use for a police whistle, and thanks to Bob the Computer Kid, here it is. For some harmless payback to a friend, Bob took a police whistle and, using a heavy-duty, metal-spring tension clamp, mounted it to the underside of his car's front bumper.

"The mount of the whistle must be perpendicular to the plane of the bumper, though," Bob says. "Mount the whistle dead center, and this will produce the rudest sounds possible at speeds of from 5 to 45 miles per hour."

Think of the fun when a mechanic charges your mark twenty bucks to remove the whistle.

Windows

If you live near a nosy neighbor who loves to peek and peer at everyone else's business but his or her own, I have a new idea to screen the view. Vaseline smeared on either plastic or aluminum screens goes on quickly and easily if warm. It makes a horrible mess and also acts like a magnet for dust and bugs. It's also hard to see through. Washing it away might be impossible, and the mark would have to replace the window screens.

Another approach, which appeals to me because it is more direct and a hell of a lot easier if you're as physically lazy as I am, is to either flash or moon the nosy peeper. Right! Simply bare and grin. You may wave or jiggle, too, if you're equipped to do so.

more

Windows

Deadeye Jordan passes along a true CIA-style act that enables you to take out a glass window without leaving evidence of any projectile. He advises you to use a Whamo wrist rocket slingshot and a small, clear-glass marble as a projectile. Both the target window and the projectile marble will shatter, leaving no evidence. Sonic boom, UFOs or the Trilateral Commission will get the blame.

Windshield Wipers

Obtain a handful of aluminum oxide micro grit from a chemistry supply source. On a drizzly, but not real rainy, day, pour a bead of this grit on the wiper blades of your mark's car. When he or she turns on the wipers, the grit will severely scratch the windshield.

Wine

After reading this trick, I'm glad I passed on pressing grapes a few seasons back, if you catch my drift. A fun guy signing himself SOFR says that when a store selling booze really irks him, he goes to the wine area, borrows a couple of jars of the types without seals and takes them to the rest-room. He empties out some of the wine and refills the jug with urine from his portable dispenser, then reseals and replaces the product.

Word for the Day

One of the worst jokes I ever heard came from the infamous Gerald Anderson, clown prince of Woodland and conductor of the Mt. Lebanon Wind Symphony, who tells you authoritatively that the word for the day is "legs." Then, with a shy smile, he says, "Help spread the word."

Wrong Numbers

No, I'm not talking about that last blind date you had. This time it's for real. You've just sat down for that wonderful roast pork dinner or with that neat Single Malt Scotch after same. You look into her/his eyes or the single eye of the boobtube. RAANNNANNNNNGGGGG. It's your telephone interrupting your life again. You answer.

"Hey, ahhh, like, ahhh, is Emilie there," dulls back a voice sounding like something growing in a crack of a mall parking lot. Your moment of shocked silence is met with a blob of "Hey, ahhh, Emilie? Is that, ahh, you?"

Your first reaction is to scream "WRONG NUMBER" and hang up.

Don't. Here's a better way. Pause another second or two, then sound as sad and distraughtly sincere as possible when you say in a slow, low voice, barely above a whisper, "Ohmigod, you don't know . . . she just died. I'm a neighbor and everyone's in shock. It's terrible. Emilie is dead (get a catch in your voice here) . . . please don't call here."

Now, you can hang up.

(Continued...)

There was a less negative approach to wrong numbers in the hilarious film *Ruthless People* in which Danny DeVito fielded a wrong number. His cheerful patter to the obviously obnoxious caller was something like, "Gee, I'm sorry, she can't come to the phone right now. You see, my *censored* is in her mouth and she'll be tied up for awhile. I'll have her call you back when she's *all* finished." He hung up immediately after the last word in that line.

You can adapt the idea for your own use. Despite dirty looks from my fellow film critics, I laughed like hell at that sequence. I also laugh at everything Mr. DeVito says and does. He's wonderful. What a grand attitude he expresses.

Yellow Pages

There are some businesses that thrive on letting people's fingers do the walking. Some businesses depend on the Yellow Pages. If your mark has such a business, you might just help him or her along to court. Here's dependable old Kilroy's advice.

"For this you need access to your mark's business telephone or at least the outside terminals. The idea is to make last-minute changes in Yellow Pages advertising. You call in the changes or the cancellation at the *very last* minute. You will probably be asked to furnish the mark's account number, too, so be prepared for that.

"In my experience with this scam, they usually call the mark's number right back to verify. Here's where you and/or an associate have to have command of that telephone or number so that you can be the one to verify the changes.

"It works. I had to use this on a professional person a few years ago as payback for some very costly things that happened to me thanks to his incompetency and absolute refusal to make good. My revenge worked perfectly," Kilroy says.

Zulu

That's the last letter in the phonetic alphabet and the last word in this collection, but not *my* last word. Please send me your contributions of nasty tricks for my next book.

Zymurgy . . . The Last Word

As Dick Smegma told his proctologist, "Well, that's about it from this end."

"Make fun where there is none."

—Gretchen Liscinsky
Sorry Charlie's
Greensburg, PA